An Early Upaniṣadic Reader

AN EARLY UPANIṢADIC READER

With notes, glossary, and an appendix of related Vedic texts

Edited for the use of Sanskrit students
as a supplement to Lanman's *Sanskrit Reader*

HANS HENRICH HOCK

MOTILAL BANARSIDASS PUBLISHERS
PRIVATE LIMITED • DELHI

First Edition : Delhi ***2007***

ISBN: 81-208-3213-2 (HB)
ISBN: 81-208-3214-0 (PB)

MOTILAL BANARSIDASS
41 U.A. Bungalow Road, Jawahar Nagar, Delhi 110 007
8 Mahalaxmi Chamber, 22 Bhulabhai Desai Road, Mumbai 400 026
203 Royapettah High Road, Mylapore, Chennai 600 004
236, 9th Main III Block, Jayanagar, Bangalore 560 011
Sanas Plaza, 1302 Baji Rao Road, Pune 411 002
8 Camac Street, Kolkata 700 017
Ashok Rajpath, Patna 800 004
Chowk, Varanasi 221 001

PRINTED IN INDIA
BY JAINENDRA PRAKASH JAIN AT SHRI JAINENDRA PRESS,
A-45 NARAINA, PHASE-I, NEW DELHI 110 028
AND PUBLISHED BY NARENDRA PRAKASH JAIN FOR
MOTILAL BANARSIDASS PUBLISHERS PRIVATE LIMITED,
BUNGALOW ROAD, DELHI 110 007

Contents

Preface

The great upaniṣads of the late Vedic period take a position in the literary and philosophical tradition of Sanskrit that can be characterized as Janus-faced in western terms or, in Indian terms, as देहलीदीप, a light on the threshold which illuminates both what is behind and in front. From one perspective the early upaniṣads constitute the end — according to some, the culmination — of the long and prolific Vedic period. From a different point of view they are the starting point for a philosophical tradition that pervades all of post-Vedic India, whether orthodox (Hindu) or heterodox (Buddhist and Jaina).

It is here that the question of the transcendental unity behind the great diversity of the phenomenal world is systematically addressed. The issue had, of course, been mooted in the earlier Vedic tradition, especially under the heading तदेकम् 'that one (entity)' from which everything has evolved. But it is in the late Vedic upaniṣads that the issue is met head-on, with various competing characterizations of तदेकम् as Brahman, Ātman, ॐ, and even more profoundly, as beyond any positive definition, describable only negatively as नेति नेति and the like.

It is here, too, that the important concepts of karman and reincarnation are first formulated, concepts that are foundational to all post-Vedic Indian religions. Again, there were earlier Vedic antecedents, especially in the later portions of the Brāhmaṇas. Most notable among these is the concept of पुनर्मृत्यु, repeated death in "yonder world" which deprives the deceased of immortality. But again, it is only in the late Vedic upaniṣads that coherent theories of पुनर्जन्म 'rebirth', based on the nature of one's कर्मन्, are beginning to be developed. (The term used by the early upaniṣads actually is पुनरावृत्ति 'returning'.)

Just as the early upaniṣads of the late Vedic era are a point of transition in Indian religious thinking, so they also constitute a transitional period in terms of their grammar and language use. Features of Vedic grammar and diction coexist with rhetorical strategies and methods of argumentation that characterize post-Vedic śāstric texts. The early upaniṣads, therefore, offer an excellent entry point to the Vedic language for students familiar with Classical Sanskrit.

It is for these reasons that some ten years ago I began preparing this Early Upaniṣadic Reader, for students who had completed the better part of two years of Classical Sanskrit instruction at the University of Illinois.

I have benefited from my students' feedback, even though — or because — in the early years it often expressed itself as deep frustration with trying to make sense of the texts, their "alien" grammar and diction, and their "arcane" subject matter. I have also profited from feedback by my teaching associates, Yasuko Suzuki and Sarah Tsiang. I am especially grateful to Sarah Tsiang who made copious suggestions for improving the explanatory Notes and the Glossary, and who painstakingly went over the entire text in search of misprints, ambiguities, and other infelicities. In fact, the idea of a self-contained Glossary came from Sarah Tsiang, and she also contributed the large majority of the entries.

If the present form of the Reader is able to accomplish its goal of providing a helpful introduction to the early upaniṣads and to the Vedic language in general, the credit must go to my students, to Yasuko Suzuki, and especially to Sarah Tsiang. I have to take the responsibility for any problems that remain.

Finally, let me express my deepest gratitude to my wife, Zarina, and to our son, Heinrich Sharad, for their love and support.

Hans Henrich Hock

(Urbana-Champaign, Summer 2005)

Introduction

असतो मा सद्गमय तमसो मा ज्योतिर्गमय मृत्योर्मामृतं गमय

Introduction*

1. The Purpose of this Reader

Since its publication in 1884, Lanman's *Sanskrit Reader*[1] has been the most widely used English-language introduction to original Sanskrit texts. What has been especially useful for beginning students are the copious notes and the glossary, as well as helpful references to Whitney's *Sanskrit Grammar*. Even so, students and teachers alike have had problems with some aspects of Lanman's *Reader*, including the fact that it refers to the first edition of Whitney's *Grammar*, not the second one, which appeared in 1889,[2] five years after Lanman's *Reader*. More important, many students today do not have the background in classical Greek and Latin that could be taken for granted in Lanman's and Whitney's times; the work of Sanskrit scholars since the 1880s has in many cases produced better editions of the texts that Lanman incorporated in his *Reader*; and even more significant, this more recent work has had a profound impact on our understanding of the texts. A new, updated edition therefore would be highly desirable. The present *Reader* has a more modest goal — to add to Lanman's Vedic selections and, in so doing, to offer beginning Sanskrit students an avenue to the Vedic language which, I hope, they will find more accessible.

Lanman's Vedic selections come mainly from the Ṛg-Veda, with some additions from the Yajur-Veda, most of which are concerned with the Vedic ritual,[3] plus a few selections from the late Vedic Gṛhya-Sūtras and from Yāska's *Nirukta*. The philological, Indo-Europeanist tendencies of the nineteenth century naturally favored Lan-

---

* A note on the transcription of the Sanskrit words ब्रह्मन् and ब्राह्मण: Following the practice of Basham's *The Wonder that Was India*, the following conventions are used when citing these words in English. In the sense of 'Ultimate Principle' ब्रह्मन् is written Brahman (with capital initial); in the sense of the priest who directs the Vedic ritual, it is written brahman (without capitalization). For ब्राह्मण in reference to one of the four castes, brahmin is used; when the word refers to a Vedic text and textual period, the transliteration brāhmaṇa is employed (with capitalization if it is part of the name of a particular text).

1 Charles Rockwell Lanman, *A Sanskrit Reader: Text and Vocabulary and Notes*, Harvard University Press, 1884.

2 William Dwight Whitney, *Sanskrit Grammar: Including both the Classical Language, and the Older Dialects, of Veda and Brahmana*, Harvard University Press, 1889.

3 Those not familiar with terms such as Ṛg-Veda, Yajur-Veda, Gṛhya-Sūtra, etc., should consult Section 5 of this Introduction which provides a brief survey of Vedic literature.

man's heavy emphasis on the Ṛg-Veda, the oldest layer of Vedic literature, because presumably it is closest to the Indo-European parent language; and the ritualist texts were included because they were considered the oldest Indo-European prose texts. The switch, however, from Lanman's epic and classical selections to the Ṛg-Veda is enormous — in time, language, and style. Even specialists find Vedic hymns notoriously difficult to interpret, because we do not have any direct access to the religious, cultural, and linguistic contexts in and for which they were composed. And as Lanman himself states, the Vedic Prose texts of the brāhmaṇas and of the prose portions of the Black Yajur-Veda saṁhitās tend to be quite "arid". (Lanman's general characterization of the texts, however, is overly uncharitable.) Whatever the merits of offering such texts to beginning Sanskrit students may have been in Lanman's times, today his selections are less than apt to attract beginning students' interest in the Vedic language.

My experience has shown that a selection of upaniṣadic texts has a better chance of arousing students' interest in the enormously rich tradition of Vedic language and literature. Because of their relative lateness these texts are closer to the language that students are familiar with from Lanman's post-Vedic selections. They reflect a time of intense intellectual speculation and discussion, out of which grew not only the later forms of philosophical Hinduism but no doubt also Buddhism, Jainism, plus other religious and philosophical systems that have since died out. Their topics and discussions therefore are of keen interest to anyone interested in the religious and philosophical traditions of India, and especially to the ever-growing number of students who want to learn Sanskrit in order to study these traditions. Moreover, the upaniṣads tend to employ a more interesting rhetorical style than the often rather turgid presentation of earlier Vedic Prose; they provide a window on aspects of the social and cultural life of their time, including the status of women; they even offer glimpses of humor.

The texts in this Reader have been selected to present as wide and representative a picture of the literature as possible. Being a selection, of course, the Reader could not possibly include all the texts that those who use it (or I, for that matter) might have wanted to see included. Selections I - XIX are presented in the same fashion as Lanman's selections, as texts to be translated by the students, aided by a glossary and notes with references to Whitney's *Grammar*. In one respect, however, this reader departs from Lanman's practice. Rather than forcing students to simultaneously wrestle with the difficulties of the Vedic language and with the complexities of Vedic ritual and philosophy, I provide at the beginning of the notes to each selection a brief content summary or in some cases a rough translation, as a guide to understanding the selection's purport and line of argument.

The Reader is supplemented by an Appendix, Selection XX, which gives related texts, mainly from the earlier Vedic literature, but including one post-Vedic upaniṣadic text that may provide a glimpse of how the different strands of thinking found in the earlier texts could be integrated into a more comprehensive, structured system of thought. These ancillary readings are presented together with translations that attempt to make it possible for readers to work out the meanings of the texts for themselves. The translations do not make any claim to providing "the" meaning of the texts, and they have no pretensions to literary elegance.

2. The Earlier Vedic Background of Upaniṣadic Thought

In his commentary on a particularly difficult passage in the Chāndogya-Upaniṣad (5:18:1), which had elicited a variety of different interpretations, the great medieval philosopher Śaṅkarācārya states, एतद्धस्तिदर्शन इव जात्यन्धाः 'that is like people blind from birth in visualizing an elephant'. This is the first occurrence of a reference that keeps recurring in attempts to discuss the early history of India, whether from the perspective of literature, of religion and philosophy, or of language and linguistics. Any attempt to establish a clear chronology of events for that period is fraught with difficulties. Partly these difficulties result from the well-known fact that the sense of historicity which characterizes modern western thinking is alien to traditional India (just as it is to much of traditional Europe). But they also result from other factors, such as the fact that the text collections that have come down to us were composed over extended periods, during which different strands of thinking could be borrowed back and forth. The following attempt to locate the upaniṣads within the Vedic tradition, therefore, must be taken with a considerable dose of salt. Moreover, it should be kept in mind that the historical approach adopted here and in the western model of scholarship in general is not accepted by many modern Hindus, whether scholars or laypeople. For them, the Vedas are eternal, अपौरुषेय (i.e., not produced by humans), and therefore beyond history. The following discussion, therefore, is meaningless to those who hold this belief. At the same time, it is deeply meaningful to those who are interested in, and concerned with, the history of Indian traditions. The best that I can ask for is that adherents of these two views respect each others' perspectives, in spite of their differences.

European and European-inspired scholarship on the Indian traditions began with scholars such as Sir William Jones, and in its early stages was often colored by ethnocentrism and worse. Lanman's discussion of the Vedic tradition (p. 352-358) very much reflects the preconceptions of western scholarship toward the end of the nineteenth century. He suggests two layers of Vedic literature: 1. An early period of hymnal poetry represented most prominently in the Ṛg-Veda and reflecting 'the life of a vigorous, active, and healthy people ... whose religion was a simple worship of the deified powers of nature.' 2. A later period in which 'the old Vedic religion was converted into an infinitely complex system of sacrifices and ceremonies. To this period belongs the belief in metempsychosis [reincarnation] ... The sultry air of Ganges-land has relaxed both the physical and the mental fibre of the Hindu, and he has become a Quietist.'[4]

Even in Lanman's times scholars were beginning to realize that his interpretation is deficient on several counts — beyond the dubious value judgments. Most scholars would now agree that in principle we need to distinguish three periods: An early stage of hymnal poetry (mantras); a second stage of Vedic Prose concerned with explaining the use of the mantras, other verbal expressions, ritual implements, etc. in an increasingly complex ritual, and with establishing the mystical significance of the ritual; finally, the stage of the āraṇyakas and upaniṣads where mystical speculation turns to questions such as the transcendental unity underlying the phenomenal world, karman and reincarnation, and release from the cycle of reincarnations.[5] Some scholars further consider the final, upaniṣadic, stage a radical departure from the ritualist concerns of Vedic Prose, a veritable revolution in thinking.

This threefold layering of Vedic literature, however, is not directly reflected in the Vedic texts. The Ṛg-Veda contains numerous hymns dealing with the ritual and the priests officiating in it, the mystical significance of the ritual (see especially Selection XX:G of this Reader), and such issues as the origin of the world and the transcendental unity that underlies it (see the selections in XX:H and I). At least one hymn (XX:G) combines these two strands of thought by portraying the creation of the world as a primeval sacrifice of a primordial human being (Puruṣa) by the Gods — who themselves are created by this sacrifice.

True, Ṛg-Vedic hymns that address more mystical and transcendental issues are quite late, to judge by aspects of their linguistic and poetic structure. Nevertheless, they must have preceded the upaniṣads and (much of) ritualist Vedic Prose, since they are referred to, or even cited, in the latter texts (see e.g. XI and XX:J). Similarly, the

---

4 As Lanman himself states, however, his two stages of development 'are not separated by hard and fast lines'.

5 In western accounts, the *a*-stem form *karma* is generally used instead of the *n*-stem form *karman*. — In a recent publication Herman W. Tull tries to show that there is no real difference between the ritualist literature and the early upaniṣads (*The Vedic Origins of Karma*, State University of New York Press, 1989). While it is certainly true that there is no clear dividing line between the two layers of tradition, it is also true that the discussion of transcendental issues is much more massive in the upaniṣads than in the ritualist literature, a fact recognized in the indigenous tradition (see Section 3 below). Moreover, in his attempt to deny the usual distinction between the two layers of tradition, Tull underplays the significance of the passages reproduced in Selections XVII and XVIII of this Reader.

assemblies at kings' courts which host important disputations regarding mystical and transcendental issues in the ritualist texts and especially in the upaniṣads (see e.g. VII - X) find their antecedents in Ṛg-Vedic references to competitions between seers at the assemblies of royal patrons (e.g. RV 2:23-26, 8:54:8, 10:61, 10:71, 10:88). And brahmodya, the upaniṣadic term for such disputations, is in the ritualist texts employed to refer to "riddles" which already appear in the Ṛg-Veda (see e.g. Selection XX:F) and which address such issues as the nature of the ritual or the origin of the world.[6]

Within the ritual texts, too, we find much that anticipates the mystical and transcendental speculations of the upaniṣads. This is especially true for the later texts which tend to shade over into passages that come to be identified as āraṇyakas or upaniṣads. Some aspects of the ritual lend themselves especially to mystical speculation.

One of these is the aśvamedha, a ritual in which the king lets a horse, protected by his warriors, roam around for a year, so as to claim whatever territory the horse covers in the course of its wanderings. From Ṛg-Vedic times there was a tradition of attributing a mystical significance to this sacrificial horse. Thus, in RV 1:163 it is identified with Yama, Trita, and Āditya, the sun, from which it is said to have been created. In the Śatapatha-Brāhmaṇa account of the aśvamedha (M 13:5:2:23), a speculative Vedic hymn on the origin of the world is recited (see Selection XX:I), no doubt to implicitly identify the sacrificial horse with the primordial "golden embryo" from which this world arose. Part of the aśvamedha consists in the recitation of traditional brahmodyas, as in Śatapatha-Brāhmaṇa (M) 13:2:6:9-17 and 13:5:2:11-22, verbal exchanges which in less ritualized form might well end in a lively disputation. In fact, as Eggeling remarks in his translation of the Śatapatha-Brāhmaṇa (introduction to volume 5), in the aśvamedha section of the Mahābhārata, 'dialecticians, eager to vanquish one another, foregather to discuss the nature and origin of things.'

A second generally recognized focus of mystical speculation is the agnicayana, another extensive, year-long rite, the building, or "piling" of a fire altar which has the shape of a giant bird. Even in the oldest ritualist texts, the saṁhitās of the Black Yajur-Veda, this ritual is given special significance. The altar is equated with Agni, the God of fire, and with Prajāpati, the 'lord of creatures', the creator God of Vedic Prose who at the end of a late Ṛg-Vedic hymn (Selection XX:I) is identified as the "golden embryo" from which all this world arose. Through the agnicayana, therefore, the sacrificer and the priests who conduct the sacrifice for him, pile not just Agni, or Prajāpati, but establish the entire world. The mystical significance of the agnicayana becomes even greater in the late ritualist text of the Śatapatha-Brāhmaṇa which devotes five of its fourteen books to the agnicayana. Especially in the introductory and concluding chap-

6 On Vedic brahmodyas, see George Thompson, 'The *brahmodya* and Vedic discourse', *Journal of the American Oriental Society* 117: 13-37, 1997.

ters (see e.g. XX:J), the discussion goes far beyond what we find in earlier ritualist literature, and draws on the most speculative of the Ṛg-Vedic hymns to bring out the full extent of the ritual as a reenactment of the creation of the world and as an instrument for its maintenance and proper understanding.

At the conclusion of its discussion of the agnicayana, the Śatapatha-Brāhmaṇa goes even further, by integrating aspects of the aśvamedha into the agnicayana, thus combining the mystical significance of both rites. It is therefore no accident that these final, integrated sections form the first part of the Bṛhad-Āraṇyaka-Upaniṣad (see also below).

Another ritual that has given rise to a great amount of mystical speculation is the pravargya, in origin no doubt a ritual connected with the sun and presenting the sun by means of a golden disk. It is not quite clear why the ritual was considered a highly esoteric one. But already the earliest Vedic Prose traditions, those of the Black Yajur-Veda, relegate the discussion of the ritual to their Āraṇyaka (Taittirīya-Āraṇyaka 5), a text that by definition is esoteric in nature. Even more explicit is the injunction of the Śatapatha-Brāhmaṇa that the pravargya should only be performed for one who is known or dear to the priest, or for one who has studied the Vedas (ŚB (M) 14:2:2:46).

The earliest explicit discussion (Aitareya-Brāhmaṇa 1:22:14) claims that those who know the significance of the pravargya are (re-)born as composed of the three Vedas and Brahman (i.e. the holy power or transcendental principle), and hence become immortal. In the Śatapatha-Brāhmaṇa (M 14:1:1:1-2) the ritual is given even greater significance. It is said to have been performed by the Gods in Kurukṣetra, lit. 'the field or land of the Kurus', but commonly interpreted as the center of the entire civilized world. The ritual is in succession equated to the year, the three worlds (earth, "ether", and heaven), the Gods, the sacrificer, and just about all the other rituals (14:3:2:22-30). And it is stated that those who learn the mystical significance of the rite or partake in it, enter eternal life and light. The latter statement occurs twice, first at 14:1:2:26, the second time at 14:3:2:32, in the last paragraph of the pravargya discussion — which immediately is followed by the main body of the Bṛhad-Āraṇyaka-Upaniṣad.[7]

Mystical speculation is not limited to the aśvamedha, agnicayana, and pravargya. All ritualist literature tries to attach special significance to whatever ritual is being discussed at the time.

The means for accomplishing this goal include equations of the ritual, or implements used in it, with phenomena of the "outside" world or with divine powers. A very interesting variant, appearing more commonly in the later brāhmaṇas, consists of defin-

---

[7] For a recent discussion of the pravargya ritual with references to earlier literature see Jan E. M. Houben, *The Pravargya Brāhmaṇa of the Taittirīya-Āraṇyaka*, Delhi, Motilal Banarsidass, 1991.

ing implements of the sacrifice as "male" or "female", based on their grammatical gender: feminine gender = female; non-feminine (i.e. masculine or neuter) = male.[8] Bringing together pairs of such "male" and "female" implements then is equated with bringing about a sexual union, whose "offspring" consists in increased power for the sacrifice and the sacrificer. (See e.g. the selections in XX:B.) In their attempts to correlate grammatical and natural gender, these accounts reflect an increasing technical concern with language and grammar.

Concern with language, especially with ritually correct language, goes back to Ṛg-Vedic times. Selection XX:F contains one brief illustration. An interesting later testimony to this concern is found in a mythological story of the Śatapatha-Brāhmaṇa (M 3.2.1.23-4) in which the Asuras, the constant enemies of the Gods, are defeated because they say हे ऽळवो हे ऽळवः instead of the correct हे (अ)रयो हे (अ)रयः 'O enemies/strangers, O enemies/strangers'.

One aspect of ritual language use is given special prominence, at a rather early time, in the brāhmaṇas of the Sāma-Veda. This is the use of particles such as वा, हो, and ओम् / ॐ in the ritual. The use is especially common in Sāma-Vedic chant, where the particles function like "filler-syllables" to support a melody (roughly like *la-la-la* in modern English or *sa-re-ga* in Indian classical music); but some of the particles are also used in Ṛg-Vedic and Yajur-Vedic recitation. (See for instance Selection XX:C3, which also gives testimony to the degree to which developments in grammatical thought can be brought to bear on such discussions.)

Of these particles, ओम् / ॐ soon becomes the most important, no doubt because it is the one particle that is shared by all three modes of recitation in the ritual, those of the Ṛg-Vedic, Yajur-Vedic, and Sāma-Vedic priests. As such it was interpreted as containing within itself the three Vedas and the sacrifice. It could therefore acquire a significance comparable to that of the aśvamedha, agnicayana, and pravargya, as representing the essence of the entire ritual, even of the entire world. (See the selections in XIII and X:C.[9])

A deeper understanding of the sacrifice and its various components — mantras, implements, recitational particles — increasingly becomes a major focus, even the major focus, of the brāhmaṇas and upaniṣads. This focus receives linguistic expression in

---

8 See e.g. Rajeshwari Pandharipande: 'Metaphor as ritualistic symbol', *Anthropological Linguistics* 29: 3: 297-318, 1987.

9 See also Hans Henrich Hock, 'On the origin and early development of the sacred Sanskrit syllable *om*'. *Perspectives on Indo-European Language, Culture, and Religion: Studies in Honor of Edgar C. Polomé* 1:89-110 (*Journal of Indo-European Studies Monographs*, 7) 1991.

the commonly used formula य एवं वेद 'who knows/understands thus or in this way.' An एवंविद् may be said to be able to wipe out all imperfections through his knowledge, including mistakes in performing the sacrifice or morally reprehensible conduct. Some, in fact, argue that this knowledge makes the actual performance of the sacrifice unnecessary; mere understanding of the sacrifice and its significance is sufficient.

3. A Brief Characterization of the Early Upaniṣads and of the Major Issues Addressed in Them

3.1. The relationship of the upaniṣads to earlier Vedic literature. In so far as the upaniṣads address the question of the transcendental unity underlying the diversity of the phenomenal world, they simply present further developments of ideas found in the earlier ritualist literature and even in the Ṛg-Veda. In fact, some of their discussions (e.g. Selections I and II) are much more "ritualist" in character than some of the more "upaniṣadic" passages of the ritualist texts (such as Selection XX:J). Note in this regard that the entire tenth book of the Śatapatha-Brāhmaṇa (M), is traditionally referred to as the अग्निरहस्य 'the secret (doctrine) about Agni (or about the agnicayana)', while only the last two sections of the book (10:6:4-5) are considered part of the Bṛhad-Āraṇyaka-Upaniṣad.

Even physically, the early upaniṣads and the slightly earlier āraṇyakas grow out of the ritualist literature, in the sense that the indigenous tradition often classifies them as parts of the earlier texts. For instance, by one method of classification, the Bṛhad-Āraṇyaka-Upaniṣad is simply a part of the Śatapatha-Brāhmaṇa. The fuzzy distinction between brāhmaṇa, āraṇyaka, and upaniṣad is frequently reflected in the mixed nature of the titles, which combine terms such as brāhmaṇa and upaniṣad. For instance, the Mādhyandina recension of the Bṛhad-Āraṇyaka-Upaniṣad is also known as Mādhyandina-Brāhmaṇa-Upaniṣad; the Kāṇva recension of the same text has the alternative title Vājasaneyi-Brāhmaṇa-Upaniṣad; and the now most common name of the text, Bṛhad-Āraṇyaka-Upaniṣad, is itself composite.

In fact, in the Mādhyandina recension there seems to have been some difference of opinion as to whether the Bṛhad-Āraṇyaka-Upaniṣad includes both Śatapatha-Brāhmaṇa 10:6:4-5 (the conclusion of the agnicayana chapters) and Śatapatha-Brāhmaṇa 14:4-9 (the sections following the pravargya discussion), or only the latter.

At the same time, the indigenous tradition came to recognize some of the upaniṣadic texts as a separate body of literature. Thus, in the Mādhyandina version of the Śatapatha-Brāhmaṇa, the great medieval commentator Sāyaṇa did not comment on 10:6:4-5, stating that it belonged with the Bṛhad-Āraṇyaka-Upaniṣad in book 14. Moreover, if he did produce a commentary on the latter text, that seems to have been lost, probably because others, such as the great philosopher-commentator Śaṅkarācārya, had composed more highly regarded, upaniṣadic explications of the text.

3.2. The upaniṣads as a genre of their own. While late upaniṣads (e.g. Selection XX:K) and philosopher-commentators such as Śaṅkarācārya, Rāmānuja, and Madhvācārya provide unified accounts of the transcendental principle underlying the phenomenal world, the early upaniṣads present a stage of flux, in which different theories are juxtaposed and compete with each other, most of them already found in earlier Vedic literature. As a consequence, the transcendental principle is variously identified as the sacrificial horse, Brahman (neuter), ātman (a difficult term, which depending on context may also refer to 'body', or is used as a reflexive pronoun), the sacred syllable ओम्, and many others. In this regard, the early upaniṣads are quite similar to their ritualist predecessors.

They differ from their predecessors in the massiveness of speculation, with ever-decreasing attention being paid to specific aspects of the ritual. In fact, some upaniṣadic texts reject the ritualist path as being inferior to the path of knowledge; see e.g. Selections IV, XI, XV, XVI, and especially the later Muṇḍaka-Upaniṣad 1:1:4-5 and 1:2:7-11 (not included in this Reader). Compared to the earlier texts, we also find much more explicit statements that assert the identity between the individual and the ultimate principle; see especially Selections XII and XIX.

Moreover, the upaniṣads increasingly employ a more elaborate, argumentative rhetoric, growing out of the Ṛg-Vedic and ritualist brahmodya and disputation tradition, but going considerably beyond. In the process they insert elements characteristic of a more natural or colloquial form of language, and they may express great anger, or even humor. For instance, in his discussion with his wife Maitreyī (Selection VI), Yājñavalkya employs the particle अरे, generally reserved for addressing persons of slightly lower social standing. (Even in modern Northern India, a husband may easily say अरे to his wife, while her addressing him with that word would be considered inappropriate.) And in Selection VII we find the same Yājñavalkya quipping that he doesn't really care who is most learned, he just wants to have the cows that King Janaka set out as a prize for the best scholar.

3.3. The upaniṣads as a mirror of their society. The upaniṣads further differ from the earlier ritualist literature by presenting a socially less restrictive environment. In ritualist literature, kings and other members of the kṣatriya caste mainly function as the "sacrificers", the persons who commission the priests to conduct the sacrifice for them and, in return, are expected to richly reward the priests. Beyond that, we have occasional references to kings holding assemblies at which brahmins compete with each other in brahmodya discussions.

In the early upaniṣads, such assemblies are a much more pervasive phenomenon. Moreover, kings may actively participate in the discussions and even force brahmins to acknowledge their superiority in spiritual matters and, more remarkable yet, to turn to them for instruction (e.g. Selections V and XVII:A, B, and XVIII).

Women play an even more subordinate role in ritualist literature than kṣatriyas. But the Bṛhad-Āraṇyaka-Upaniṣad presents several passages in which women participate in philosophical discussions. And while in Selection V, Maitreyī is addressed by Yājñavalkya using the somewhat condescending particle अरे, in Selection IX, another woman, Vācaknavī Gārgī, challenges him in very bold language, and Yājñavalkya does not respond to her by using अरे. One reason for this different treatment may be that she is not his wife; but the fact that Yājñavalkya's other learned opponents assent to her questioning him suggests that she was recognized as a scholar in her own right. The fact that she eventually has to admit defeat by Yājñavalkya does not diminish her status. All of Yājñavalkya's learned opponents suffer this fate, or worse — and most of them are men.

3.4. The doctrine of karman and reincarnation — a kṣatriya revolution? What most distinguishes the early upaniṣads from the preceding ritualist literature is that three of them, the Bṛhad-Āraṇyaka-Upaniṣad, the Chāndogya-Upaniṣad, and the Kauṣītaki-(Brāhmaṇa-)Upaniṣad, for the first time provide explicit accounts of the doctrine of karman and reincarnation, a doctrine which underlies virtually all of later Indian religion and philosophy, whether "orthodox" (Hindu) or "hetorodox" (most notably Buddhist and Jain). The three passages usually considered relevant, two of which are closely related to each other, are presented in Selections XVII and XVIII.

According to two of the passages, the knowledge of this doctrine originally was limited to the kṣatriyas; and in all three of the passages the new doctrine is propounded by kings, to brahmins who have to admit that they do not know it. Moreover, as is well known, the founders of the heterodox traditions of the Buddhists and Jains were kṣatriyas.

This combination of facts has been taken by some scholars, especially in the late nineteenth century, to indicate that the doctrine originated in non-brahmin circles, may even have been "non-Aryan", and that its acceptance by the brahmins constituted a major revolution. This view is sometimes considered to be supported by the fact that at the end of his disputations at the court of King Janaka, the great brahmin-sage Yājñavalkya seems to state explicitly that there is no such thing as rebirth for human beings (see Selection X, paragraphs 33-34; but contrast sections 3.6 and 4 below, as well as the notes on X, paragraphs 33-34).

3.5. Ritualist precedents of the doctrine of karman and reincarnation? Other scholars do find precedents for the notion of karman and reincarnation in the ritualist literature.

Most relevant in this regard is the fact that late ritualist texts offer increasing references to पुनर्मृत्यु 're-death', which might suggest a counterpart of पुनर्जन्म 'rebirth'. However, though the latter term is widely used in later literature, it is curiously absent in ritualist texts and in the early upaniṣads. Moreover, the exact significance of पुनर्मृत्यु in the early texts is far from certain. This is largely because most passages in which the term is used are too brief to tell us anything helpful about the nature and implications of पुनर्मृत्यु. (This is true even for upaniṣadic passages that talk of पुनर्मृत्यु, such as Selection VIII.)

The few slightly longer passages turn out to be just as unhelpful. For instance, Śatapatha-Brāhmaṇa (M) 13:3:5:1 states that every world has its own death and that if the sacrificer does not sacrifice to all of these deaths, death will defeat him in every world that he may attain as a result of the sacrifice. This may appear to be an account of rebirth and re-death in different worlds, but given the ritualist context and the absence of further elaboration, a more likely interpretation is the following. The ritual is often assumed to help the sacrificer attain the world of heaven after death. Some passages suggest the existence of more than one such higher world; for instance, Śatapatha-Brāhmaṇa (M) 11:2:3:1-2 postulates higher worlds for certain deities, with a topmost world for Brahman, the transcendental principle. If the sacrificer fails to propitiate death, then he will again fall victim to death in these higher worlds and thus fail to attain his goal of immortality.

Similarly, the Jaiminīya-Brāhmaṇa tells two related stories (1:18 and 1:46) about a person's fate after death. In both stories, the deceased are met by a guardian who asks them a question. If they answer the question correctly they go to an immortal world; if not, they fall down and stay in an apparently intermediate world in which (re-)death eventually reaches them.

In both cases, re-death takes place in a higher world, not here on earth. Moreover, none of the ritualist texts informs us whether पुनर्मृत्यु in one of the higher worlds entails rebirth in this world. As one scholar remarked about the Jaiminīya-Brāhmaṇa passages, 'If ... a transmigration doctrine were to be assumed here, one might expect that the author ... would have expounded this quite new rebirth theory more clearly.'[10] This is in marked contrast to the upaniṣadic Selections XVII and XVIII which are very explicit on this matter.

---

10 Hendrik Wilhelm Bodewitz, *Jaiminīya-Brāhmaṇa I, 1-65: Translation and Commentary with a Study: Agnihotra and Prāṇāgnihotra*, Leiden: Brill, 1973.

The situation is similar as regards a passage in Bṛhad-Āraṇyaka-Upaniṣad (M) 3:2:14 (K 3:2:13). At the end of a disputation, Ārtabhāga asks Yājñavalkya to tell him what happens to human beings when they die and when their physical body is dissolved into the elements. Yājñavalkya responds, saying, 'Take my hand, we two shall know this alone.' The passage concludes: 'They talked about karman, and they praised karman. One becomes meritorious by meritorious karman, bad by bad karman.' Some scholars believe that this passage deals with the "karman" that determines reincarnation. If this in fact should be the case, then we would here have a brahmin propounding the karman doctrine (see also 3.6 and 4 below). Unfortunately, the passage is exceedingly cryptic, and the term कर्मन् can be interpreted in several different ways — as simple 'action, deed', as ritual action (which is the claim of Tull's publication, referred to in footnote 5 above), or as the karman of the doctrine of reincarnation. Most important, however, there is nothing in this passage that informs us how — or even whether — those who become bad by bad karman are reincarnated.

There are difficulties, too, in trying to find precedents for the doctrine of the cycle of reincarnations in earlier "cyclical" theories. One theory of this type goes back to the Ṛg-Veda, which offers the following verse in a "brahmodya" hymn, suggesting something like a "rain cycle".

> समानमेतदुदकमुच्चैत्यव चाहभिः ।
> भूमिं पर्जन्या जिन्वन्ति दिवं जिन्वन्त्यग्नयः (RV 1:164:51)
> This same water rises up and goes down with the (passage of) days;
> The rain Gods quicken the earth, the fires quicken the heaven (through the oblations that they carry to the Gods and/or through their smoke which turns into clouds).

A more elaborate cyclical theory is proposed in a relatively late ritualist passage of the Śatapatha-Brāhmaṇa (M 11:6:2:6-10). The two libations offered in the agnihotra ritual rise to the air and satiate it; from the air they rise to the sky and satiate it; from there they return to earth, satiate it, and rise up from it; they enter man, satiate him, and rise up from him; they enter woman, satiate her, and from her arises a son who is the लोकः प्रत्युत्थायी 'the world (that is) rising again'. While this secret doctrine, too, is told by a kṣatriya, King Janaka, to a brahmin, Yājñavalkya, it does not clearly propound a new theory of reincarnation, but seems to merely provide a cyclic foundation for the old belief that reincarnation lies in one's propagation through offspring. (But see also §3.6.)

There is thus no conclusive evidence that the doctrine of karman and reincarnation was known to the pre-upaniṣadic ritualist tradition. The selections in XVII and XVIII seem to be the first explicit and unambiguous statements of this doctrine. And as noted, in two of these texts the doctrine is said to have previously been the exclusive property of the kṣatriyas.

The view, however, that the doctrine of karman and reincarnation originated among kṣatriyas and was unknown to brahmins runs into the difficulty that the doctrine is also espoused by Yājñavalkya, brahmiṣṭha ('most brahmin') of the brahmins, in one early upaniṣadic text, Bṛhad-Āraṇyaka-Upaniṣad (K,M) 3-4 — quite explicitly toward the end of this entire "Yājñavalkya Cycle" (BAU 4:3-4), for which see section 4 below, and arguably also in the passage given in Selection X, paragraphs 33 and 34 (see the notes on this selection).

There is, however, good reason to believe that the concluding passage of the Yājñavalkya Cycle (BAU 4:3-4) is quite late and presents the culmination of a long period of development in the thinking of Yājñavalkya — or perhaps rather, of the school of thought that he represents.

First, the passage contrasts with the "kṣatriya" passages of BAU (M) 6:1, ChU 5:3-10, and KU 1 along several parameters. The kṣatriya versions are fairly simple, presenting the doctrine as something novel, and giving a rather rudimentary outline of the relationship between karman and reincarnation. The "Yājñavalkya" text presents a much more elaborate discussion and ends in an excellent example of what may be called a śāstric argument: Two "pūrvapakṣin" theories on karman and reincarnation are implicitly refuted by a final "siddhāntin" argument that release from rebirth only comes through realizing the identity of the self with the transcendental principle.[11] Moreover, in citing a large number of earlier ślokas that deal with the doctrine, the "Yājñavalkya" passage suggests that when this text was composed the doctrine of karman and reincarnation had been current for a considerable time.

Even more significant, the "Yājñavalkya Cycle" exhibits all the characteristics of a deliberate and quite elaborate composition (see section 4 below). By contrast, the "kṣatriya" versions of the Bṛhad-Āraṇyaka-Upaniṣad, Chāndogya-Upaniṣad, and especially the Kauṣītaki-Upaniṣad are very simple in their rhetorical organization.

It is thus likely that the "kṣatriya" episodes are earlier versions of the doctrine of karman and reincarnation and that the "Yājñavalkya Cycle" version represents a later elaboration.

---

11 The term *pūrvapakṣin* refers to those holding earlier positions in an argument, which need to be refuted, and *siddhāntin* designates one who proposes the final, correct position. According to the first pūrvapakṣin view in our text, good vs. bad karman determines the nature of reincarnation; the second pūrvapakṣin position is similar to that of Buddhism and the Bhagavad-Gītā — attachment vs. non-attachment to karman correlates with reincarnation vs. release from reincarnation.

Further support for the view that the doctrine did indeed originate among the kṣatriyas may be based on the following reasoning.

3.6. A reappraisal of the role of kṣatriyas and ritualist brahmins. Although kṣatriyas (and women) are permitted to play a greater role in the upaniṣads than in earlier ritualist literature, and although kṣatriyas may occasionally defeat brahmins in debate, our texts and the society they reflect are heavily dominated by brahmins who tend to consider themselves the sole legitimate authorities on spiritual matters. Even some kṣatriyas concede the brahmins' claim of superiority, in so far as they do not want to accept brahmins' requests to become their students, since that would require the brahmins to show deference to them. (See e.g. Selection V.)

The brahmins' attitude of superiority is also reflected in the use of the deprecatory term राजन्यबन्धु 'second-rate kṣatriya' in Selection XVII, to refer to the king who eventually discloses the doctrine of karman and reincarnation. Similarly, in §5 of Śatapatha-Brāhmaṇa (M 11:6:2), mentioned in the preceding section, most of the brahmins avoid a disputation with King Janaka after the following, quite telling, verbal exchange:

> The other brahmins said, 'This राजन्यबन्धु has outtalked us. Come let us challenge him to a disputation.' Yājñavalkya replied, 'We are brahmins, he is a राजन्यबन्धु. If we were to defeat him, what would we win? But if he should defeat us, then they would say that we were defeated by a राजन्यबन्धु. Do not (even) think of this.' (11:6:2:5)

Interestingly, Yājñavalkya then secretly goes back to Janaka in order to learn from him. And to resolve any remaining social problems, Janaka is said to have become a brahmin after that.

The fact that in such a brahmin-dominated context the new and explicitly stated theory of karman and reincarnation is repeatedly acknowledged as coming from kṣatriyas, then, is something quite remarkable, if not extraordinary, and would seem to preclude the explanation proposed by some scholars that attributing the doctrine to kṣatriyas merely served the purpose of flattering royal patrons. (If royal patrons were indeed supposed to be flattered, the use of the deprecatory term राजन्यबन्धु seems hardly apt to serve the purpose.) In this regard it may be significant that the kṣatriya version of the doctrine in the Bṛhad-Āraṇyaka-Upaniṣad seems to occur in a position of the text that frequently accommodates khilas, i.e. secondarily added, originally non-canonical material, a fact which suggests that the passage was only secondarily accepted in the brahmin-dominated tradition.

It may therefore well be true that this particular doctrine did originate in kṣatriya circles. And it is completely certain that it was promulgated in a context of intensive interaction between kṣatriyas and brahmins. From this, however, it does not follow that it was an exclusive invention of the kṣatriyas or that it originated in "non-Aryan" circles.

In fact, it can be argued that the details of the new doctrine of karman and reincarnation are not as revolutionary as often assumed. The notion of reincarnation has precedents in the earlier ideas of "cyclicity" and पुनर्मृत्यु; and the notion karman may be precedented by the wide-spread ritualist use of the term karman (for which see the publication by Tull referred to in footnote 5).

What is novel — and in a sense, revolutionary — is the manner in which these earlier strands of thought have been reinterpreted and integrated into a coherent doctrine, a doctrine which moreover, unlike the ritualist tradition, provided an explanation for social inequality and human misery (which are said to be the result of karman accumulated in earlier incarnations), and a possible release which, in principle, is open to everyone — the path of proper knowledge.

The relatedness and indebtedness of the early upaniṣadic texts on karman and reincarnation to the earlier ritualist tradition goes beyond similarities in ideas and thought. In their frame story and major themes, the three passages presented in Selections XVII and XVIII bear strong resemblances to Jaiminīya-Brāhmaṇa 1:45-46, continued in 1:49-50, a passage from which comes one of the two Jaiminīya-Brāhmaṇa stories briefly summarized in §3.5 above.

Selection XVIII shares with this passage the idea of a heavenly guardian or gate keeper whose question must be properly answered by a deceased person to become immortal; if it is not properly answered, then the deceased descends from the heavenly world and is subject to पुनर्मृत्यु. The main difference is that in the Jaiminīya-Brāhmaṇa the descent is to an intermediate world, and पुनर्मृत्यु merely prevents the deceased from reaching immortality, while in the Kauṣītaki-Upaniṣad the descent is explicitly stated to be to this earth, to be born again, with the precise kind of incarnation being determined by karman and knowledge.

The two closely related selections in XVII share with the Jaiminīya-Brāhmaṇa passage the fact that they start out with the "cyclic" पञ्चाग्निविद्या, the 'doctrine of five fires', which postulates a descent of human beings from the world of heaven, through the world of rain, to the earth, from there to man, and from man to woman. What completes the cycle is a sixth fire, that of cremation which through its smoke transports human beings back toward heaven (for a precedent of this idea see the Ṛg-Vedic passage cited in §3.5). While the Jaiminīya-Brāhmaṇa version is content with letting a heavenly guardian or doorkeeper decide whether the deceased will reach immortality or not, the selections in XVII establish a dual — or actually triple — path, one leading to immortality, the other(s) to eventual reincarnation on this earth, with the precise kind of incarnation, again, determined by knowledge and/or karman.

What makes things even more complex — and interesting — is that the prototype of the पञ्चाग्निविद्या, which truly deserves the name because it talks only about **five** fires, is the Śatapatha-Brāhmaṇa passage (11:2:6-10) referred to in §3.5 and again early in this section. Here, too, the doctrine is proclaimed by a kṣatriya (Janaka) to a brahmin (Yājñavalkya). It appears, then, as if there is a cyclic tradition behind the cyclic doctrine of the पञ्चाग्निविद्या — from the kṣatriya-dominated Śatapatha-Brāhmaṇa version, via the brahmin-dominated Jaiminīya-Brāhmaṇa version, to the kṣatriya-dominated versions in the Bṛhad-Āraṇyaka-Upaniṣad and Chāndogya-Upaniṣad — with each layer of the tradition making its own additions and contributions.

Whatever its origin, however, the explicit statement of the doctrine is what most clearly distinguishes the upaniṣads from earlier Vedic literature and justifies considering them a separate tradition.[12] And, as noted earlier, the doctrine forms the foundation of all later Indian religion and philosophy.

3.7. The nature of the transcendental principle. Most of the early upaniṣads focus on "impersonal" transcendental principles, often expressed in neuter gender (especially in the form of ब्रह्मन्) or characterized as being beyond our senses and experience; see e.g. Selections IX, and XII. Note especially Selection X, the culmination of Yājñavalkya's disputations at the court of King Janaka, where Yājñavalkya uses the entirely negative expression नेति नेति 'not, not' to characterize the transcendental principle as being totally different from anything that we can experience, or express in words.

By contrast, the Kauṣītaki-Upaniṣad (Selection XVIII) and the Kāṇva recension of the Bṛhad-Āraṇyaka-Upaniṣad (Selection XIX) implicitly or explicitly identify a per-

---

12 Recent discussions, presenting rather different views and approaches, can be found in Hendrik Wilhelm Bodewitz's *Jaiminīya-Brāhmaṇa I, 1-65: Translation and Commentary with a Study: Agnihotra and Prāṇāgnihotra*, Leiden: Brill, 1973; Erhardt Hanefeld's *Philosophische Haupttexte der älteren Upaniṣaden* (Harrassowitz, Wiesbaden, 1976); Herman W. Tull's *The Vedic Origins of Karma* (State University of New York Press, 1989; see also footnote 5 above); and A. L. Basham's *The Origins and Development of Classical Hinduism*, edited and annotated by K. G. Zysk (Beacon Press, 1989); see also Wendy Doniger O'Flaherty (ed.), *Karma and Rebirth in Classical Indian Traditions* (Motilal Banarsidass, Delhi, 1983). Bodewitz's, Hanefeld's, and Tull's monographs also contain ample references to earlier literature. In addition to these books and monographs, note the following recent articles. H. W. Bodewitz, 'The Pañcāgnividyā and the Pitṛyāna/Devayāna,' *Studies in Indology: Professor Mukunda Madhava Felicitation Volume*, ed. by Goswami and Chutia, pp. 51-57, Delhi: Satguru Publications, 1996; L. Schmithausen, 'Zur Textgeschichte der Pañcāgnividyā,' *Wiener Zeitschrift für die Kunde Südasiens* 38: 43-60, 1994; Renate Söhnen, 'Die Einleitungsgeschichte der Belehrung des Uddālaka Āruṇi: Ein Vergleich der drei Fassungen KauṣU 1.1, ChU 5.3 und BṛU 6.2.1-8,' *Studien zur Indologie und Iranistik* 7: 177-213, 1981; and Patrick Olivelle, 'Young Śvetaketu: A literary study of an upaniṣadic story,' *Journal of the American Oriental Society* 119: 46-70, 1999.

sonal God as the ultimate principle and proclaim the transcendental identity of the individual with that principle.[13] This is a theme that becomes more dominant in the later upaniṣads and in the Bhagavad-Gītā, where devotion to a personal God is offered as one of the roads toward release from the cycle of reincarnations.

From a historical perspective, passages identifying the ultimate principle as ओम् / ॐ (see the selections in XIII) may likewise be important. The transcendental significance assigned to a "mere particle" has striking counterparts in the Tantric tradition (beginning to be clearly attested by the middle of the first millennium AD), where ओम् / ॐ and similar bīja-mantras serve as one of several means to direct one's attention to the underlying identity between oneself and the ultimate principle.

4. The "Yājñavalkya-Cycle" as a literary composition

As already noted, the "Yājñavalkya Cycle" exhibits all the characteristics of a deliberate and quite elaborate composition. This section presents a closer look at the structure of the composition.[14] The core of the Cycle consists of two parts. In the first one (BAU 3), Yājñavalkya engages in open disputations with various other scholars assembled at the court of King Janaka. In each case, he defeats his opponent, see e.g. selections VII - IX. This part concludes with a dramatic episode (Selection X) in which the head of Yājñavalkya's last opponent, Vidagdha Śākalya, flies apart. While there are references to पुनर्मृत्यु and possibly an acknowledgment of the concept of karman and reincarnation, they are oblique or ambiguous at best; see §3.5 above and the notes on Selections VIII and X.

The second part of the cycle (BAU 4:1-4) consists of discussions between Yājñavalkya and King Janaka. Since these discussions are one-on-one, without the presence of other scholars, the ideas presented in this section can be considered to be more esoteric and also to more accurately reflect the final views of Yājñavalkya (or perhaps rather of his school). This part ends with the śāstric argument mentioned in §3.5 above, in which Yājñavalkya clearly accepts the concept of karman and reincarnation, refutes earlier views on the release from the cycle of reincarnations, and adopts a strict advaita, i.e. monistic or non-dualist, theory of release through realization of the self's identity with the ultimate principle.

---

13 These passages, too, appear to be related to the Jaiminīya-Brāhmaṇa passage that seems to have been the source for the upaniṣadic texts dealing with karman and reincarnation.

14 See Hans Henrich Hock, 'The Yājñavalkya Cycle in the Bṛhad Āraṇyaka Upaniṣad', *Stanley Insler Festschrift* (*Journal of the American Oriental Society* 122: 2: 278-286, 2002). A detailed discussion of part of this cycle (BAU 3) is presented by Joel P. Brereton, 'Why is a sleeping dog like the Vedic Sacrifice?' *Beyond the Texts: New Approaches to Vedic Studies*, ed. by Michael Witzel, pp. 1-14 (Harvard Oriental Series, Opera Minora, 2) 1997.

That these two sections form a larger cycle is shown by the fact that they are framed by the famous Maitreyī-episode (BAU 2:4, Selection VI), which precedes the cycle,[15] and a more elaborate retelling of the same episode, which forms the finale (BAU 4:5). This (near-)repetition of episodes at the beginning and end of a larger composition is a characteristic of many early Indo-European, and especially Indo-Iranian texts and has come to be known as "ring composition".[16]

The episode in BAU 2:1 (Selection V), narrating a dispute between King Ajātaśatru and a brahmin named (Dṛpta) Bālāki Gārgya, together with its extensions in BAU 2:2-3, seems to form a prelude to the entire Cycle, which may have been added later. This episode introduces a number of concepts that recur in the Yājñavalkya Cycle, including the idea of Sleep/Dream and Deep Sleep as approximations to realizing the identity between the self and the transcendental principle. This idea plays a significant role in the concluding śāstric argument of the Cycle. Consider further the important advaita refrain नेति नेति introduced at BAU 2:3:11, a refrain which, as noted in §3.7 above, characterizes the ultimate principle in purely negative terms, and which recurs in the conclusions of both major core parts (BAU 3:9 and BAU 4:4[17]), as well as in the finale, the expanded Maitreyī-episode in BAU 4:5.[18] The equation of King Ajātaśatru with King Janaka in the first paragraph of BAU 2:1 establishes an additional thematic link with the King Janaka of the two core parts of the Yājñavalkya Cycle. Finally, note the recurrence of the concept हिता नाम नाड्यः 'the arteries named *hitā*' in the Ajātaśatru episode (BAU 2:1:19), and in BAU (K) 4:2:4, toward the end of the Cycle.

The overall structure of the Yājñavalkya Cycle, then, is as follows:

1. Prelude: The Ajātaśatru and (Dṛpta) Bālāki Gārgya episode and extensions (BAU 2:1-3). Introduction of the concepts Sleep/Deep Sleep and नेति नेति
2. Introduction: Maitreyī-episode I and extensions (BAU 2:4-6)
3. Core, Part I: Open disputations of Yājñavalkya with different scholars at King Janaka's court (BAU 3). Dramatic conclusion, which includes नेति नेति

15 Between the Maitreyī-episode and the first part of the cycle are found two paragraphs (BAU 2:5-6), which may function as something like an extension of the Maitreyī-episode or as an interlude.

16 For the concept of ring composition see Calvert Watkins, 'Aspects of Indo-European poetics', *The Indo-Europeans in the Fourth and Third Millennia,* ed. by E. C. Polomé, pp. 109-111. Ann Arbor: Karoma, 1982. See also Michael Witzel, 'On the origin of the literary device of the "frame story" in Old Indian literature', *Hinduismus und Buddhismus: Festschrift für Ulrich Schneider*, ed. by H. Falk, 380-414, Freiburg, 1987.

17 The latter only in the Kāṇva version.

18 Again, only in the Kāṇva version.

4. Core, Part II: More esoteric discussions of Yājñavalkya with King Janaka alone (BAU 4:1-4). Overt acknowledgment of the doctrine of karman and reincarnation. Advaita conclusion, including नेति नेति.
5. Finale: Maitreyī-episode II (BAU 4:5), more elaborate, and more clearly advaita than the first version, including नेति नेति.

5. A Note on the Affiliation of the Text Selections with the "Branches" of Vedic Literature

The majority of the passages in Selections I - XIX come from the Bṛhad-Āraṇyaka-Upaniṣad (Mādhyandina recension) and from the Chāndogya-Upaniṣad, the two most voluminous and interesting texts among the early upaniṣads which, moreover, offer the first explicit statements of the doctrine of karman and reincarnation. Additional selections are taken from other Vedic texts, as well as from one post-Vedic upaniṣad.

What follows is a brief outline of the "branches" and historical development of Vedic literature which may help the beginning reader to place the selected passages in their historical context. A tabular summary is presented toward the end of this section.

Early Vedic texts recognize three major "branches" of the Veda, each affiliated with a different aspect of the ritual and with the priests performing that part of the ritual. These three branches and their ritual affiliations are as follows:

The Ṛg-Veda, the tradition of the Hotṛ, the 'libator' or 'invoker' priest, and his assistants who perform the śastra and other types of recitation;

The Sāma-Veda, the tradition of the Udgātṛ, the 'chanter', and his assistants who perform stotras and other types of chant;

The Yajur-Veda, the tradition of the Adhvaryu, the 'pathmaker' (or 'ritualist' ?), and his assistants who recite yajuses and other formulas, respond to the other priests, and perform other duties in the ritual.

These three branches are often referred to as the त्रयी विद्या, the 'threefold knowledge or Veda'. By late Vedic times a fourth branch of the Veda is beginning to be recognized:

The Atharva-Veda, originally a priestly tradition connected with simpler, more domestic rituals, with charms and incantations, but also with a fair amount of mystical speculation (a trait shared with the other three traditions). According to the very late text of the Gopatha-Brāhmaṇa, the Atharva-Vedic priest performs the role of the "brahman", the priest who oversees the ritual;

but earlier Vedic texts suggest that this office was not specifically relegated to any branch of the Veda.

Each of these major branches has sub-branches. For instance, in the Yajur-Veda we have a major division between the "Black" and "White" Yajur-Veda traditions. The Black Yajur-Veda has several further sub-branches; the two drawn on in this Reader are the Maitrāyaṇī- and Taittirīya-branches. The texts of the White or Vājasaneyi-tradition come in two "recensions", the Mādhyandina and Kāṇva ones. The Sāma-Vedic tradition has two major sub-branches, the Jaiminīya and the Kauthuma-Rāṇāyanīya ones. And so on.

In principle, each branch has its own saṁhitā and brāhmaṇa, plus an āraṇyaka and/or upaniṣad, as well as other ancillary texts, such as the Śrauta- and Gṛhya-Sūtras which present summaries of the grand and domestic rituals respectively. To judge by the names of the sages to whom the Sūtras are traditionally ascribed, these texts are roughly contemporary with the late Vedic texts of brahmodya disputations.

The saṁhitās of the Ṛg- and Sāma-Veda consist entirely of mantras or verses. The Atharva-Veda mainly contains mantras; but there are a few prose passages. The saṁhitās of the Black Yajur-Veda consist both of mantras, yajuses, and other formulas, and of prose texts explaining the performance and significance of the sacrifice. In the younger tradition of the White Yajur-Veda, the two different types of text have been taken apart, so that the saṁhitā contains only mantras, yajuses, and other formulas, while the explanatory prose texts are relegated to the Śatapatha-Brāhmaṇa. In this respect, the White Yajur-Veda follows the example of the Ṛg-, Sāma-, and Atharva-Vedas which likewise relegate the explanation of the ritual to their brāhmaṇas.

Among the different Vedic texts, the Ṛg-Veda saṁhitā is the oldest, but other saṁhitās contain mantras of equal (or nearly equal) age, and conversely, some of the Ṛg-Vedic hymns are quite late. Disregarding such complications, which result from the fact that all of the texts were composed over extended periods of time, the approximate chronological relation of the texts to each other can be presented as in the diagram below, focusing on those texts which have been drawn on as sources for selections in this Reader. The diagram is followed by a key to the abbreviations. Those which are marked by a bullet (•) will be employed in the remainder of this Reader.

Approximate Chronology of Vedic Literature

Tradition:	Ṛg-Vedic	Atharva-Vedic	Sāma-Vedic	Yajur-Vedic
Sub-branches			Kau.-Rā. Jai.	Black White
Saṁhitās (Early Vedic; ca. 2000-1000 BC)	RV	AV	(SV)	MS, TS VS (M), VS (K)
Brāhmaṇas (ca. 1000-700 BC)	AB		JB	(TB) ŚB (M), ŚB (K)
Āraṇyakas and Early Upaniṣads Sūtras (ca. 700-500 BC)	KU ĀŚS, ĀGS		ChU JUB	TA/TU BAU (M), BAU (K)
Post-Vedic Upaniṣads				Su.U

Abbreviations

•AB	Aitareya-Brāhmaṇa
ĀGS	Āśvalāyana Gṛhya-Sūtra
•ĀŚS	Āśvalāyana Śrauta-Sūtra
•AV	Atharva-Veda
•BAU (K)	Bṛhad-Āraṇyaka-Upaniṣad (Kāṇva recension)
•BAU (M)	Bṛhad-Āraṇyaka-Upaniṣad (Mādhyandina recension)
•ChU	Chāndogya-Upaniṣad
Jai.	Jaiminiya
•JB	Jaiminiya-Brāhmaṇa
•JUB	Jaiminiya-Upaniṣad-Brāhmaṇa
Kau.-Rā.	Kauthuma-Rāṇāyaniya
•KU	Kauṣītaki-(Brāhmaṇa-)Upaniṣad
•MS	Maitrāyaṇī-Saṁhitā
•RV	Ṛg-Veda
•ŚB (K)	Śatapatha-Brāhmaṇa (Mādhyandina recension)
•ŚB (M	Śatapatha-Brāhmaṇa (Mādhyandina recension)
Su.U	Subāla-Upaniṣad
SV	Sāma-Veda
•TA	Taittiriya-Āraṇyaka
TB	Taittiriya-Brāhmaṇa
•TS	Taittiriya-Saṁhitā
•TU	Taittiriya-Upaniṣad
•VS (K)	Vājasaneyi-Saṁhitā (Kāṇva recension)
•VS (M)	Vājasaneyi-Saṁhitā (Mādhyandina recension)

The Texts*

For typographical reasons, variant readings and other textual comments are presented at the end of each selection.

I: The mystical significance of the sacrificial horse (BAU (M) 1:1)

Fully “Vedic” version with Śatapatha-Brāhmaṇa accentuation, Vedic sandhi, and sandhi across sentences; followed by a more usual “upaniṣadic” version of the text without accentuation, with classical sandhi, and with sentence separation.

उषा वा ऽअश्वस्य मेध्यस्य शिरः । सूर्य्यश्चक्षुर्व्वातः प्राणो व्व्यात्तमग्निर्व्वैश्वानरः संव्वत्सर ऽआत्मा ऽश्वस्य मेध्यस्य द्यौष्पृष्ठमन्तरिक्षमुदरं पृथिवी पाजस्यं दिशः पार्श्वे ऽअवान्तरदिशः पर्शव ऽऋतवो ऽङ्गानि मासाश्चार्द्धमासाश्च पर्व्वाण्यहोरात्राणि प्रतिष्ठा नक्षत्राण्यस्थीनि नभो माꣳसान्यूवध्यꣳ सिकताः सिन्धवो गुदा यकृच्च क्लोमानश्च पर्व्वता ऽओषधयश्च व्वनस्पतयश्च लोमान्युद्यन्पूर्व्वार्द्धो निम्लोचञ्जघनार्द्धो यद्विजृम्भते तद्विद्योतते यद्विधूनुते तत्स्तनयति यन्मेहति तद्वर्षति व्वागेवास्य व्वागहर्व्वा ऽअश्वं पुरस्तान्महिमा ऽन्वजायत तस्य पूर्व्वे समुद्रे योनी रात्रिरेनं पश्चान्महिमा ऽन्वजायत तस्यापरे समुद्रे योनिरेतौ वा ऽअश्वं महिमानावभितः सम्बभूवतुर्हयो भूत्वा देवानवहद्वाजी गन्धर्व्वानर्व्वा ऽसुरानश्वो मनुष्यान्त्समुद्र ऽएवास्य बन्धुः समुद्रो योनिः ॥ १ ॥

उषा वा अश्वस्य मेध्यस्य शिरः ' सूर्यश्चक्षुः ' वातः प्राणः ' व्यात्तमग्निर्वैश्वानरः ' संवत्सर आत्माश्वस्य मेध्यस्य ' द्यौष्पृष्ठम् ' अन्तरिक्षमुदरम् ' पृथिवी पाजस्यम् ' दिशः पार्श्वे ' अवान्तरदिशः पर्शवः ' ऋतवो ऽङ्गानि ' मासाश्चार्धमासाश्च पर्वाणि ' अहोरात्राणि प्रतिष्ठा ' नक्षत्राण्यस्थीनि ' नभो मांसानि ' ऊवध्यं सिकताः ' सिन्धवो गुदाः ' यकृच्च क्लोमानश्च पर्वताः ' ओषधयश्च वनस्पतयश्च लोमानि ' उद्यन्पूर्वार्धः ' निम्लोचञ्जघनार्धः ' यद्विजृम्भते तद्विद्योतते ' यद्विधूनुते तत्स्तनयति ' यन्मेहति तद्वर्षति ' वागेवास्य वाक् ' अहर्वा अश्वं पुरस्तान्महिमान्वजायत ' तस्य पूर्वे समुद्रे योनिः ' रात्रिरेनं पश्चान्महिमान्वजायत ' तस्यापरे समुद्रे योनिः ' एतौ वा अश्वं महिमानावभितः संबभूवतुः ' हयो भूत्वा देवानवहत् ' वाजी गन्धर्वान् ' अर्वासुरान् ' अश्वो मनुष्यान् ' समुद्र एवास्य बन्धुः ' समुद्रो योनिः ॥ १ ॥

II: A creation myth associated with the agnicayana and aśvamedha (from BAU (M) 1:2)

नैवेह किं चनाग्र आसीत् ' मृत्युनैवेदमावृतमासीदशनायया ' अशनाया हि मृत्युः ' तन्मनो ऽकुरुत ' आत्मन्वी स्यामिति ' सो ऽर्चन्नचरत् ' तस्यार्चत आपो ऽजायन्त ' अर्चते वै मे कमभूदिति ' तदेवार्कस्यार्कत्वम्[1] ' कं ह वा अस्मै भवति य एवमेतदर्कस्यार्कत्वं[1] वेद ॥ १ ॥

आपो वा अर्कः ' तद्यदपां शर आसीत्तत्समहन्यत ' सा पृथिव्यभवत् ' तस्यामश्राम्यत् ' तस्य श्रान्तस्य तप्तस्य तेजो रसो निरवर्तताग्निः ॥ २ ॥

स त्रेधात्मानं व्यकुरुत ' आदित्यं तृतीयम् ' वायुं तृतीयम् ' स एष प्राणस्त्रेधा विहितः ' तस्य प्राची दिक् शिरः ' असौ चासौ चेर्मौ ' अथास्य प्रतीची दिक् पुच्छम् ' असौ चासौ च सक्थ्यौ ' दक्षिणा चोदीची च पार्श्वे ' द्यौष्पृष्ठम् ' अन्तरिक्षमुदरम् ' इयमुरः ' स एषो ऽप्सु प्रतिष्ठितः ' यत्र क्व चैति तदेव प्रतितिष्ठत्येवं विद्वान् ॥ ३ ॥

सो ऽकामयत ' द्वितीयो म आत्मा जायेतेति ' स मनसा वाचं मिथुनं समभवदशनाया[2] मृत्युः ' तद्यद्रेत आसीत्स संवत्सरो ऽभवत् ' न ह पुरा ततः संवत्सर आस ' तमेतावन्तं कालमबिभर्यावान्संवत्सरः ' तमेतावतः कालस्य परस्तादसृजत ' तं जातमभिव्याददात् ' स भाणकरोत् ' सैव वागभवत् ॥ ४ ॥

स ऐक्षत ' यदि वा इममभिमंस्ये कनीयो ऽन्नं करिष्य इति ' स तया वाचा तेनात्मनेदं सर्वमसृजत यदिदं किं च ' ऋचो यजूंषि सामानि च्छन्दांसि यज्ञान्प्रजां पशून् ' स यद्यदेवासृजत तत्तदत्तुमध्रियत ' सर्वं वा अत्तीति ' तददितेरदितित्वम् ' सर्वस्यात्ता भवति सर्वमस्यान्नं भवति य एवमेतददितेरदितित्वं वेद ॥ ५ ॥

सो ऽकामयत ' भूयसा यज्ञेन भूयो यजेयेति ' सो ऽश्राम्यत् ' स तपो ऽतप्यत ' तस्य श्रान्तस्य तप्तस्य यशो वीर्यमुदक्रामत् ' प्राणो वै यशो वीर्यम् ' तत्प्राणेषूत्क्रान्तेषु शरीरं श्वयितुमध्रियत ' तस्य शरीर एव मन आसीत् ॥ ६ ॥

सो ऽकामयत ' मेध्यं म इदं स्यात् ' आत्मन्व्यनेन स्यामिति ' ततो ऽश्वः समभवत् ' यदश्वत्तन्मेध्यमभूदिति ' तदेवाश्वमेधस्याश्वमेधत्वम् ' एष ह वा अश्वमेधं वेद य एनमेवं वेद ॥ ७ ॥

1 Most manuscripts have अर्क्यस्य; but the context requires अर्कस्य, and this is the form read by the commentary.

2 Weber's and Böhtlingk's editions have अशनायां; the present reading, found in the Gian Publishing House edition, is supported by the commentary.

III: ‘Lead me from untruth to truth …’ (from BAU (M) 1:3)

तस्य हैतस्य साम्नो यः प्रतिष्ठां वेद प्रति ह तिष्ठति ' तस्य वै वागेव प्रतिष्ठा ' वाचि हि खल्वेष एतत्प्राणः प्रतिष्ठितो गीयते ' अन्न इत्यु हैक आहुः ॥ २९ ॥

अथातः पवमानानामेवाभ्यारोहः ' स वै खलु प्रस्तोता साम प्रस्तौति ' स यत्र प्रस्तुयात्तदेतानि जपेत् '

असतो मा सद्गमय ' तमसो मा ज्योतिर्गमय ' मृत्योर्मामृतं गमय '

इति ॥ ३० ॥

स यदाह ' असतो मा सद्गमयेति ' मृत्युर्वा असत् ' सदमृतम् ' मृत्योर्मामृतं गमय ' अमृतं मा कुरु ' इत्येवैतदाह ॥ ३१ ॥

तमसो मा ज्योतिर्गमयेति ' मृत्युर्वै तमः ' ज्योतिरमृतम् ' मृत्योर्मामृतं गमय ' अमृतं मा कुरु ' इत्येवैतदाह ' मृत्योर्मामृतं गमयेति ' नात्र तिरोहितमिवास्ति ॥ ३२ ॥

अथ यानीतराणि स्तोत्राणि तेष्वात्मने ऽन्नाद्यमागायेत् ' तस्मादु तेषु वरं वृणीत यं कामं कामयेत तम् ' स एष एवंविदुद्गातात्मने वा यजमानाय वा यं कामं कामयते तमागायति ' तद्धैतल्लोकजिदेव ' न हैवालोक्यताया आशास्ति य एवमेतत्साम वेद ॥ ३३ ॥

IV: Another creation myth: The underlying oneness (BAU (M) 1:4)

आत्मैवेदमग्र आसीत् पुरुषविधः ' सो ऽनुवीक्ष्य नान्यदात्मनो ऽपश्यत् ' सो ऽहमस्मीत्यग्रे व्याहरत् ' ततो ऽहंनामाभवत् ' तस्मादप्येतर्ह्यामन्त्रितो ऽहमयमित्येवाग्र उक्त्वाथान्यन्नाम प्रब्रूते यदस्य भवति ॥ १ ॥

स यत्पूर्वो ऽस्मात्सर्वस्मात् सर्वान्पाप्मन औषत्तस्मात्पुरुषः ' ओषति ह वै स तं यो ऽस्मात्पूर्वो बुभूषति य एवं वेद ॥ २ ॥

सो ऽबिभेत् ' तस्मादेकाकी बिभेति ' स हायमीक्षां चक्रे ' यन्मदन्यन्नास्ति कस्मान्नु बिभेमीति ' तत एवास्य भयं वीयाय ' कस्माद्ध्यभेष्यत् ' द्वितीयाद्वै भयं भवति ॥ ३ ॥

स वै नैव रेमे ' तस्मादेकाकी न रमते ' स द्वितीयमैच्छत् ' स हैतावानास यथा स्त्रीपुमांसौ संपरिष्वक्तौ ॥ ४ ॥

स इममेवात्मानं द्वेधापातयत् ' ततः पतिश्च पत्नी चाभवताम् ' तस्मादिदमर्धबृगलमिव स्वः ' इति ह स्माह याज्ञवल्क्यः ' तस्मादयमाकाशः स्त्रिया पूर्यत एव ' तां समभवत् ' ततो मनुष्या अजायन्त ॥ ५ ॥

सो हेयमीक्षां चक्रे ' कथं नु मात्मन एव जनयित्वा संभवति ' हन्त तिरो ऽसानीति ॥ ६ ॥

सा गौरभवत् ' वृषभ इतरः ' तां समेवाभवत् ' ततो गावो ऽजायन्त ॥ ७ ॥

वडवेतराभवत् ' अश्ववृष इतरः ' गर्दभीतरा गर्दभ इतरः ' तां समेवाभवत् ' तत एकशफमजायत ॥ ८ ॥

अजेतराभवत् ' बस्त इतरः ' अविरितरा[1] मेष इतरः ' तां समेवाभवत् ' ततो ऽजावयो ऽजायन्त ' एवमेव यदिदं किं च मिथुनमा पिपीलिकाभ्यस्तत्सर्वमसृजत ॥ ९ ॥

सो ऽवेत् ' अहं वाव सृष्टिरस्मि ' अहं हीदं सर्वमसृक्षीति ' ततः सृष्टिरभवत् ' सृष्ट्यां हास्यैतस्यां भवति य एवं वेद ॥ १० ॥

अथेत्यभ्यमन्थत् ' स मुखाच्च योनेर्हस्ताभ्यां चाग्निमसृजत ' तस्मादेतदुभयमलोमकमन्तरतः ' अलोमका हि योनिरन्तरतः ॥ ११ ॥

तद्यदिदमाहुः ' अमुं यजामुं यजेत्येकैकं देवम् ' एतस्यैव सा विसृष्टिः ' एष उ ह्येव सर्वे देवाः ॥ १२ ॥

अथ यत्किं चेदमार्द्रं तद्रेतसो ऽसृजत ' तदु सोमः ' एतावद्वा इदं सर्वम् ' अन्नं चैवान्नादश्च ' सोम एवान्नमग्निरन्नादः ॥ १३ ॥

सैषा ब्रह्मणो ऽतिसृष्टिर्यच्छ्रेयसो देवानसृजत ' अथ यन्मर्त्यः सन्नमृतानसृजत तस्मादतिसृष्टिः ' अतिसृष्ट्यां हास्यैतस्यां भवति य एवं वेद ॥ १४ ॥

तद्धेदं तर्ह्यव्याकृतमासीत् ' तन्नामरूपाभ्यामेव व्याक्रियत ' असौनामायमिदंरूप इति ' तदिदमप्येतर्हि नामरूपाभ्यामेव व्याक्रियते ' असौनामायमिदंरूप इति ॥ १५ ॥

स एष इह प्रविष्ट आ नखाग्रेभ्यो यथा क्षुरः क्षुरधाने ऽवहितः स्याद्विश्वंभरो वा विश्वंभरकुलाये ' तं न पश्यति ' अकृत्स्नो हि सः ॥ १६ ॥

प्राणन्नेव प्राणो नाम भवति ' वदन्वाक् ' पश्यंश्चक्षुः ' शृण्वञ्छ्रोत्रम् ' मन्वानो मनः ' तान्यस्यैतानि कर्मनामान्येव ' स यो ऽत एकैकमुपास्ते न स वेद ' अकृत्स्नो ह्येषो ऽत एकैकेन भवति ॥ १७ ॥

आत्मेत्येवोपासीत ' अत्र ह्येते सर्वं एकं भवन्ति ' तदेतत्पदनीयमस्य सर्वस्य यदयमात्मा ' अनेन ह्येतत्सर्वं वेद यथा ह वै पदेनानुविन्देदेवम् ' कीर्तिं श्लोकं विन्दते य एवं वेद ॥ १८ ॥

तदेतत्प्रेयः पुत्रात् प्रेयो वित्तात् प्रेयो ऽन्यस्मात्सर्वस्मादन्तरतरं यदयमात्मा ' स यो ऽन्यमात्मनः प्रियं ब्रुवाणं ब्रूयात् प्रियं रोत्स्यतीतीश्वरो ह तथैव स्यात् ' आत्मानमेव प्रियमुपासीत ' स य आत्मानमेव प्रियमुपास्ते न हास्य प्रियं प्रमायुकं भवति ॥ १९ ॥

तदाहुः ' यद् ब्रह्मविद्यया सर्वं भविष्यन्तो मनुष्या मन्यन्ते किमु तद् ब्रह्मावेद् यस्मात्तत्सर्वमभवदिति ॥ २० ॥

ब्रह्म वा इदमग्र आसीत् ' तदात्मानमेवावेत् ' अहं ब्रह्मास्मीति ' तस्मात्तत्सर्वमभवत् ' तद्यो यो देवानां प्रत्यबुध्यत स एव तदभवत् तथर्षीणां तथा मनुष्याणाम् ॥ २१ ॥

तद्धैतत्पश्यन्नृषिर्वामदेवः प्रतिपेदे ' अहं मनुरभवं सूर्यश्चेति ' तदिदमप्येतर्हि य एवं वेदाहं ब्रह्मास्मीति स इदं सर्वं भवति ' तस्य ह न देवाश्चनाभूत्या ईशते ' आत्मा ह्येषां स भवति ' अथ यो ऽन्यां देवतामुपास्ते ऽन्यो ऽसावन्यो ऽहमस्मीति न स वेद ' यथा पशुरेवं स देवानाम् ' यथा ह वै बहवः पशवो मनुष्यं भुञ्ज्युरेवमेकैकः पुरुषो देवान्भुनक्ति ' एकस्मिन्नेव पशावादीयमाने ऽप्रियं भवति किमु बहुषु ' तस्मादेषां तन्न प्रियं यदेतन्मनुष्या विद्युः ॥ २२ ॥

ब्रह्म वा इदमग्र आसीदेकमेव ' तदेकं सन्न व्यभवत् ' तच्छ्रेयो रूपमत्यसृजत क्षत्रम् ' यान्येतानि देवत्रा क्षत्राणीन्द्रो वरुणः सोमो रुद्रः पर्जन्यो यमो मृत्युरीशान इति ' तस्मात्क्षत्रात्परं नास्ति ' तस्माद् ब्राह्मणः क्षत्रियमधस्तादुपास्ते राजसूये ' क्षत्र एव तद्यशो दधाति ' सैषा क्षत्रस्य योनिर्यद् ब्रह्म ' तस्माद्यद्यपि राजा परमतां गच्छति ब्रह्मैवान्तत उपनिश्रयति स्वां योनिम् ' य उ एनं हिनस्ति स्वां स योनिमृच्छति ' स पापीयान्भवति यथा श्रेयांसं हिंसित्वा ॥ २३ ॥

स नैव व्यभवत् ' स विशमसृजत ' यान्येतानि देवजातानि गणश आख्यायन्ते वसवो रुद्रा आदित्या विश्वे देवा मरुत इति ॥ २४ ॥

स नैव व्यभवत् ' स शौद्रं वर्णमसृजत पूषणम् ' इयं वै पूषा ' इयं हीदं सर्वं पुष्यति यदिदं किं च ॥ २५ ॥

स नैव व्यभवत् ' तच्छ्रेयो रूपमत्यसृजत धर्मम् ' तदेतत्क्षत्रस्य क्षत्रं यद्धर्मः ' तस्माद्धर्मात्परं नास्ति ' अथो अबलीयान्बलीयांसमाशंसते धर्मेण यथा राज्ञैवम् ' यो वै स धर्मः सत्यं वै तत् ' तस्मात्सत्यं वदन्तमाहुर्धर्मं वदतीति धर्मं वा वदन्तं सत्यं वदतीति ' एतद्ध्येवैतदुभयं भवति ॥ २६ ॥

तदेतद् ब्रह्म क्षत्रं विट् छूद्रः ' तदग्निनैव देवेषु ब्रह्माभवद् ब्राह्मणो मनुष्येषु ' क्षत्रियेण क्षत्रियः ' वैश्येन वैश्यः ' शूद्रेण शूद्रः ' तस्मादग्नावेव देवेषु लोकमिच्छन्ते ब्राह्मणे मनुष्येषु ' एताभ्यां हि रूपाभ्यां ब्रह्माभवत् ॥ २७ ॥

अथ यो ह वा अस्माल्लोकात्स्वं लोकमदृष्ट्वा प्रैति स एनमविदितो न भुनक्ति यथा वेदो वाननूक्तो ऽन्यद्वा कर्माकृतम् ' यदु ह वा अप्यनेवंविन्महत्पुण्यं कर्म करोति तद्धास्यान्ततः क्षीयत एव ' आत्मानमेव लोकमुपासीत ' स य आत्मानमेव लोकमुपास्ते न हास्य कर्म क्षीयते ' अस्माद्ध्येवात्मनो यद्यत्कामयते तत्तत्सृजते ॥ २८ ॥

अथो अयं वा आत्मा सर्वेषां भूतानां लोकः ' स यज्जुहोति यद्यजते तेन देवानां लोकः ' अथ यदनुब्रूते तेनर्षीणाम् ' अथ यत्प्रजामिच्छते यत्पितृभ्यो निपृणाति तेन पितृणाम् ' अथ यन्मनुष्यान्वासयते यदेभ्यो ऽशनं ददाति तेन मनुष्याणाम् ' अथ यत्पशुभ्यस्तृणोदकं विन्दति तेन पशूनाम् ' यदस्य गृहेषु श्वापदा वयांस्या पिपीलिकाभ्य उपजीवन्ति तेन तेषां लोकः ' यथा ह वै स्वाय लोकायारिष्टिमिच्छेदेवं हैवंविदे सर्वदा सर्वाणि भूतान्यरिष्टिमिच्छन्ति ' तद्वा एतद्विदितं मीमांसितम् ॥ २९ ॥

आत्मैवेदमग्र आसीदेक एव ' सो ऽकामयत जाया मे स्यादथ प्रजायेयाथ वित्तं मे स्यादथ कर्म कुर्वीयेति ' एतावान्वै कामः ' नेच्छंश्चनातो भूयो विन्देत् ' तस्मादप्येतर्ह्येकाकी कामयते जाया मे स्यादथ प्रजायेयाथ वित्तं मे स्यादथ कर्म कुर्वीयेति ' स यावदप्येतेषामेकैकं न प्राप्नोत्यकृत्स्न एव तावन्मन्यते ' तस्यो कृत्स्नता ॥ ३० ॥

मन एवास्यात्मा ' वाग्जाया ' प्राणः प्रजा ' चक्षुर्मानुषं वित्तं चक्षुषा हि तद्विन्दति ' श्रोत्रं दैवं श्रोत्रेण हि तच्छृणोति ' आत्मैवास्य कर्मात्मना हि कर्म करोति ' स एष पाङ्क्तो यज्ञः ' पाङ्क्तः पशुः ' पाङ्क्तः पुरुषः ' पाङ्क्तमिदं सर्वं यदिदं किं च ' तदिदं सर्वमाप्नोति यदिदं किं च य एवं वेद ॥ ३१ ॥

1 Weber and Böhtlingk have इतरो = इतरा + conjunctive particle उ.

V: A brahmin turns to a kṣatriya as teacher, and the parable of the sleeping man (from BAU (M) 2:1)

दृप्तबालाकिर्हानूचानो गार्ग्य आस ' स होवाचाजातशत्रुं काश्यम् ' ब्रह्म ते ब्रवाणीति ' स होवाचाजातशत्रुः ' सहस्रमेतस्यां वाचि दद्मः ' जनको जनक इति वै जना धावन्तीति ॥ १ ॥

स होवाच गार्ग्यः ' य एवासावादित्ये पुरुष एतमेवाहं ब्रह्मोपास इति ' स होवाचाजातशत्रुः ' मा मैतस्मिन्संवदिष्ठाः ' अतिष्ठाः सर्वेषां भूतानां मूर्धा राजेति वा अहमेतमुपास इति ' स य एतमेवमुपास्ते ऽतिष्ठाः सर्वेषां भूतानां मूर्धा राजा भवति ॥ २ ॥

स होवाच गार्ग्यः ' य एवायमात्मनि[1] पुरुष एतमेवाहं ब्रह्मोपास इति ' स होवाचाजातशत्रुः ' मा मैतस्मिन्संवदिष्ठाः ' आत्मन्वीति वा अहमेतमुपास इति ' स य एतमेवमुपास्त आत्मन्वी ह भवति ' आत्मन्विनी हास्य प्रजा भवति ' स ह तूष्णीमास गार्ग्यः ॥ १३ ॥

स होवाचाजातशत्रुः ' एतावन्नू३ इति ' एतावद्धीति ' नैतावता विदितं भवतीति ' स होवाच गार्ग्यः ' उप त्वायानीति ॥ १४ ॥

स होवाचाजातशत्रुः ' प्रतिलोमं वै तद्यद् ब्राह्मणः क्षत्रियमुपेयाद् ब्रह्म मे वक्ष्यतीति ' व्येव त्वा ज्ञपयिष्यामीति ' तं पाणावादायोत्तस्थौ ' तौ ह पुरुषं सुप्तमाजग्मतुः ' तमेतैर्नामभिरामन्त्रयां चक्रे ' बृहन्पाण्डुरवासः सोम राजन्निति ' स नोत्तस्थौ ' तं पाणिनापेषं बोधयां चकार ' स होत्तस्थौ ॥ १५ ॥

स होवाचाजातशत्रुः ' यत्रैष एतत्सुप्तो ऽभूद्य एष विज्ञानमयः पुरुषः क्वैष तदाभूत् ' कुत एतदागादिति ' तदु ह न मेने गार्ग्यः ॥ १६ ॥

स होवाचाजातशत्रुः ' यत्रैष एतत् सुप्तो ऽभूद्य एष विज्ञानमयः पुरुषस् तदेषां प्राणानां विज्ञानेन विज्ञानमादाय य एषो ऽन्तर्हृदय आकाशस् तस्मिञ्छेते ॥ १७ ॥

तानि यदा गृह्णात्यथ हैतत्पुरुषः स्वपिति नाम ' तद् गृहीत एव प्राणो भवति ' गृहीता वाक् ' गृहीतं चक्षुः ' गृहीतं श्रोत्रम् ' गृहीतं मनः ॥ १८ ॥

स यत्रैतत्स्वप्न्यया चरति ते हास्य लोकाः ' तदुतेव महाराजो भवति ' उतेव महाब्राह्मणः ' उतेवोच्चावचं निगच्छति ॥ १९ ॥

स यथा महाराजो जानपदान्गृहीत्वा स्वे जनपदे यथाकामं परिवर्तेतैवमेवैष एतत्प्राणान्गृहीत्वा स्वे शरीरे यथाकामं परिवर्तते ॥ २० ॥

अथ यदा सुषुप्तो भवति ' यदा न कस्य चन वेद ' हिता नाम नाड्यो द्वासप्ततिः सहस्राणि हृदयात्पुरीततमभिप्रतिष्ठन्ते ' ताभिः प्रत्यवसृप्य पुरीतति शेते ॥ २१ ॥

स यथा कुमारो वा महाब्राह्मणो वातिघ्नीमानन्दस्य गत्वा शयीतैवमेवैष एतच्छेते ॥ २२ ॥

स यथोर्णवाभिस्तन्तुनोच्चरेत् ' यथाग्नेः क्षुद्रा विष्फुलिङ्गा व्युच्चरन्त्येवमेवास्मादात्मनः सर्वे प्राणाः सर्वे लोकाः सर्वे देवाः सर्वाणि भूतानि सर्व एत आत्मानो व्युच्चरन्ति ' तस्योपनिषत्सत्यस्य सत्यमिति ' प्राणा वै सत्यम् ' तेषामेष सत्यम् ॥ २३ ॥

1 Weber and Böhtlingk have यश्चायमात्मनि.

VI: Yājñavalkya and Maitreyi (BAU (M) 2:4)

मैत्रेयीति होवाच याज्ञवल्क्यः ' उद्यास्यन्वा अरे ऽहमस्मात्स्थानादस्मि ' हन्त ते ऽनया कात्यायन्यान्तं करवाणीति ॥ १ ॥

सा होवाच मैत्रेयी ' यन्म इयं भगोः सर्वा पृथिवी वित्तेन पूर्णा स्यात्कथं तेनामृता स्यामिति ' नेति होवाच याज्ञवल्क्यः ' यथैवोपकरणवतां जीवितं तथैव ते जीवितं स्यात् ' अमृतत्वस्य तु नाशास्ति वित्तेनेति ॥ २ ॥

सा होवाच मैत्रेयी ' येनाहं नामृता स्यां किमहं तेन कुर्याम् ' यदेव भगवान् वेद तदेव मे ब्रूहीति ॥ ३ ॥

स होवाच याज्ञवल्क्यः ' प्रिया बतारे नः सती प्रियं भाषसे ' एह्यास्स्व व्याख्यास्यामि ते ' व्याचक्षाणस्य तु मे निदिध्यासस्वेति ' ब्रवीतु भगवानिति ॥ ४ ॥

स होवाच याज्ञवल्क्यः ' न वा अरे पत्युः कामाय पतिः प्रियो भवति ' आत्मनस्तु कामाय पतिः प्रियो भवति ' न वा अरे जायायै कामाय जाया प्रिया भवति ' आत्मनस्तु कामाय जाया प्रिया भवति ' न वा अरे पुत्राणां कामाय पुत्राः प्रिया भवन्ति ' आत्मनस्तु कामाय पुत्राः प्रिया भवन्ति ' न वा अरे वित्तस्य कामाय वित्तं प्रियं भवति ' आत्मनस्तु कामाय वित्तं प्रियं भव-

ति ' न वा अरे ब्रह्मणः कामाय ब्रह्म प्रियं भवति ' आत्मनस्तु कामाय ब्रह्म प्रियं भवति ' न वा अरे क्षत्रस्य कामाय क्षत्रं प्रियं भवति ' आत्मनस्तु कामाय क्षत्रं प्रियं भवति ' न वा अरे लोकानां कामाय लोकाः प्रिया भवन्ति ' आत्मनस्तु कामाय लोकाः प्रिया भवन्ति ' न वा अरे देवानां कामाय देवाः प्रिया भवन्ति ' आत्मनस्तु कामाय देवाः प्रिया भवन्ति ' न वा अरे भूतानां कामाय भूतानि प्रियाणि भवन्ति ' आत्मनस्तु कामाय भूतानि प्रियाणि भवन्ति ' न वा अरे सर्वस्य कामाय सर्वं प्रियं भवति ' आत्मनस्तु कामाय सर्वं प्रियं भवति ' आत्मा वा अरे द्रष्टव्यः श्रोतव्यो मन्तव्यो निदिध्यासितव्यो मैत्रेयि ' आत्मनो वा अरे दर्शनेन श्रवणेन मत्या विज्ञानेनेदं सर्वं विदितम् ॥ ५ ॥

ब्रह्म तं परादाद्यो ऽन्यत्रात्मनो ब्रह्म वेद ' क्षत्रं तं परादाद्यो ऽन्यत्रात्मनः क्षत्रं वेद ' लोकास्तं परादुर्यो ऽन्यत्रात्मनो लोकान्वेद ' देवास्तं परादुर्यो ऽन्यत्रात्मनो देवान्वेद ' भूतानि तं परादुर्यो ऽन्यत्रात्मनो भूतानि वेद ' सर्वं तं परादाद्यो ऽन्यत्रात्मनः सर्वं वेद ' इदं ब्रह्मेदं क्षत्रमिमे लोका इमे देवा इमानि भूतानीदं सर्वं यदयमात्मा ॥ ६ ॥

स यथा दुन्दुभेर्हन्यमानस्य न बाह्याञ्छब्दाञ्छक्नुयाद् ग्रहणाय दुन्दुभेस्तु ग्रहणेन दुन्दुभ्याघातस्य वा शब्दो गृहीतः ॥ ७ ॥

स यथा वीणायै वाद्यमानायै न बाह्याञ्छब्दाञ्छक्नुयाद् ग्रहणाय वीणायै तु ग्रहणेन वीणावादस्य वा शब्दो गृहीतः ॥ ८ ॥

स यथा शङ्खस्य ध्मायमानस्य न बाह्याञ्छब्दाञ्छक्नुयाद् ग्रहणाय शङ्खस्य तु ग्रहणेन शङ्खध्मस्य वा शब्दो गृहीतः ॥ ९ ॥

स यथार्द्रैधाग्नेरभ्याहितस्य पृथग्धूमा विनिश्चरन्ति ' एवं वा अरे ऽस्य महतो भूतस्य निःश्वसितमेतद् यदृग्वेदो यजुर्वेदः सामवेदो ऽथर्वाङ्गिरस इतिहासः पुराणं विद्या उपनिषदः श्लोकाः सूत्राण्यनुव्याख्यानानि व्याख्यानानि ' अस्यैवैतानि सर्वाणि निःश्वसितानि ॥ १० ॥

स यथा सर्वासामपां समुद्र एकायनम् ' एवं सर्वेषां स्पर्शानां त्वगेकायनम् ' एवं सर्वेषां गन्धानां नासिके एकायनम् ' एवं सर्वेषां रसानां जिह्वैकायनम् ' एवं सर्वेषां रूपाणां चक्षुरेकायनम् ' एवं सर्वेषां शब्दानां श्रोत्रमेकायनम् ' एवं सर्वेषां संकल्पानां मन एकायनम् ' एवं सर्वेषां वेदानां हृदयमेकायनम् ' एवं

सर्वेषां कर्मणां हस्तावेकायनम् ' एवं सर्वेषामध्वनां पादावेकायनम् ' एवं सर्वेषामानन्दानामुपस्थ एकायनम् ' एवं सर्वेषां विसर्गाणां पायुरेकायनम् ' एवं सर्वासां विद्यानां वागेकायनम् ॥ ११ ॥

स यथा सैन्धवखिल्य उदके प्रास्त उदकमेवानुविलीयेत न हास्योद्ग्रहणायेव[1] स्याद्यतो यतस्त्वाददीत लवणमेवैवं वा अर इदं महद्भूतमनन्तमपारं विज्ञानघन एवैतेभ्यो भूतेभ्यः समुत्थाय तान्येवानुविनश्यति ' न प्रेत्य संज्ञास्तीत्यरे ब्रवीमि ' इति होवाच याज्ञवल्क्यः ॥ १२ ॥

सा होवाच मैत्रेयी ' अत्रैव मा भगवानमूमुहत् ' न प्रेत्य संज्ञास्तीति ॥ १३ ॥

स होवाच याज्ञवल्क्यः ' न वा अरे ऽहं मोहं ब्रवीमि ' अलं वा अर इदं विज्ञानाय ॥ १४ ॥

यत्र हि द्वैतमिव भवति तदितर इतरं पश्यति ' तदितर इतरं जिघ्रति ' तदितर इतरमभिवदति ' तदितर इतरं शृणोति ' तदितर इतरं मनुते ' तदितर इतरं विजानाति ॥ १५ ॥

यत्र त्वस्य सर्वमात्मैवाभूत् तत्केन कं पश्येत् ' तत्केन कं जिघ्रेत् ' तत्केन कमभिवदेत् ' तत्केन कं शृणुयात् ' तत्केन कं मन्वीत ' तत्केन कं विजानीयात् ' येनेदं सर्वं विजानाति तं केन विजानीयात् ' विज्ञातारमरे केन विजानीयादिति ॥ १६ ॥

1 Weber and Böhtlingk have नाहास्य-, with the particle अह rather than the ह of the Gian Publishing House edition. The latter reading is supported by the commentary.

VII: Yājñavalkya's disputations at the assembly of King Janaka, 1: The cows and the hotṛ Aśvala (BAU (M) 3:1)

जनको ह वैदेहो बहुदक्षिणेन यज्ञेनेजे ' तत्र ह कुरुपञ्चालानां ब्राह्मणा अभिसमेता बभूवुः ' तस्य ह जनकस्य वैदेहस्य विजिज्ञासा बभूव ' कः स्विदेषां ब्राह्मणानामनूचानतम इति ॥ १ ॥

स ह गवां सहस्रमवरुरोध ' दशदश पादा एकैकस्याः शृङ्गयोराबद्धा बभूवुः ' तान्होवाच ' ब्राह्मणा भगवन्तो यो वो ब्रह्मिष्ठः स एता गा उदजतामिति ' ते ह ब्राह्मणा न दधृषुः ॥ २ ॥

अथ याज्ञवल्क्यः स्वमेव ब्रह्मचारिणमुवाच ' एताः सौम्योदज सामश्रवा३ इति ' ता होदाचकार ' ते ह ब्राह्मणाश्चुक्रुधुः ' कथं नु नो ब्रह्मिष्ठो ब्रुवीतेति ॥ ३ ॥

अथ ह जनकस्य वैदेहस्य होताश्वलो बभूव ' स हैनं पप्रच्छ ' त्वं नु खलु नो याज्ञवल्क्य ब्रह्मिष्ठो ऽसी३ इति ' स होवाच ' नमो वयं ब्रह्मिष्ठाय कुर्मः ' गोकामा एव वयं स्म इति ' तं ह तत एव प्रष्टुं दध्रे होताश्वलः ॥ ४ ॥

याज्ञवल्क्येति होवाच ' यदिदं सर्वं मृत्युनाप्तं सर्वं मृत्युनाभिपन्नं केन यजमानो मृत्योराप्तिमतिमुच्यत इति ' होत्रर्त्विजाग्निना वाचा ' वाग्वै यज्ञस्य होता ' तद्येयं वाक्सो ऽयमग्निः ' स होता ' सा मुक्तिः ' सातिमुक्तिः ॥ ५ ॥

याज्ञवल्क्येति होवाच ' यदिदं सर्वमहोरात्राभ्यामाप्तं सर्वमहोरात्राभ्यामभिपन्नं केन यजमानो ऽहोरात्रयोराप्तिमतिमुच्यत इति ' अध्वर्युणर्त्विजा चक्षुषादित्येन ' चक्षुर्वै यज्ञस्याध्वर्युः ' तद्यदिदं चक्षुः सो ऽसावादित्यः ' सो ऽध्वर्युः ' सा मुक्तिः ' सातिमुक्तिः ॥ ६ ॥

याज्ञवल्क्येति होवाच ' यदिदं सर्वं पूर्वपक्षापरपक्षाभ्यामाप्तं सर्वं पूर्वपक्षापरपक्षाभ्यामभिपन्नं केन यजमानः पूर्वपक्षापरपक्षयोराप्तिमतिमुच्यत इति ' ब्रह्मणर्त्विजा मनसा चन्द्रेण ' मनो वै यज्ञस्य ब्रह्मा ' तद्यदिदं मनः सो ऽसौ चन्द्रः ' स ब्रह्मा ' सा मुक्तिः ' सातिमुक्तिः ॥ ७ ॥

याज्ञवल्क्येति होवाच ' यदिदमन्तरिक्षमनारम्बणमिवाथ केनाक्रमेण यजमानः स्वर्गं लोकमाक्रमत इति ' उद्गात्रर्त्विजा वायुना प्राणेन ' प्राणो वै यज्ञस्योद्गाता ' तद्यो ऽयं प्राणः स वायुः ' स उद्गाता ' सा मुक्तिः ' सातिमुक्तिः ' इत्यतिमोक्षाः ' अथ संपदः ॥ ८ ॥

याज्ञवल्क्येति होवाच ' कतिभिरयमद्यर्ग्भिर्होतास्मिन्यज्ञे करिष्यतीति ' तिसृभिरिति ' कतमास्तास्तिस्र इति ' पुरोनुवाक्या च याज्या च शस्यैव तृतीया ' किं ताभिर्जयतीति ' पृथिवीलोकमेव पुरोनुवाक्यया जयति ' अन्तरिक्षलोकं याज्यया ' द्यौर्लोकं शस्यया ॥ ९ ॥

याज्ञवल्क्येति होवाच ' कत्ययमद्याध्वर्युरस्मिन्यज्ञ आहुतीर्होष्यतीति ' तिस्र इति ' कतमास्तास्तिस्र इति ' या हुता उज्ज्वलन्ति ' या हुता अतिनेदन्ति ' या हुता अधिशेरते ' किं ताभिर्जयतीति ' या हुता उज्ज्वलन्ति देवलोकमेव ताभिर्जयति ' दीप्यत इव हि देवलोकः ' या हुता अतिनेदन्ति मनुष्यलोकमेव

ताभिर्जयति ' अतीव हि मनुष्यलोकः ' या हुता अधिशेरते पितृलोकमेव ताभिर्जयति ' अध इव हि पितृलोकः ॥ १० ॥

याज्ञवल्क्येति होवाच ' कतिभिरयमद्य ब्रह्मा यज्ञं दक्षिणतो देवताभिर्गोपायिष्यतीति ' एकयेति ' कतमा सैकेति ' मन एवेति ' अनन्तं वै मनः ' अनन्ता विश्वे देवाः ' अनन्तमेव स तेन लोकं जयति ॥ ११ ॥

याज्ञवल्क्येति होवाच ' कत्ययमद्योद्गातास्मिन्यज्ञे स्तोत्रियाः स्तोष्यतीति ' तिस्र इति ' कतमास्तास्तिस्र इति ' पुरोनुवाक्या च याज्या च शस्यैव तृतीया ' इत्यधिदेवतम्[1] ' अथाध्यात्मम् ' कतमास्ता या अध्यात्ममिति ' प्राण एव पुरोनुवाक्या ' अपानो याज्या ' व्यानः शस्या ' किं ताभिर्जयतीति ' यत्किंचेदं प्राणभृदिति ' ततो ह होताश्वल उपरराम ॥ १२ ॥

[1] Weber and the Gian Publishing House edition do not have the इति.

VIII: Yājñavalkya's disputations at the assembly of King Janaka, 2: Release from "re-death" (BAU (M) 3:3)

अथ हैनं भुज्युर्लाह्यायनिः पप्रच्छ ' याज्ञवल्क्येति होवाच मद्रेषु चरकाः पर्यव्रजाम ' ते पतञ्चलस्य काप्यस्य गृहानैम ' तस्यासीद्दुहिता गन्धर्वगृहीता ' तमपृच्छाम ' को ऽसीति ' सो ऽब्रवीत् ' सुधन्वाङ्गिरस इति ' तं यदा लोकानामन्तानपृच्छामाथैनमब्रूम ' क्व पारिक्षिता अभवन्क्व पारिक्षिता अभवन्निति ' तत्त्वा पृच्छामि याज्ञवल्क्य ' क्व पारिक्षिता अभवन्निति ॥ १ ॥

स होवाच ' उवाच वै स तत् ' अगच्छन्वै ते तत्र यत्राश्वमेधयाजिनो गच्छन्तीति ' क्व न्वश्वमेधयाजिनो गच्छन्तीति ' द्वात्रिंशतं वै देवरथाह्न्यान्ययं लोकः ' तं समन्तं लोकं द्विस्तावत्पृथिवी पर्यैति ' तां पृथिवीं द्विस्तावत्समुद्रः पर्यैति ' तद्यावती क्षुरस्य धारा यावद्वा मक्षिकायाः पत्रं तावानन्तरेणाकाशः ' तानिन्द्रः सुपर्णो भूत्वा वायवे प्रायच्छत् ' तान्वायुरात्मनि धित्वा तत्रागमयत्र पारिक्षिता अभवन्निति ' एवमिव वै स वायुमेव प्रशशंस ' तस्माद्वायुरेव व्यष्टिः ' वायुः समष्टिः ' अप पुनर्मृत्युं जयति सर्वमायुरेति य एवं वेद ' ततो ह भुज्युर्लाह्यायनिरुपरराम ॥ २ ॥

IX: Yājñavalkya's disputations at the assembly of King Janaka, 3: Vācaknavī Gārgī challenges Yājñavalkya (BAU (M) 3:8)

अथ ह वाचक्नव्युवाच ' ब्राह्मणा भगवन्तो हन्ताहमिमं याज्ञवल्क्यं द्वौ प्रश्नौ प्रक्ष्यामि ' तौ चेन्मे विवक्ष्यति न वै जातु युष्माकमिमं कश्चिद् ब्रह्मोद्यं जेतेति ' तौ चेन्मे न विवक्ष्यति मूर्धास्य विपतिष्यतीति ' पृच्छ गार्गीति ॥ १ ॥

सा होवाच ' अहं वै त्वा याज्ञवल्क्य यथा काश्यो वा वैदेहो वोग्रपुत्र उद्यं[1] धनुरधिज्यं कृत्वा द्वौ बाणवन्तौ सपत्नातिव्याधिनौ[2] हस्ते कृत्वोपोत्तिष्ठेद् एवमेवाहं त्वा द्वाभ्यां प्रश्नाभ्यामुपोदस्थाम् ' तौ मे ब्रूहीति ' पृच्छ गार्गीति ॥ २ ॥

सा होवाच ' यदूर्ध्वं याज्ञवल्क्य दिवो यदवाक्पृथिव्या यदन्तरा द्यावापृथिवी इमे यद् भूतं च भवच्च भविष्यच्चेत्याचक्षते कस्मिंस्तदोतं च प्रोतं चेति ॥ ३ ॥

स होवाच ' यदूर्ध्वं गार्गि दिवो यदवाक्पृथिव्या यदन्तरा द्यावापृथिवी इमे यद्भूतं च भवच्च भविष्यच्चेत्याचक्षत आकाशे तदोतं च प्रोतं चेति ॥ ४ ॥

सा होवाच ' नमस्ते याज्ञवल्क्य यो म एतं व्यवोचः ' अपरस्मै धारयस्वेति ' पृच्छ गार्गीति ॥ ५ ॥

सा होवाच ' यदूर्ध्वं याज्ञवल्क्य दिवो यदवाक्पृथिव्या यदन्तरा द्यावापृथिवी इमे यद्भूतं च भवच्च भविष्यच्चेत्याचक्षते कस्मिन्नेव तदोतं च प्रोतं चेति ॥ ६ ॥

स होवाच ' यदूर्ध्वं गार्गि दिवो यदवाक्पृथिव्या यदन्तरा द्यावापृथिवी इमे यद्भूतं च भवच्च भविष्यच्चेत्याचक्षत आकाश एव तदोतं च प्रोतं चेति ' कस्मिन्न्वाकाश ओतश्च प्रोतश्चेति ॥ ७ ॥

स होवाच ' एतद्वै तदक्षरं गार्गि ब्राह्मणा अभिवदन्त्यस्थूलमनण्वह्रस्वमदीर्घमलोहितमस्नेहमच्छायमतमो ऽवाय्वनाकाशमसङ्गमस्पर्शमगन्धमरसमचक्षुष्कमश्रोत्रमवागमनो ऽतेजस्कमप्राणममुखमनामागोत्रमजरममरमभयममृतमरजो ऽशब्दमविवृतमसंवृतमपूर्वमनपरमनन्तरमबाह्यम् ' न तदश्नोति कं चन ' न तदश्नोति कश्चन ॥ ८ ॥

एतस्य वा अक्षरस्य प्रशासने गार्गि द्यावापृथिवी विधृते तिष्ठतः ' एतस्य वा अक्षरस्य प्रशासने गार्गि सूर्यचन्द्रमसौ विधृतौ तिष्ठतः ' एतस्य वा अक्षरस्य प्रशासने गार्ग्यहोरात्राण्यर्धमासा मासा ऋतवः संवत्सरा विधृतास्तिष्ठन्ति ' एतस्य वा अक्षरस्य प्रशासने गार्गि प्राच्यो ऽन्या नद्यः स्यन्दन्ते श्वेतेभ्यः पर्वतेभ्यः ' प्रतीच्यो ऽन्या यां यां च दिशम् ' एतस्य वा अक्षरस्य प्रशासने गार्गि ददतं मनुष्याः प्रशंसन्ति यजमानं देवा दर्व्यं पितरो ऽन्वायत्ताः ॥ ९ ॥

यो वा एतदक्षरमविदित्वा गार्ग्यस्मिंल्लोके जुहोति ददाति तपस्यत्यपि बहूनि वर्षसहस्राण्यन्तवानेवास्य स लोको भवति ' यो वा एतदक्षरमविदित्वा गार्ग्यस्माल्लोकात्प्रैति स कृपणः ' अथ य एतदक्षरं गार्गि विदित्वास्माल्लोकात्प्रैति स ब्राह्मणः ॥ १० ॥

तद्वा एतदक्षरं गार्गि ' अदृष्टं द्रष्टृ ' अश्रुतं श्रोतृ ' अमतं मन्तृ ' अविज्ञातं विज्ञातृ ' नान्यदस्ति द्रष्टृ ' नान्यदस्ति श्रोतृ ' नान्यदस्ति मन्तृ ' नान्यदस्ति विज्ञातृ ' एतद्वै तदक्षरं गार्गि यस्मिन्नाकाश ओतश्च प्रोतश्चेति ॥ ११ ॥

सा होवाच ' ब्राह्मणा भगवन्तस्तदेव बहु मन्यध्वं यदस्मान्नमस्कारेण मुच्याध्वै ' न वै जातु युष्माकमिमं कश्चिद् ब्रह्मोद्यं जेतेति ' ततो ह वाचक्नव्युपरराम ॥ १२ ॥

1 Böhtlingk has the more transparent reading उज्ज्यं 'with the bowstring up'; but the reading उद्यं of Weber and of the Gian Publishing House edition is supported by the commentary.

2 Here, Weber differs from the other two editions and the commentary by having सपत्नाधि° व्याधिनौ.

X: Yājñavalkya's disputations at the assembly of King Janaka, 4: नेति नेति, and Vidagdha Śākalya's head flies apart (from BAU (M) 3:9)

अथ हैनं विदग्धः शाकल्यः पप्रच्छ ' कति देवा याज्ञवल्क्येति ' स हैतयैव निविदा प्रतिपेदे '

यावन्तो वैश्वदेवस्य निविद्युच्यन्ते '
त्रयश्च त्री च शता त्रयश्च त्री च सहस्रा

इति ' ओमिति होवाच ॥ १ ॥

कत्येव देवा याज्ञवल्क्येति ' त्रयस्त्रिंशदिति ' ओमिति होवाच कत्येव देवा याज्ञवल्क्येति ' षडिति ' ओमिति होवाच कत्येव देवा याज्ञवल्क्येति ' त्रय इति ' ओमिति होवाच कत्येव देवा याज्ञवल्क्येति ' द्वाविति ' ओमिति होवाच कत्येव देवा याज्ञवल्क्येति ' अध्यर्ध इति ' ओमिति होवाच कत्येव देवा याज्ञवल्क्येति ' एक इति ' ओमिति होवाच कतमे ते त्रयश्च त्री च शता त्रयश्च त्री च सहस्रेति ॥ २ ॥

स होवाच ' महिमान एवैषामेते ' त्रयस्त्रिंशत्त्वेव देवा इति ' कतमे ते त्रयस्त्रिंशदिति ' अष्टौ वसव एकादश रुद्रा द्वादशादित्यास्त एकत्रिंशत् ' इन्द्रश्चैव प्रजापतिश्च त्रयस्त्रिंशाविति ॥ ३ ॥

कतमे वसव इति ' अग्निश्च पृथिवी च वायुश्चान्तरिक्षं चादित्यश्च द्यौश्च चन्द्रमाश्च नक्षत्राणि चैते वसवः ' एतेषु हीदं सर्वं वसु हितम् ' एते हीदं सर्वं वासयन्ते ' तद्यदिदं सर्वं वासयन्ते तस्माद्वसव इति ॥ ४ ॥ ···

कतमे ते त्रयो देवा इति ' इम एव त्रयो लोकाः ' एषु हीमे सर्वे देवा इति ' कतमौ द्वौ देवाविति ' अन्नं चैव प्राणश्चेति ' कतमो ऽध्यर्ध इति ' यो ऽयं पवत इति ॥ ९ ॥

तदाहुः ' यदयमेक एव पवते ऽथ कथमध्यर्ध इति ' यदस्मिन्निदं सर्वमध्यार्ध्नोत्तेनाध्यर्ध इति ' कतम एको देव इति ' स ब्रह्म त्यदित्याचक्षते ॥ १० ॥

··· शाकल्येति होवाच याज्ञवल्क्यः ' त्वां स्विदिमे ब्राह्मणा अङ्गारावक्षयणमक्रता३ इति ॥ १९ ॥

याज्ञवल्क्येति होवाच शाकल्यः ' यदिदं कुरुपञ्चालानां ब्राह्मणानत्यवादीः किं ब्रह्म विद्वानिति ' दिशो वेद सदेवाः सप्रतिष्ठा इति ··· ॥ २० ॥

··· कस्मिन्नु हृदयं प्रतिष्ठितं भवतीति ॥ २५ ॥

अहल्लिकेति होवाच याज्ञवल्क्यः ' यत्रैतदन्यत्रास्मन्मन्यासै ' यत्रैतदन्यत्रास्मत् स्याच्छ्वानो वैनदद्युर्वयांसि वैनद्विमथ्नीरन्निति ॥ २६ ॥

कस्मिन्नु त्वं चात्मा च प्रतिष्ठितौ स्थ इति ' प्राण इति ' कस्मिन्नु प्राणः प्रतिष्ठित इति ' अपान इति ' कस्मिन्न्वपानः प्रतिष्ठित इति ' व्यान इति ' कस्मिन्नु व्यानः प्रतिष्ठित इति ' उदान इति ' कस्मिन्नूदानः प्रतिष्ठित इति ' समान इति ॥ २७ ॥

स एष नेति नेत्यात्मा ' अगृह्यो न हि गृह्यते ' अशीर्यो न हि शीर्यते ' असङ्गो ऽसितो न सज्यते न व्यथत इति ' एतान्यष्टावायतनान्यष्टौ लोका अष्टौ पुरुषाः ' स यस्तान्पुरुषान्व्युदुह्य प्रत्युह्यात्यक्रामीत् तं त्वौपनिषदं पुरुषं पृच्छामि ' तं चेन्मे न विवक्ष्यसि मूर्धा ते विपतिष्यतीति ' तं ह शाकल्यो न मेने ' तस्य ह मूर्धा विपपात ' तस्य हाप्यन्यन्मन्यमानाः परिमोषिणो ऽस्थीन्यपजह्रुः ॥ २८ ॥

अथ ह याज्ञवल्क्य उवाच ' ब्राह्मणा भगवन्तो यो वः कामयते स मा पृच्छतु ' सर्वे वा मा पृच्छत ' यो वः कामयते तं वः पृच्छानि ' सर्वान्वा वः पृच्छानीति ' ते ह ब्राह्मणा न दधृषुः ॥ २९ ॥

तान्हैतैः श्लोकैः पप्रच्छ ' … ॥ ३० ॥ …

यद् वृक्षो वृक्णो रोहति ' मूलान्नवतरः पुनः ।
मर्त्यः स्विन्मृत्युना वृक्णः कस्मान्मूलात्प्ररोहति ॥ ३३ ॥
रेतस इति मा वोचत ' जीवतस्तत्प्रजायते ।
जात एव न जायते को न्वेनं जनयेत्पुनः ॥
धानारुह उ वै वृक्षो ऽन्यतः प्रेत्य सम्भवः ।
यत्समूलमुद्वृहेयुर्वृक्षं न पुनराभवेत् ।
मर्त्यः स्विन्मृत्युना वृक्णः कस्मान्मूलात्प्ररोहति ॥

विज्ञानमानन्दं ब्रह्म रातेर्दातुः परायणम् ॥ तिष्ठमानस्य तद्विद इति ॥ ३४ ॥

XI: The beginning of Śvetaketu's instruction in the transcendental unity of everything (from ChU 6:1-2)

श्वेतकेतुर्हारुणेय आस ' तं ह पितोवच ' श्वेतकेतो वस ब्रह्मचर्यम् ' न वै सोम्यास्मत्कुलीनो [1] ऽननूच्य ब्रह्मबन्धुरिव भवतीति ॥ १/१ ॥

स ह द्वादशवर्ष उपेत्य चतुर्विंशतिवर्षः सर्वान्वेदानधीत्य महामना अनूचानमानी स्तब्ध एयाय ' तं ह पितोवाच ' श्वेतकेतो यन्नु सोम्येदं महामना अनूचानमानी स्तब्धो ऽस्युत तमादेशमप्राक्षीः [2] ॥ २ ॥

येनाश्रुतं श्रुतं भवति ' अमतं मतम् ' अविज्ञातं विज्ञातमिति ' कथं नु भगवः स आदेशो भवतीति ॥ ३ ॥

यथा सोम्यैकेन मृत्पिण्डेन सर्वं मृन्मयं विज्ञातं स्यात् ' वाचारम्भणं विकारो नामधेयम् ' मृत्तिकेत्येव सत्यम् ॥ ४ ॥

यथा सोम्यैकेन लोहमणिना सर्वं लोहमयं विज्ञातं स्यात् ' वाचारम्भणं विकारो नामधेयम् ' लोहमित्येव सत्यम् ॥ ५ ॥

यथा सोम्यैकेन नखनिकृन्तनेन सर्वं कार्ष्णायसं विज्ञातं स्यात् ' वाचारम्भणं विकारो नामधेयम् ' कार्ष्णायसमित्येव सत्यम् ' एवं सोम्य स आदेशो भवतीति ॥ ६ ॥

न वै नूनं भगवन्तस्त एतदवेदिषुः ' यद्ध्येतदवेदिष्यन्कथं मे नावक्ष्यन्निति भगवांस्त्वेव मे तद् ब्रवीत्विति ' तथा सोम्येति होवाच ॥ ७ ॥

सदेव सोम्येदमग्र आसीदेकमेवाद्वितीयम् ' तद्धैक आहुः ' असदेवेदमग्र आसीदेकमेवाद्वितीयम् ' तस्मादसतः सज्जायत ॥ २/१ ॥

कुतस्तु खलु सोम्यैवं स्यादिति होवाच कथमसतः सज्जायेतेति ' सत्त्वेव सोम्येदमग्र आसीदेकमेवाद्वितीयम् ॥ २ ॥

तदैक्षत ' बहु स्यां प्रजायेयेति ' तत्तेजो ऽसृजत ' तत्तेज ऐक्षत ' बहु स्यां प्रजायेयेति ' तदपो ऽसृजत ' तस्माद्यत्र क्व च शोचति स्वेदते वा पुरुषस्तेजस एव तदध्यापो जायन्ते ॥ ३ ॥

[1] The nagari editions tend to have the form सोम्य, the Bibliotheca Indica and Kumbakona editions vary between सोम्य and the more correct सौम्य, Radhakrishnan regularly has *saumya*.

[2] All consulted editions have the monstrous form अप्राक्ष्यः.

XII: The parables of the fig tree and of the salt, and तत्त्वमसि (ChU 6:12 and 13)

न्यग्रोधफलमत आहरेति ' इदं भगव इति ' भिन्द्धीति ' भिन्नं भगव इति ' किमत्र पश्यसीति ' अण्व्य इवेमा धाना भगव इति ' आसामङ्गैकां भिन्द्धीति ' भिन्ना भगव इति ' किमत्र पश्यसीति ' न किं चन भगव इति ॥ १२/१ ॥

तं होवाच ' यं वै सोम्यैतमणिमानं न निभालयस एतस्य वै सोम्यैषो ऽणिम्न एवं महान् न्यग्रोधस्तिष्ठति ' श्रद्धत्स्व सोम्य ॥ २ ॥

स य एषो ऽणिमैतदात्म्यमिदं सर्वम् ' तत्सत्यं स आत्मा ' तत्त्वमसि श्वेतकेतो इति ' भूय एव मा भगवान्विज्ञापयत्विति ' तथा सोम्येति होवाच ॥ ३ ॥

लवणमेतदुदके ऽवधायाथ मा प्रातरुपसीदथा इति ' स ह तथा चकार ' तं होवाच ' यद्दोषा लवणमुदके ऽवाधा अङ्ग तदाहरेति ' तद्धावमृश्य न विवेद ' यथा विलीनमेवम् ॥ १३/१ ॥

अङ्गास्यान्तादाचामेति ' कथमिति ' लवणमिति ' मध्यादाचामेति ' कथमिति ' लवणमिति ' अन्तादाचामेति ' कथमिति ' लवणमिति ' अभिप्रास्यैतदथ मोपसीदथा इति ' तद्ध तथा चकार ' तच्छश्वत्संवर्तते ' तं होवाच ' अत्र वाव किल सत्सोम्य न निभालयसे ' अत्रैव किलेति[1] ॥ २ ॥

स य एषो ऽणिमैतदात्म्यमिदं सर्वम् ' तत्सत्यं स आत्मा ' तत्त्वमसि श्वेतकेतो इति ' भूय एव मा भगवान्विज्ञापयत्विति ' तथा सोम्येति होवाच ॥ ३ ॥

[1] Radhakrishnan omits the इति.

XIII: The significance of ॐ (ChU 1:1 with parallels from the Jaiminiya-, Jaiminiya-Upaniṣad-, and Aitareya-Brāhmaṇas, and from the Taittiriya-Āraṇyaka)

1. Chāndogya-Upaniṣad 1:1

ओमित्येतदक्षरमुद्गीथमुपासीत ' ओमिति ह्युद्गायति ' तस्योपव्याख्यानम् ॥ १ ॥

एषां भूतानां पृथिवी रसः ' पृथिव्या आपो रसः ' अपामोषधयो रसः ' ओषधीनां पुरुषो रसः ' पुरुषस्य वाग्रसः ' वाच ऋग्रसः ' ऋचः साम रसः ' साम्न उद्गीथो रसः ॥ २ ॥

स एष रसानां रसतमः परमः परार्ध्यो ऽष्टमो यदुद्गीथः ॥ ३ ॥

कतमा कतमर्क् ' कतमत्कतमत् साम ' कतमः कतम उद्गीथ इति विमृष्टं भवति ॥ ४ ॥

वागेवर्क् ' प्राणः साम ' ओमित्येतदक्षरमुद्गीथः ' तद्वा एतन्मिथुनं यद्वाक्च प्राणश्च ' ऋक्च साम च ॥ ५ ॥

तदेतन्मिथुनमोमित्येतस्मिन्नक्षरे संसृज्यते ' यदा वै मिथुनौ समागच्छत आपयतो वै तावन्योन्यस्य कामम् ॥ ६ ॥

आपयिता ह वै कामानां भवति य एतदेवं विद्वानक्षरमुद्गीथमुपास्ते ॥ ७ ॥

तद्वा एतदनुज्ञाक्षरं ' यद्धि किं चानुजानात्योमित्येव तदाह ' एषो एव समृद्धिर्यदनुज्ञा ' समर्धयिता ह वै कामानां भवति य एतदेवं विद्वानक्षरमुद्गीथमुपास्ते ॥ ८ ॥

तेनेयं त्रयी विद्या वर्तते ' ओमित्याश्रावयति ' ओमिति शंसति ' ओमित्युद्गायति ' एतस्यैवाक्षरस्यापचित्यै महिम्ना रसेन ॥ ९ ॥

तेनोभौ कुरुतो यश्चैतदेवं वेद यश्च न वेद ' नाना तु विद्या चाविद्या च ' यदेव विद्यया करोति श्रद्धयोपनिषदा तदेव वीर्यवत्तरं भवति ' इति खल्वेतस्यैवाक्षरस्योपव्याख्यानं भवति ॥ १० ॥

2. Jaiminiya-Brāhmaṇa 3:321-322

प्रजापतिर्वाव इदमग्र आसीत् । सो ऽकामयत बहु स्यां प्रजायेय भूमानं गच्छेयमिति ··· अथ गायत्री प्रणवनवमासीत् ··· तामब्रवीत् ··· यत्त एतन्नवममक्षरं तदुदूहस्वेति ··· तथेति ' तदुदौहत् । स एव प्रणवो ऽभवत् ॥ ३२१ ॥ स प्रतिगरस्स उद्गीथस्तदाश्रावणम् । तस्मादोमिति प्रणौत्योमिति प्रत्यागृणात्योमित्युद्गायत्योमित्याश्रावयति ···॥ ३२२ ॥

3. Jaiminiya-Upaniṣad-Brāhmaṇa 1:1:1:1-5 and 3:4:5:6-7

प्रजापतिर्वा इदं त्रयेण वेदेनाजयत् । यदस्येदं जितं तत् (।) स ऐक्षत । इत्थं चेद् वा अन्ये देवा अनेन वेदेन यक्ष्यन्त । इमां वाव ते जितिं जेष्यन्ति येयं मम ॥ १/१/१/१ ॥

हन्तास्य त्रयस्य वेदस्य रसमाददा इति स भूरित्येव ऋग्वेदस्य रसमादत्त । सेयं पृथिव्यभवत् । तस्या[1] यो रसः प्राणेदत्सो ऽग्निरभवद्रसस्य रसः ॥ २ ॥

भुव इत्येव यजुर्वेदस्य रसमादत्त । तदिदमन्तरिक्षमभवत् । तस्य यो रसः प्राणेदत्स वायुरभवद्रसस्य रसः ॥ ३ ॥

स्वरित्येव सामवेदस्य रसमादत्त । सासौ द्यौरभवत् । तस्या[1] यो रसः प्राणेदत् स आदित्यो ऽभवद्रसस्य रसः ॥ ४ ॥

अथैकस्यैवाक्षरस्य रसं नाशक्नोदादातुम् । ओमित्येतस्यैव । सेयं वागभवत् । ओमेव नामैषा । तस्या उ प्राण एव रसः ॥ ५ ॥

एतद्ध वा अक्षरं त्रय्यै विद्यायै प्रतिष्ठा । ओमिति वै होता प्रतिष्ठितः । ओमित्यध्वर्युः । ओमित्युद्गाता ॥ ३/४/५/६ ॥

एतद्ध वा अक्षरं वेदानां त्रिविष्टपम् । एतस्मिन्वा अक्षर ऋत्विजो यजमानमाधाय स्वर्गे लोके समुदूहन्ति । तस्मादोमित्येवानुमन्त्रयेत ॥ ७ ॥

[1] The Tirupati edition and Rama Deva's edition (based on that of Oertel) incorrectly have तस्य.

4. Aitareya-Brāhmaṇa 5:31:1-2

प्रजापतिरकामयत प्रजायेय भूयान्स्यामिति स तपो ऽतप्यत स तपस्तप्त्वेमांल्लोकानसृजत पृथिवीमन्तरिक्षं दिवं तांल्लोकानभ्यतपत्तेभ्यो ऽभितप्तेभ्यस्त्रीणि ज्योतींष्यजायन्ताग्निरेव पृथिव्या अजायत वायुरन्तरिक्षादादित्यो दिवस्तानि ज्योतींष्यभ्यतपत्तेभ्यो ऽभितप्तेभ्यस्त्रयो वेदा अजायन्त ऋग्वेद एवाग्नेरजायत यजुर्वेदो वायोः सामवेद आदित्यात्तान्वेदानभ्यतपत्तेभ्यो ऽभितप्तेभ्यस्त्रीणि शुक्राण्यजायन्त भूरित्येव ऋग्वेदादजायत भुव इति यजुर्वेदात्स्वरिति सामवेदात् ॥ १ ॥

तानि शुक्राण्यभ्यतपत्तेभ्यो ऽभितप्तेभ्यस्त्रयो वर्णा अजायन्ताकार उकारो मकार इति तानेकधा समभरत्तदेतदो३मिति तस्मादोमोमिति प्रणौत्योमिति वै स्वर्गो लोक ओमित्यसौ यो ऽसौ तपति ॥ २ ॥

5. Taittirīya-Āraṇyaka 7:8:1 (Taittirīya-Upaniṣad 1:8:1)

ओमिति ब्रह्म । ओमितीदं सर्वम् । ओमित्येतदनुकृति ह स्म वा अप्योश्रावयेत्याश्रावयन्ति । ओमिति सामानि गायन्ति । ओं शोमिति शस्त्राणि शंसन्ति । ओमित्यध्वर्युः प्रतिगरं प्रतिगृणाति । ओमिति ब्रह्मा प्रसौति । ओमित्यग्निहोत्रमनुजानाति । ओमिति ब्राह्मणः प्रवक्ष्यन्नाह । ब्रह्मोपाप्नवानीति । ब्रह्मैवोपाप्नोति ॥ ७/८/१ ॥

XIV: Mystical passages (BAU (M) 5:1 and 5:2)

ॐ३ ' पूर्णमदः पूर्णमिदं पूर्णात्पूर्णमुदच्यते ।
पूर्णस्य पूर्णमादाय पूर्णमेवावशिष्यते ॥

ॐ३ खं ब्रह्म ' खं पुराणम् ' वायुरं खम् ' इति स्माह कौरव्यायणीपुत्रः ' वेदो ऽयम् ' ब्राह्मणा विदुः ' वेदैनेन यद्वेदितव्यम् ॥ १/१ ॥

त्रयाः प्राजापत्याः प्रजापतौ पितरि ब्रह्मचर्यमूषुर्देवा मनुष्या असुराः ॥२/१॥

उषित्वा ब्रह्मचर्यं देवा ऊचुः ' ब्रवीतु नो भवानिति ' तेभ्यो हैतदक्षरमुवाच द इति ' व्यज्ञासिष्टा३ इति ' व्यज्ञासिष्मेति होचुः ' दाम्यतेति न आत्थेति ' ओमिति होवाच व्यज्ञासिष्टेति ॥ २ ॥

अथ हैनं मनुष्या ऊचुः ' ब्रवीतु नो भवानिति ' तेभ्यो हैतदेवाक्षरमुवाच द इति ' व्यज्ञासिष्टा३ इति ' व्यज्ञासिष्मेति होचुः ' दत्तेति न आत्थेति ' ओमिति होवाच व्यज्ञासिष्टेति ॥ ३ ॥

अथ हैनमसुरा ऊचुः ' ब्रवीतु नो भवानिति ' तेभ्यो हैतदेवाक्षरमुवाच द इति ' व्यज्ञासिष्टा३ इति ' व्यज्ञासिष्मेति होचुः ' दयध्वमिति न आत्थेति ' ओमिति होवाच व्यज्ञासिष्टेति ' तदेतदेवैषा दैवी वागनुवदति स्तनयित्नुः ' दद द इति ' दाम्यत दत्त दयध्वमिति ' तदेतत्त्रयं शिक्षेत् ' दमं दानं दयामिति ॥ ४ ॥

XV: The significance of the Gāyatri, and mystical knowledge saves even the sinner (from BAU (M) 5:15)

भूमिरन्तरिक्षं द्यौरित्यष्टावक्षराणि ' अष्टाक्षरं ह वा एकं गायत्र्यै पदम् ' एतदु हास्या एतत् ' स यावदेषु लोकेषु तावद्ध जयति यो ऽस्या एतदेवं पदं वेद ॥ १ ॥

ऋचो यजूंषि सामानीत्यष्टावक्षराणि ' अष्टाक्षरं ह वा एकं गायत्र्यै पदम् ' एतदु हैवास्या एतत् ' स यावतीयं त्रयी विद्या तावद्ध जयति यो ऽस्या एतदेवं पदं वेद ॥ २ ॥

प्राणो ऽपानो व्यान इत्यष्टावक्षराणि ' अष्टाक्षरं ह वा एकं गायत्र्यै पदम् ' स यावदिदं प्राणि तावद्ध जयति यो ऽस्या एतदेवं पदं वेद ॥ ३ ॥

एतद्ध वै तज्जनको वैदेहो बुडिलमाश्वतराश्विमुवाच ' यन्नु हो तद्गायत्रीविदब्रूथा अथ कथं हस्ती भूतो वहसीति ' मुखं ह्यस्याः सम्राण्न विदां चकर ' इति होवाच ॥ ११ ॥

तस्या अग्निरेव मुखम् ' यदि ह वा अपि बह्विवाग्नावभ्यादधति सर्वमेव तत्संदहति ' एवं हैवैवंविद्यद्यपि बह्विव पापं करोति सर्वमेव तत्संप्साय शुद्धः पूतो ऽजरो ऽमृतः संभवति ॥ १२ ॥

XVI: The dogs' sacrifice: a satirical view of ritual (ChU 1:12)

अथातः शौव उद्गीथः ' तद्ध बको दाल्भ्यो ग्लावो वा मैत्रेयः स्वाध्यायमुद्वव्राज ॥१ ॥

तस्मै श्वा श्वेतः प्रादुर्बभूव ' तमन्ये श्वान उपसमेत्योचुः ' अन्नं नो भगवानागायतु ' अशनायाम वा इति ॥ २ ॥

तान्होवाच ' इहैव मा प्रातरुपसमीयातेति ' तद्ध बको दाल्भ्यो ग्लावो वा मैत्रेयः प्रतिपालयां चकार ॥ ३ ॥

ते ह यथैवेदं बहिष्पवमानेन स्तोष्यमाणाः संरब्धाः सर्पन्तीत्येवमाससृपुः ' ते ह समुपविश्य हिंचक्रुः ॥ ४ ॥

१ २१ २ १ १ २१ २१२१२० १ २
ओम्[1] अदामों पिबामों देवो वरुणः प्रजापतिः सवितान्नमिहाहरदन्नपते ऽन्नम्
१
इहाहराहरोमिति ॥ ५ ॥

[1] Here as elsewhere, Radhakrishnan has *aum* for ओम्, against all the other editions.

XVII: Reincarnation and karman, 1:
Two closely related passages from BAU (M) 6:1 and ChU 5:3-10

A: The Bṛhad-Āraṇyaka-Upaniṣad version

श्वेतकेतुर्ह वा आरुणेयः पञ्चालानां परिषदमाजगाम ' स आजगाम जैवलं प्रवाहणं परिचारयमाणम् ' तमुदीक्ष्याभ्युवाद ' कुमारा३ इति ' स भो३ इति प्रतिशुश्राव ' अनुशिष्टो न्वसि पित्रेति ' ओमिति होवाच ॥ १ ॥

वेत्थ यथेमाः प्रजाः प्रयत्यो विप्रतिपद्यान्ता३ इति ' नेति होवाच ' वेत्थ यथेमं लोकं पुनरापद्यान्ता३ इति ' नेति हैवोवाच ' वेत्थ यथासौ लोक एवं बहुभिः पुनःपुनः प्रयद्भिर्न संपूर्यता३ इति ' नेति हैवोवाच ॥ २ ॥

वेत्थ यतिथ्यामाहुत्यां हुतायामापः पुरुषवाचो भूत्वा समुत्थाय वदन्ती३ इति ' नेति हैवोवाच ' वेत्थो देवयानस्य वा पथः प्रतिपदं पितृयाणस्य वा यत्कृत्वा देवयानं वा पन्थानं प्रतिपद्यते पितृयाणं वा ॥ ३ ॥

अपि हि न ऋषेर्वचः श्रुतम् ।

द्वे सृती अशृणवं पितॄणामहं देवानामुत मर्त्यानाम् ।
ताभ्यामिदं विश्वमेजत्समेति यदन्तरा पितरं मातरं च ॥

इति ' नाहमत एकं चन वेदेति होवाच ॥ ४ ॥

अथ हैनं वसत्योपमन्त्रयां चक्रे ' अनादृत्य वसतिं कुमारः प्रदुद्राव ' स आजगाम पितरम् ' तं होवाच ' इति वाव किल नो भवान्पुरानुशिष्टानवोच इति ' कथं सुमेध इति ' पञ्च मा प्रश्नान्राजन्यबन्धुरप्राक्षीत्ततो नैकं चन वेदेति होवाच ' कतमे त इति ' इम इति ह प्रतीकान्युदाजहार ॥ ५ ॥

स होवाच ' तथा नस्त्वं तात जानीथा यथा यदहं किं च वेद सर्वमहं तत्तुभ्यमवोचम् ' प्रेहि तु तत्र प्रतीत्य ब्रह्मचर्यं वत्स्याव इति ' भवानेव गच्छत्विति ॥ ६ ॥

स आजगाम गौतमो यत्र प्रवाहणस्य जैवलेरास ' तस्मा आसनमाहार्योदकमाहारयां चकार ' अथ हास्मा अर्घं चकार ॥ ७ ॥

स होवाच ' वरं भवते गौतमाय दद्म इति ' स होवाच ' प्रतिज्ञातो म एष वरः ' यां तु कुमारस्यान्ते वाचमभाषथास्तां मे ब्रूहीति ॥ ८ ॥

स होवाच ' दैवेषु वै गौतम तद्वरेषु ' मानुषाणां ब्रूहीति ॥ ९ ॥

स होवाच ' विज्ञायते ह ' अस्ति हिरण्यस्यापात्तं गोअश्वानां दासीनां प्रवराणां परिधानानाम् ' मा नो भवान्बहोरनन्तस्यापर्यन्तस्याभ्यवदान्यो भूदिति ' स वै गौतम तीर्थेनेच्छासा इति ' उपैम्यहं भवन्तमिति वाचा ह स्मैव पूर्व उपयन्ति ॥ १० ॥

स होपायनकीर्ता उवाच ' तथा नस्त्वं गौतम मापराधास्तव च पितामहा यथेयं विद्येतः पूर्वं न कस्मिंश्चन ब्राह्मण उवास ' तां त्वहं तुभ्यं वक्ष्यामि ' को हि त्वैवं ब्रुवन्तमर्हति प्रत्याख्यातुमिति ॥ ११ ॥

असौ वै लोको ऽग्निर्गौतम ' तस्यादित्य एव समित् ' रश्मयो धूमः ' अहरर्चिः ' चन्द्रमा अङ्गाराः ' नक्षत्राणि विष्फुलिङ्गाः ' तस्मिन्नेतस्मिन्नग्नौ देवाः श्रद्धां जुह्वति ' तस्या आहुतेः सोमो राजा संभवति ॥ १२ ॥

पर्जन्यो वा अग्निर्गौतम ' तस्य संवत्सर एव समित् ' अभ्राणि धूमः ' विद्युदर्चिः ' अशनिरङ्गाराः ' ह्रादुनयो विष्फुलिङ्गाः ' तस्मिन्नेतस्मिन्नग्नौ देवा सोमं जुह्वति ' तस्या आहुतेर्वृष्टिः संभवति ॥ १३ ॥

अयं वै लोको ऽग्निर्गौतम ' तस्य पृथिव्येव समित् ' वायुर्धूमः ' रात्रिरर्चिः ' दिशो ऽङ्गाराः ' अवान्तरदिशो विष्फुलिङ्गाः ' तस्मिन्नेतस्मिन्नग्नौ देवा वृष्टिं जुह्वति ' तस्या आहुतेरन्नं संभवति ॥ १४ ॥

पुरुषो वा अग्निर्गौतम ' तस्य व्यात्तमेव समित् ' प्राणो धूमः ' वागर्चिः ' चक्षुरङ्गाराः ' श्रोत्रं विष्फुलिङ्गाः ' तस्मिन्नेतस्मिन्नग्नौ देवा अन्नं जुह्वति ' तस्या आहुते रेतः संभवति ॥ १५ ॥

योषा वा अग्निर्गौतम ' तस्या उपस्थ एव समित् ' लोमानि धूमः ' योनिरर्चिः ' यदन्तः करोति ते ऽङ्गाराः ' अभिनन्दा विष्फुलिङ्गाः ' तस्मिन्नेतस्मिन्नग्नौ देवा रेतो जुह्वति ' तस्या आहुतेः पुरुषः संभवति ' स जायते ' स जीवति यावज्जीवति ' अथ यदा म्रियते ऽथैनमग्नये हरन्ति ॥ १६ ॥

तस्याग्निरेवाग्निर्भवति ' समित्समित् ' धूमो धूमः ' अर्चिरर्चिः ' अङ्गारा अङ्गाराः ' विष्फुलिङ्गा विष्फुलिङ्गाः ' तस्मिन्नेतस्मिन्नग्नौ देवा पुरुषं जुह्वति ' तस्या आहुतेः पुरुषो भास्वरवर्णः संभवति ॥ १७ ॥

ते य एवमेतद्विदुर्ये चामी अरण्ये श्रद्धां सत्यमुपासते ते ऽर्चिरभिसंभवन्ति ' अर्चिषो ऽहः ' अह्न आपूर्यमाणपक्षम् ' आपूर्यमाणपक्षाद्यान्षण्मासानुदङ्ङादित्य एति ' मासेभ्यो देवलोकम् ' देवलोकादादित्यम् ' आदित्याद्वैद्युतम् ' तान्वैद्युतात्पुरुषो मानस एत्य ब्रह्मलोकान्गमयति ' ते तेषु ब्रह्मलोकेषु पराः परावतो वसन्ति ' तेषामिह न पुनरावृत्तिरस्ति ॥ १८ ॥

अथ ये यज्ञेन दानेन तपसा लोकं जयन्ति ते धूममभिसंभवन्ति ' धूमाद्रात्रिम् ' रात्रेरपक्षीयमाणपक्षम् ' अपक्षीयमाणपक्षाद्यान्षण्मासान्दक्षिणादित्य एति ' मासेभ्यः पितृलोकम् ' पितृलोकाच्चन्द्रम् ' ते चन्द्रं प्राप्यान्नं भवन्ति ' तांस्तत्र देवा यथा सोमं राजानम् ' आप्यायस्व ' अपक्षीयस्वेति ' एवमेनांस्तत्र भक्षयन्ति ' तेषां यदा तत्पर्यवैति ' अथेममेवाकाशमभिनिष्पद्यन्ते ' आकाशाद्वायुम् ' वायोर्वृष्टिम् ' वृष्टेः पृथिवीम् ' ते पृथिवीं प्राप्यान्नं भवन्ति ' त एवमेवानुपरिवर्तन्ते ' अथ य एतौ पन्थानौ न विदुस्ते कीटाः पतङ्गा यदिदं दन्दशूकम् ॥ १९ ॥

B: Selections from the Chāndogya-Upaniṣad version

श्वेतकेतुर्हारुणेयः पञ्चालानां समितिमेयाय ' तं ह प्रवाहणो जैवलिरुवाच ' कुमारानु त्वाशिषत्पितेति ' अनु हि भगव इति ॥ ३/१ ॥

वेत्थ यदितो ऽधि प्रजाः प्रयन्तीति ' न भगव इति ' वेत्थ यथा पुनरावर्तन्ता३ [1] इति ' न भगव इति ' वेत्थ पथोर्देवयानस्य पितृयाणस्य च व्यावर्तना३ इति ' न भगव इति ॥ २ ॥

वेत्थ यथासौ लोको न संपूर्यता३ इति ' न भगव इति ' वेत्थ यथा पञ्चम्यामाहुतावापः पुरुषवचसो भवन्तीति ' नैव भगव इति ॥ ३ ॥

अथानु [2] किमनुशिष्टो ऽवोचथाः ' यो हीमानि न विद्यात्कथं सो ऽनुशिष्टो ब्रुवीतेति ' स हायस्तः पितुरर्धमेयाय ' तं होवाच ' अननुशिष्य वाव किल मा भगवानब्रवीदनु त्वाशिषमिति ॥ ४ ॥

पञ्च मा राजन्यबन्धुः प्रश्नानप्राक्षीत् ' तेषां नैकं चनाशकं विवक्तुमिति ' स होवाच ' यथा मा त्वं तातैतानवदस्तथाहमेषां [3] नैकं चन वेद ' यद्यहमिमानवेदिष्यं कथं ते नावक्ष्यमिति ॥ ५ ॥

स ह गौतमो राज्ञो ऽर्धमेयाय ' तस्मै ह प्राप्तायार्हां चकार ' स ह प्रातः सभाग उदेयाय ' तं होवाच ' मानुषस्य भगवन्गौतम वित्तस्य वरं वृणीथा इति ' स होवाच ' तवैव राजन्मानुषं वित्तम् ' यामेव कुमारस्यान्ते वाचमभाषथास्तामेव मे ब्रूहीति ' स ह कृच्छ्रीबभूव ॥ ६ ॥

तं ह चिरं वसेत्याज्ञापयां चकार ' तं होवाच ' यथा मा त्वं गौतमावदो यथेयं न प्राक्त्वत्तः पुरा विद्या ब्राह्मणान्गच्छति तस्मादु सर्वेषु लोकेषु क्षत्रस्यैव प्रशासनमभूदिति ' तस्मै होवाच ॥ ७ ॥

असौ वाव लोको गौतमाग्निः ' तस्यादित्य एव समित् ' रश्मयो धूमः ' अहरर्चिः ' चन्द्रमा अङ्गाराः ' नक्षत्राणि विष्फुलिङ्गाः ॥ ४/१ ॥

तस्मिन्नेतस्मिन्नग्नौ देवाः श्रद्धां जुह्वति ' तस्या आहुतेः सोमो राजा संभवति ॥ २ ॥ ⋯

पुरुषो वाव गौतमाग्निः ' तस्य वागेव समित् ' प्राणो धूमः ' जिह्वार्चिः ' चक्षुरङ्गाराः ' श्रोत्रं विष्फुलिङ्गाः ॥ ७/१ ॥

तस्मिन्नेतस्मिन्नग्नौ देवा अन्नं जुह्वति ' तस्या आहुते रेतः संभवति ॥ २ ॥

योषा वाव गौतमाग्निः ' तस्या उपस्थ एव समित् ' यदुपमन्त्रयते स धूमः ' योनिरर्चिः ' यदन्तः करोति ते ऽङ्गाराः ' अभिनन्दा विष्फुलिङ्गाः ॥ ८/१ ॥

तस्मिन्नेतस्मिन्नग्नौ देवा रेतो जुह्वति ' तस्या आहुतेर्गर्भः संभवति ॥ २ ॥

इति तु पञ्चम्यामाहुतावापः पुरुषवचसो भवन्तीति ' स उल्बावृतो गर्भो दश वा नव वा मासानन्तः शयित्वा यावद्वाथ जायते ॥ ९/१ ॥

स जातो यावदायुषं जीवति ' तं प्रेतं दिष्टमितो ऽग्नय एव हरन्ति यत एवेतो यतः संभूतो भवति ॥ २ ॥

तद्य इत्थं विदुर्ये चेमे ऽरण्ये श्रद्धा तप इत्युपासते ते ऽर्चिषमभिसंभवन्ति ' अर्चिषो ऽहः ' अह्न आपूर्यमाणपक्षम् ' आपूर्यमाणपक्षाद्यान्षडुदङ्ङेति मासांस्तान् ॥ १०/१ ॥

मासेभ्यः संवत्सरम् ' संवत्सरादादित्यम् ' आदित्याच्चन्द्रमसम् ' चन्द्रमसो विद्युतम् ' तत् पुरुषो ऽमानवः ' स एनान्ब्रह्म गमयति ' एष देवयानः पन्था इति ॥ २ ॥

अथ य इमे ग्राम इष्टपूर्ते दत्तमित्युपासते ते धूममभिसंभवन्ति ' धूमाद्रात्रिम् ' रात्रेरपरपक्षम् ' अपरपक्षाद्यान्षड् दक्षिणैति मासांस्तान् ' नैते संवत्सरमभिप्राप्नुवन्ति ॥ ३ ॥

मासेभ्यः पितृलोकम् ' पितृलोकादाकाशम् ' आकाशाच्चन्द्रमसम् ' एष सोमो राजा ' तद्देवानामन्नम् ' तं देवा भक्षयन्ति ॥ ४ ॥

तस्मिन्यावत्संपातमुषित्वाथैतमेवाध्वानं पुनर्निवर्तन्ते यथेतमाकाशम् ' आकाशाद्वायुम् ' वायुर्भूत्वा धूमो भवति ' धूमो भूत्वाभ्रं भवति ॥ ५ ॥

अभ्रं भूत्वा मेघो भवति ' मेघो भूत्वा प्रवर्षति ' त इह व्रीहियवा ओषधिवनस्पतयस्तिलमाषा इति जायन्ते ' अतो वै खलु दुर्निष्प्रपतरम् ' यो यो ह्यन्नमत्ति यो रेतः सिञ्चति तद्भूय एव भवति ॥ ६ ॥

तद्य इह रमणीयचरणा अभ्याशो ह यत्ते रमणीयां योनिमापद्येरन् ' ब्राह्मणयोनिं वा क्षत्रिययोनिं वा वैश्ययोनिं वा ' अथ य इह कपूयचरणा अभ्याशो ह यत् ते कपुयां योनिमापद्येरन् ' श्वयोनिं वा सूकरयोनिं वा चण्डालयोनिं वा ॥ ७ ॥

अथैतयोः पथोर्न कतरेण चन तानीमानि क्षुद्राण्यसकृदावर्तीनि भूतानि भवन्ति ' जायस्व म्रियस्वेति ' एतत्तृतीयं स्थानम् ' तेनासौ लोको न संपूर्यते ' तस्माज्जुगुप्सेत ' तदेष श्लोकः ॥ ८ ॥

स्तेनो हिरण्यस्य सुरां पिबंश्च
गुरोस्तल्पमावसन्ब्रह्महा च ।
एते पतन्ति चत्वारः
पञ्चमश्चाचरंस्तैः ' इति ॥ ९ ॥

अथ ह य एतानेवं पञ्चाग्नीन्वेद न सह तैरप्याचरन्पाप्मना लिप्यते ' शुद्धः पूतः पुण्यलोको भवति य एवं वेद य एवं वेद ॥ १० ॥

[1] This is the (correct) reading in the Bibliotheca Indica edition. All other consulted editions have the incorrect पुनरावर्तन्त३.

[2] Bibliotheca Indica and Radhakrishnan: अथ नु.

[3] The consulted nagari editions all have तातैतानवदो यथाहमेषां; but Radhakrishnan's ··· तथा ··· makes better sense.

XVIII: Reincarnation and karman, 2: Selections from KU 1

चित्रो ह वै गाङ्ग्यायनिर्यक्ष्यमाण [1] आरुणिं वव्रे ' स ह पुत्रं श्वेतकेतुं प्रजिघाय याजयेति ' तं हाभ्यागतं [2] पप्रच्छ ' गौतमस्य पुत्रास्ति [3] संवृतं लोके यस्मिन् मा धास्यस्यन्यतमो [4] वाध्वा ' तस्य मा लोके धास्यसीति ' स होवाच ' नाहमेतद्वेद ' हन्ताचार्यं पृच्छानीति ' स ह पितरमासाद्य पप्रच्छ ' इतीति माप्राक्षीत् ' कथं प्रतिब्रवाणीति ' स होवाच ' अहमप्येतन्न वेद ' सदस्येव वयं स्वाध्यायमधीत्य हरामहे यन्नः परे ददति ' एह्युभौ गमिष्याव इति ' स ह समित्पाणिश्चित्रं गाङ्ग्यायनिं [1] प्रतिचक्रमे ' उपायानीति ' तं होवाच ' ब्रह्मग्राह्यसि [5] गौतम यो न मानमुपागाः ' एहि व्येव त्वा ज्ञपयिष्यामीति ॥ १ ॥

स होवाच ' ये वै के चास्माल्लोकात्प्रयन्ति चन्द्रमसमेव ते सर्वे गच्छन्ति ' तेषां प्राणैः पूर्वपक्ष आप्यायते ' तानपरपक्षेण [6] प्रजनयति ' एतद्वै स्वर्गस्य लोकस्य द्वारं यच्चन्द्रमाः [7] ' तं यः प्रत्याह तमतिसृजते ' अथ यो [8] न प्रत्याह तमिह वृष्टिर्भूत्वा वर्षति ' स इह कीटो वा पतङ्गो वा मत्स्यो वा शकुनिर्वा सिंहो वा वराहो वा परश्वान्वा शार्दूलो [9] वा पुरुषो वान्यो वा तेषु तेषु [10]

स्थानेषु प्रत्याजायते यथाकर्म यथाविद्यम् ' तमागतं पृच्छति को ऽसीति ' तं प्रतिब्रूयात् '

विचक्षणादृतवो रेत आभृतं पञ्चदशात्प्रसूतात्पित्र्यावतः ।
तन्मा[11] पुंसि कर्तर्येरयध्वं पुंसा कर्त्रा मातरि मासिषिक्त[12] ॥
स जाय[13] उपजायमानो द्वादशत्रयोदशोपमासः[14] ।
द्वादशत्रयोदशेन पित्रा[15] सं तद्विदे ऽहं प्रति तद्विदे ऽहम् ॥
तन्म ऋतवो ऽमृत्यव[16] आभरध्वम् ।
तेन सत्येन तेन तपसा ऋतुरस्म्यार्तवो ऽस्मि ॥

को ऽसि[17] त्वमस्मीति ' तमतिसृजते ॥ २ ॥

स एतं देवयानं पन्थानमापद्याग्निलोकमागच्छति ' स वायुलोकम्[18] ' स वरुणलोकम् ' स इन्द्रलोकम् ' स प्रजापतिलोकम् ' स ब्रह्मलोकम् ' तस्य ह वा एतस्य लोकस्यारो[19] ह्रदो ··· विजरा नदी ··· इन्द्रप्रजापती द्वारगोपौ ··· ' तमित्थंविदागच्छति ' तं ब्रह्मा हाभिधावत ' मम यशसा विजरां वा अयं नदीं प्रापन्न वा अयं जरयिष्यतीति ॥ ३ ॥

··· यस्त्वमसि सो ऽहमस्मि ··· ॥ ६ ॥

1 Variant: गार्ग्यायनि

2 Variant: तं हासीनं 'him sitting' (i.e. after he had been asked to sit down)

3 Variant: पुत्रो ऽसि — an inferior reading; the context requires the verb अस्ति.

4 Variant: अन्यमुताहो — an inferior reading; अन्यम् (acc.) does not agree with अध्वा (nom.).

5 Variant: ब्रह्मार्चो ऽसि; Radhakrishnan: ब्रह्मार्हो ऽसि.

6 Variant: तानपरपक्षे न प्रजनयति — an important variant, which gives a very different interpretation: According to the commentary, the moon does not produce them because it has waned and thereby has been diminished. (This actually is an attractive interpretation.)

7 Śāstrī: यश्चन्द्रमाः, but the normal structure of this type has invariable यद् (see the note on Selection IV, lines 40-41).

8 Variant: य एनं, a reading supported by the commentary.

9 Śāstrī and the commentary have a different order for some of these beings, but this does not affect the overall logic of the arrangement.

10 Śāstrī and the commentary offer एतेषु instead of तेषु तेषु; but the latter reading is more appealing in the present context.

11 Radhakrishnan: तं म.

12 This reading follows the suggestion of Bodewitz (1973, p. 59, n. 23). The manuscripts and consulted editions offer निषिञ्च (with unexpected singular), निषिक्त, and सिषिक्त.

13 उपजाय is Bodewitz's emendation (1973, p. 59, n. 24) for the जाय of all the manuscripts and consulted editions. The emendation is supported by the meter, and by the parallel in JB 1:18.

14 Variants: द्वादशत्रयोदशो मासः, द्वादशत्रयोदश उपमासः.

15 All consulted editions read पित्रासं = पित्रा + आसम्. Bodewitz (1973, p. 60, n. 26) and Keith (p.17, fn. 2) plausibly suggest to read सं as a prefix (with tmesis), going with the first विदे.

16 Śāstri and Radhakrishnan: (अ)मर्त्यव. (The commentary reads मर्त्यवो, as a vocative; but that is not a likely interpretation.)

17 Variants: (को ऽसि) को ऽस्मि.

18 Śāstri adds आदित्यलोकम्, and the commentary offers a few additional worlds.

19 Śāstri: ब्रह्मलोकस्य.

XIX: Identification with a personal God and सो ऽहमस्मि (BAU (K) 5:15 = VS (K) 40:1:15-18)

हिरण्मयेन पात्रेण सत्यस्यापिहितं मुखम् ।
तत्त्वं पूषनपावृणु सत्यधर्माय दृष्टये ॥ १ ॥
पूषन्नेकर्षे यम सूर्य प्राजापत्य व्यूह रश्मीन्समूह ' तेजो यत्ते रूपं कल्याण-
तमं तत्ते पश्यामि ' यो ऽसावसौ पुरुषस्सो ऽहमस्मि ॥ २ ॥
वायुरनिलममृतम् ' अथेदं भस्मान्तं शरीरम् ।
ओं३ क्रतो स्मर ' कृतं स्मर ' क्रतो स्मर ' कृतं स्मर ॥ ३ ॥
अग्ने नय सुपथा राये अस्मान् विश्वानि देव वयुनानि विद्वान् ।
युयोध्यस्मज्जुहुराणमेनो भूयिष्ठां ते नमउक्तिं विधेम ॥ ४ ॥

XX: APPENDIX

Related texts, mainly from earlier Vedic literature, with translations

A. Wedding mantras

In Selection XIII, the Chāndogya-Upaniṣad alludes to a mantra of the wedding ritual to expound on the mystical significance of ओम्. Below are given two variants of the mantra, followed by a passage from the Jaiminiya-Upaniṣad-Brāhmaṇa which makes more explicit use of the mantra, in a passage concerned with another favorite theme of the upaniṣads, the creation of this world from 'being' and 'non-being' (for which see e.g. Selection XI and the selections in XX:H below). The translations of those parts of the passages that are relevant to Selection XIII are highlighted.

1. Atharva-Veda 14:2:71

अमो ऽहमस्मि सा त्वं सामाहमस्म्यृक्त्वं द्यौरहं पृथिवी त्वम् ।
ताविह सं भवाव प्रजामा जनयावहै ॥ ७१ ॥

This one am I, that one are you; **I am the sāman, you are the ṛc**. I am heaven, you are earth.
So let us two unite here; let us beget offspring.

2. Āśvalāyana Gṛhya-Sūtra 1:7

अमो ऽहमस्मि सा त्वं सा त्वमस्यमो ऽहम् । द्यौरहं पृथिवी त्वं सामाहमृक्त्वम् ॥
तावेहि विवहावहै प्रजां प्रजनयावहै । संप्रियौ रोचिष्णू सुमनस्यमानौ जीवेव शरदः शतम् ॥

This one am I, that one are you; that one are you, this one am I.
I am heaven, you are earth; **I am the sāman, you are the ṛc**.
So come, let us two marry; let us beget offspring.
Dear together, shining, with good intentions, may we two live a hundred autumns (= years).

3. Jaiminiya-Upaniṣad-Brāhmaṇa 1:17:1

द्वयं वावेदमग्र आसीत्सच्चैवासच्च ॥ १ ॥

There was duality here in the beginning: Being and non-being.

तयोर्यत्सत्तत्साम तन्मनः स प्राणः । अथ यदसत्तदृक्[1] सा वाक् सो ऽपानः ॥ २ ॥

Of the two what was the being, that is the sāman, that is the mind, that is the up-breathing. Now what was the non-being, that is the ṛc, that is speech, that is the down-breathing.

तद्यन्मनश्च प्राणश्च तत्समानम् । अथ या वाक् चापानश्च तत्समानम् । इदमायतनं मनश्च प्राणश्चेदमायतनं वाक् चापानश्च । तस्मात्पुमान् दक्षिणतो योषामुपशेते ॥ ३ ॥

Now, what is the mind and the up-breathing, that is alike; and what is the speech and the down-breathing, that is alike. Mind and up-breathing are of this abode; speech and down-breathing are of this abode. Therefore the man (identified with the non-feminine मनस्[2]) sleeps to the right of the woman (identified with the feminine वाच्[2]).

सेयमृगस्मिन्सामन्मिथुनमैच्छत । तामपृच्छत् । का त्वमसीति । साहमस्मीत्यब्रवीत् । अथ वा अहममो ऽस्मीति ॥ ४ ॥

This ṛc desired a sexual union with (lit. in) this sāman.[3] He asked her: 'Who are you?' **'I am that one** (साहमस्मि),' she said. Then (he said) **'I am this one** (अहममो ऽस्मि).'

तद्यत्सा चामश्च तत्सामाभवत् । तत्साम्नः सामत्वम् ॥ ५ ॥

Now, what is सा 'that (fem.)' and अम(:) 'this (masc.)', that became the sāman (सा + अम = साम). That is the sāman-hood of the sāman.

तौ वै संभवावेति ··· ॥ ६ ॥

(She said:) **'So, let us unite.'** ...

[1] The manuscripts have सर्क् and स ऋ(म्य)क्, which the Tirupati edition unnecessarily resolves into सम्यक् (सेयमृक् ?). Oertel's and Rama Deva's edition have the correct interpretation.

[2] See the introduction to the next selection.

[3] A Vedic endingless locative singular form (see Whitney §425c).

B. Ritual "coupling"

In addition to explaining the mantras, yajuses, and other expressions used in the ritual, one of the major purposes of the brāhmaṇas is to expound on the significance of the ritual and of the यज्ञायुधानि, the "instruments of the ritual" (lit. 'weapons of the sacrifice'). Especially in later texts, one of the prominent ideas is that the pair-wise use of these "instruments" is not just comparable, but identical, to the production of a sexual union whose offspring ensures the vitality and success of the sacrifice and thereby of the sacrificer, the priests, and even the entire world. In this context, instruments that are feminine in gender are identified as female, instruments that are masculine or neuter (non-feminine) as male (see the notes on l. 8 of Selection XIII: 1). While clearly ritualist in outlook, this ideology, combined with the wedding ritual, has been alluded to in Selection XIII for explaining the significance of the particle ओम्; and it has been more explicitly utilized in Selection XX:A.3.

1. An ordinary ritualist example (from ŚB (M) 1:1:1)

ता ऽउत्तरेणाहवनीयम्प्रणयति । योषा वा ऽआपो व्वृषाग्निर्मिथुनमेवैतत्प्रजननं क्रियत ऽएवमिव हि मिथुनं क्लृप्तमुत्तरतो हि स्त्री पुमाँऽसमुपशेते ॥ २० ॥

He then carries it (the water) to the north of the āhavanīya fire. The water is a woman (अप् is feminine), fire is a man (अग्नि is masculine). A copulation, a procreation is produced at this time. Thus, as it were, a copulation is (properly) accomplished, for the woman lies on the left of the man (उत्तर means both 'left' and 'north').

ता नान्तरेण सञ्चरेयुः । नेन्मिथुनञ्चर्यमाणमन्तरेण सञ्चचरानिति ··· ॥ २१ ॥

They should not pass in between, lest they pass in between the copulation (as it is) taking place …

··· अथ यद् द्वन्द्वं द्वन्द्वं वै व्वीर्य्यं यदा वै द्वौ सँऽरभेते ऽअथ तद्वीर्य्यम्भवति द्वन्द्वं वै मिथुनं प्रजननम्मिथुनमेवैतत्प्रजननं क्रियते ॥ २२ ॥

… Now, as to why (he takes) a pair (of ritual utensils at a time) — a pair is strength. When two copulate, then there is strength. A pair is a copulation, a procreation. A copulation, a procreation is thus produced.

2. An interesting variant: The pairing of numbers (Jaiminiya-Brāhmaṇa 2:291-292)

This story exists in several variants, of which the JB version (given here) and the ŚB version (M 1:5:4:6-11) are the most complete. The story is a variant of an extremely widespread story type, used throughout the ritualist literature, in which the Gods and the Asuras fight or contend over one or another issue of ritual significance and in which, one way or the other, the Gods always triumph over the Asuras.

देवासुरा अस्पर्धन्त । ते नैव दण्डैर्नेषुभिर्व्यजयन्त । ते ऽब्रुवन्न वै दण्डैर्नेषुभिर्विजयामहे । वाच्येव वाव नो व्रह्मन्विजयो ऽस्त्विति । त ऐक्षन्त यतरे नो यतरान्पूर्वे ऽभिव्याहरिष्यन्ति ते संजेष्यन्त इति । ते देवा असुरानब्रुवन्यूयं पूर्वे ब्रूध्वमिति । यूयमिद्वा इत्यसुरा देवान् । ते देवा एतद्वाचो मिथुनमपश्यन् ॥ २९१ ॥

The Gods and the Asuras were contending. They did not win (either) by clubs (or) by arrows. They said, 'We are not winning either by clubs or by arrows. Let our victory be in speech, in brahman[1] (neuter, here probably 'sacred speech').' They reflected, 'Whoever of us will speak before whomever of us, they will win.' The Gods said to the Asuras, 'You speak first.' 'You indeed,' (said) the Asuras to the Gods. The Gods saw this coupling of speech.

एको ऽस्माकमिति देवा अब्रुवतैकास्माकमित्यसुराः । मन एव देवा अब्रुवत वाचमसुराः । ते देवा मनसैव वाचमसुराणामवृञ्जत । तस्माद्यन्मनसाधिगच्छति तद्वाचा वदति । द्वावस्माकमिति देवा अब्रुवत द्वे अस्माकमित्यसुराः । प्राणापानावेव देवा अब्रुवताहोरात्रे असुराः । ते देवाः प्राणापानाभ्यामेवाहोरात्रे असुराणामवृञ्जत । तस्माज्ज्योग्जीवन्बहून्यहोरात्राण्यवनयति । त्रयो ऽस्माकमिति देवा अब्रुवत तिस्रो ऽस्माकमित्यसुराः । इमानेव त्रीँल्लोकान्देवा अब्रुवत तिस्रो विद्या असुराः । ते देवा एभिरेव लोकैस्तिस्रो विद्या असुराणामवृञ्जत । तस्मादेता विद्या एष्वेव लोकेषु प्रोच्यन्ते । चत्वारो ऽस्माकमिति देवा अब्रुवत चतस्रो ऽस्माकमित्यसुराः । चतुष्पद एव पशून्देवा अब्रुवत चतस्रो दिशो ऽसुराः । ते देवाश्चतुष्पद्भिरेव पशुभिश्चतस्रो दिशो ऽसुराणामवृञ्जत । तस्माद्यां कां चन दिशं पशुमानयति सर्वामेव जितां क्लृप्तां प्रतिष्ठामन्वेति । पञ्चास्माकमिति देवा ऋतूनेवाब्रुवताथासुरा न प्राविन्दन् । न हि पञ्चि किं चनास्ति । ते ऽसुरा आरम्भमविन्दन्तः पञ्च पञ्चेत्येव वदन्तः पराजयन्त । ततो वै देवा अभवन् परासुराः । भवत्यात्मना परास्य द्विषन् भ्रातृव्यो भवति य एवं वेद ॥ २९२ ॥

'One (masc.) of us,' said the Gods; 'One (fem.) of us,' the Asuras. The Gods spoke (of) mind (non-fem.), the Asuras of speech (fem.). By mind, the Gods appropriated the speech of the Asuras. Therefore, what one conceives by mind, that one utters by speech. 'Two (masc.) of us,' said the Gods; 'Two (fem.) of us,' the Asuras. The Gods spoke of up-breathing and out-breathing (du. masc.), the Asuras of day and night (du. neut.; but रात्रि fem. is the final member of the compound). By up-breathing and down-breathing the Gods appropriated the day and night of the Asuras. Therefore, one living long spends many days and nights. 'Three (masc.) of us,' said the Gods; 'Three (fem.) of us,' the Asuras. The Gods spoke of these three worlds (masc.; heaven, ether, and earth), the Asuras of the three sciences/Vedas (fem.; Ṛg-Veda, Sāma-Veda, Yajur-Veda). By these three worlds the Gods appropriated the Vedas of the Asuras. Therefore these Vedas are proclaimed in these worlds. 'Four (masc.),' said the Gods; 'Four (fem.),' the Asuras. The Gods spoke of the four-legged animals (masc.), the Asuras of the four quarters (of the world; fem.). By the fourlegged animals the Gods appropriated the four quarters of the Asuras. Therefore, to whatever quarter one takes one's cattle, one reaches a complete, victorious, (and) proper support. 'Five of us,' the Gods said, (meaning) the seasons. Then the Asuras did not find a counterpart, for there is nothing (like) पञ्चि ("fem."). The Asuras, not finding a hold, saying पञ्च पञ्च 'five, five', lost. Then the Gods prospered, the Asuras (came) to naught.[2] He prospers himself, his hateful rival comes to naught,[3] who knows thus.

1 For the form see Selection A:3, note 3 above.

2,3 These two passages are highly formulaic and recur, with minor variations, throughout the ritualist literature. Note the idiomatic use of अभवन्, भवति to convey the meaning 'prosper' and its counterpart परा . . . अभवन्, भवति (with "tmesis"; see Whitney §1081), meaning 'come to naught, perish'. The द्विषन्भ्रातृव्यः 'hateful enemy', too, is a stock expression.

C. More on ॐ and other "ritual particles"

1. Some early uses of *Om*

The first two passages illustrate the use of *om* with imperatives and vocatives. (The first type, with "preposed" *om*, is more common.) The second set of examples illustrates the use of *o/om* in certain types of Vedic recitation.

a. From Maitrāyaṇī-Saṁhitā 4:9, 4:5, and 1:4/4:1

ओमिन्द्रवन्तः प्रचरत ॥ ४/९/२ ॥

'*Om*, proceed with Indra.'

अवेरपो ऽध्वर्या३ ओम् ॥ इत्यंविदो यज्ञां३मिति वा एतदाह ॥ · · · ॥ ४/५/२ ॥

'Have you seen the waters, Adhvaryu, *om*?' Thereby he says 'Have you seen the sacrifice?'

ओं श्रावय · · · ॥ १/४/११ ॥   ओँ श्रावय · · · ॥ ४/१/११ ॥

(A formula which calls on the adhvaryu to make the श्रौषट् call, through which he invites the deities to hear the prayers. The usual version of the formula is आ श्रावय, lit. 'make (the deity) hear (our prayers)'. The padapāṭha on Maitrāyaṇī-Saṁhitā 4:1:1, in fact, glosses the passage as ओं श्रावयेति आ३ श्रा३वय.)

b. From Aitareya-Brāhmaṇa 3:12:1-4

This passage begins a section of the Aitareya-Brāhmaṇa dealing with a śastra, a form of recitation in which *o/om* regularly is substituted for the vowel of the last syllable of the line or verse (and where any following consonant is deleted). The hotṛ, who is to perform the śastra, calls on (आह्वयते) the adhvaryu, who in turn responds (प्रतिगृणाति). In our passage, the ओ(म्) marked by double underlining substitutes for original *a*-vowels.

शोंसावोमित्याह्वयते · · · शंसामोदैवोमित्यध्वर्युः प्रतिगृणाति · · · ॥

= शंसाव[1] · · · शंसा[2] मदैव · · ·

'Let us two praise,' he invites … 'Praise, rejoice (indeed),' the adhvaryu responds …

1 Compare the normal form शंसाव in the closely related Ṛg-Vedic passage शंसावाध्वर्यो प्रति मे गृणीहि (RV 3:53:3) 'Let us two praise, Adhvaryu, respond to me'.

2 शंसा is an early Vedic variant of second singular imperative शंस 'praise'.

c. The "nyūṅkha", from Āśvalāyana-Śrauta-Sūtra 7:11:7

The nyūṅkha is a more elaborate and rather complex variant of the śastra recitation. The vowel of the second syllable in each (double-)line is replaced by ओ; the vowel and any following consonant of the verse-final syllable are replaced by ओम्, and then the first two syllables of the verse are repeated, again with substitution of ओ for the vowel of the second syllable. What is probably significant is that "attenuation" of the second-syllable ओ in the process of prolongation yields an ॐ (characterized as 'half-ओम्'). One suspects that this is the source for the wide-spread alternate notation ॐ for ओम्. For greater clarity, the substituted ओ, ओम्, and ॐ are highlighted by double underlining.

आपो३ ॐ ॐ ॐ ॐ ॐ ॐ ओ३ ॐ ॐ ॐ ॐ ॐ ओ३ ॐ ॐ रेवतीः
··· वयो धो३म् आपो३ ॥ ७ ॥

= आपो रेवतीः ··· वयो धात् (RV 10:30:12)

'O wealthy waters ..., may she bestow vigor.'

2. Some other ritual particles (JB 1:141)

Particles of this type are especially common in the Sāma-Veda, where they serve as something like "filler syllables" to sustain the melody when a verse is to be chanted. The example given here comes from a Sāma-Vedic brāhmaṇa and exhibits an extreme abundance of particles. Usually, the number of particles in a given line of text is more limited, even in Sāma-Vedic chant. (For greater clarity, the particles are highlighted by double underlining.)

अविता जरायितृणाम् आ औ हो हा यि शतं भवस्य् ओ हो हुं मा ताया हुं मा इत्युत्तमाया उत्तरार्धे कुर्यात् ॥ १४१ ॥

He should perform the second half of the last (verse) [as above] instead of the original अविता जरायितृणां शतं भवसि ..., a variant of the mantra found in RV 4:31:3bc अविता जरितॄणां शतं भवास्यूतये 'may you be for the singers a helper with a hundred favors for support.'

3. Mystical speculations on some ritual particles I: हो (JB 2:244-245)

In the following selection, the major focus is on the Sāma-Vedic "filler syllable" हो, the third particle in the first stretch of filler syllables in the preceding passage. Here the particle is characterized as the essence of speech, i.e., no doubt of sacred Speech. In addition, the selection evidently presupposes a fairly advanced stage in linguistic thinking, at which the speech sounds were already classified in terms of their phonetic characteristics, with vowels preceding the consonants, with the consonant series beginning with क, and with ह concluding the listing of consonants, and thus of speech sounds in general.

प्रजापतिर्वा इदमग्र आसीत् ' नान्यं द्वितीयं पश्यमानः · · · स ऐक्षत हन्तेमां वाचं विसृजे · · · इति ' तां वागित्येव व्यसृजत ' · · · तस्या एत्येकमक्षरमच्छिनत् ' तदिदमभवत् ' अभूद् वा इदमिति ' तद् भूमेर्भूमित्वम् ' केति द्वितीयम् ' तदिदमन्तरिक्षमभवत् ' अन्तरेव वा इदमुभयमभूदिति ' तदन्तरिक्षस्यान्तरिक्षत्वम् ' हो इति तृतीयमूर्ध्वमुदास्यत् ' तददो ऽभवत् ' अद्युतदिव वा अद इति ' तद्दिवो दिवत्वम् · · · ॥ २४४ ॥

Prajāpati was here/this world in the beginning. Not seeing another, a second … he reflected, 'Come on, let me create[1] this speech …' He created her as 'speech' … He cut off one sound of it, अ[2] [the beginning of the traditional recitation of the sound system and also the first of the vowels]. That became this (world). 'This (world) has come about (अभूत्),' that is the earth-hood of earth (भूमि). (He cut off) a second (sound), क[3] [the first of the consonants in the sound system]. That became this ether (अन्तरिक्षम्). 'This came about in between (अन्तरा) both, as it were,' that is the ether-hood of ether. 'हो,' he cast up high the third [where *ho* is ritual particle and also stands for ह, the last sound of the sound system]. That became yonder (world). 'In yonder world there was lightning as it were (अद्युतत् from द्युत् ≈ दिव्/द्यु + त्),' that is the sky/heaven-hood of the sky/ heaven (दिव्) …

· · · एषा ह खलु वै प्रत्यक्षं वाग्यज्जिह्वाग्रेणैतद्वाचो वदति यदेति ' मध्येनैतद्वाचो वदति यत्केति ' सर्वस्या[4] एतद्वाचो रसो ऽध्युद्वदति यद्धो इति ' हो इति हि सर्वा वाक् · · · ॥ २४५ ॥

What of speech one speaks with the tip of the tongue (or at the beginning), that indeed manifestly is speech, viz. अ.[2] With the middle of speech (or in the middle of the sound system) one speaks that which is क.[3] The essence of all speech speaks up which is हो, for हो is all Speech [because ह is the end and therefore the culmination of the sound system]

1 Indicative used for the imperative (or subjunctive), a common feature in more "relaxed" Sanskrit.
2 एति = अ + इति.
3 केति = क + इति.
4 The edited text has सर्वयैतद्वाचो, with सर्वया (instr.) not agreeing with वाचः (gen.).

4. Mystical speculations on some ritual particles, II: ओ वा (JUB 3:3:7-12)

In this passage from the Jaiminīya-Upaniṣad-Brāhmaṇa, ओ evidently is equated with the syllable ओम्, and वा with sacred Speech, वाच्. The latter equation is found even in the earlier Sāma-Vedic brāhmaṇas, where instead of the chant "finale" वा we frequently find वाच्.

अथ वा अतो निधनमेव । ओ वा इति द्वे अक्षरे । अन्तो वै साम्नो निधनम् । अन्तः स्वर्गो लोकानाम् । अन्तो ब्रध्नस्य विष्टपम् ॥ ७ ॥

Now then the finale: ओ वा, two syllables. The finale is the end of the sāman. The end of the worlds is heaven. The acme of the sun is the end.

तमेतदुद्गाता यजमानमोमित्यक्षरेणान्ते स्वर्गे लोके दधाति ॥ ८ ॥ ...

At this time the udgātṛ places the sacrificer in the end, in the heavenly world (by saying) ओम् (= the ओ of the finale).

ते ह वा एते अक्षरे देवलोकश्चैव मनुष्यलोकश्च । आदित्यश्च ह वा एते अक्षरे चन्द्रमाश्च ॥ ११ ॥

These two syllables are the world of the Gods and the world of human beings; these two syllables are the sun and the moon.

आदित्य एव देवलोकः । चन्द्रमा मनुष्यलोकः । ओमित्यादित्यो वागिति चन्द्रमाः ॥ १२ ॥

The world of the Gods is the sun; the world of human beings, the moon. ओ(म्) is the sun; वा(च्), the moon.

D. The Gāyatri or Sāvitri (from RV 3:62; see also Lanman p. 74)

Verses 10–12 of this hymn to various deities are a request for divine inspiration. The most important of these is verse 10, which is to be recited by every practicing Hindu at dawn and at dusk, with ओम् भूर्भुवः स्वः preceding, and with ओम् following; see Manu 2:78. The fact that the recitation is to be preceded and followed by these expressions is especially significant, because of the great importance attached to them in the tradition that began with the upaniṣads.

तत्स॑वि॒तुर्वरे॑ण्यं॒ भर्गो॑ दे॒वस्य॑ धीमहि । धियो॒ यो नः॑ प्रचो॒दया॑त् ॥ १० ॥
दे॒वस्य॑ सवि॒तु॒र्व॒यं वा॑ज॒यन्तः॒ पुर॑न्ध्या । भग॑स्य रा॒तिमी॑महे ॥ ११ ॥
दे॒वं नरः॑ सवि॒तारं॒ विप्रा॑ य॒ज्ञैः सु॑वृ॒क्तिभिः॑ । न॒म॒स्यन्ति॑ धि॒येषि॒ताः ॥ १२ ॥

We meditate on this desirable splendor of God Savitṛ who shall inspire our thoughts.
Being powerful through the graciousness of God Savitṛ, we ask for the liberality of Bhaga.
The inspired men (i.e. the brahmins), incited by meditation, honor God Savitṛ with sacrifices (and) well-prepared (hymns).

E. 'Lead me from untruth to truth …'

1. Ṛg-Veda 7:59:12

This verse, dedicated to Rudra Tryambaka (lit. 'having three mothers'), also known as मृत्युंजय 'defeating death', is appended to a hymn otherwise addressed to the Maruts. As Geldner observes, the verse is quite popular. It recurs in the Vājasaneyi-Saṁhitā (M), the Taittirīya-Saṁhitā and other early Black Yajur-Veda Saṁhitās, the Śatapatha-Brāhmaṇa (M), the Taittirīya-Brāhmaṇa, and many other texts, including the Śivasaṁkalpa-Upaniṣad.

त्र्य॑म्बकं यजामहे सु॒गन्धिं॑ पु॒ष्टि॒वर्ध॑नम् ।
उ॒र्वा॒रु॒कमि॑व॒ बन्ध॑नान् मृ॒त्योर्मु॑क्षीय॒ मामृता॑त् ॥ १२ ॥

We sacrifice to Tryambaka, the fragrant one, increaser of prosperity.
Like the gourd from its vine, may I be free from death, not from immortality.

2. Ṛg-Veda 8:48:3

This verse likewise recurs in a number of other Vedic texts, including the Taittirīya-Saṁhitā and the Śiras-Upaniṣad.

अपा॑म॒ सोम॑म॒मृता॑ अभू॒माग॑न्म॒ ज्योति॒रवि॑दाम दे॒वान् ।
किं नू॒नम॒स्मान्कृ॑णव॒दरा॑ति॒ः किमु॑ धू॒र्तिर॑मृत॒ मर्त्य॑स्य ॥

We have drunk Soma, have become immortal, have gone to light, and we have seen the Gods.
What indeed can enmity do to us and what the knavery of a mortal, O immortal one?

3. A ritualist passage (from Maitrāyaṇī-Saṁhitā 1:4:2)

Though ritualist, this passage employs mantras in wide circulation in Vedic literature. The first part, for instance, recurs with some variations in the Atharva-Veda, the Taittirīya-Saṁhitā, and the Vājasaneyi-Saṁhitā (M); the second part also occurs in the Taittirīya-Saṁhitā and the Vājasaneyi-Saṁhitā (M); in the latter (2:25), both parts occur together, just as they do in the present selection, but without the surrounding ritualist text.

विष्णुमुखा वै देवा असुरानेभ्यो लोकेभ्यः प्रणुद्य स्वर्गं लोकमायँस्तद्विष्णुमुखो वा
एतद्यजमानो भ्रातृव्यमेभ्यो लोकेभ्यः प्रणुद्य स्वर्गं लोकमेत्यगन्म ३स्वरिति
स्वर्गमेव लोकमेति सं ज्योतिषाभूमेति ज्योतिर्हि स्वर्गो लोकः(:) ... ॥ ७ ॥

With Viṣṇu as their leader the Gods, having ousted the Asuras from these worlds, went to the heavenly world. So, with Viṣṇu as his leader, the sacrificer now, having ousted his rival from these worlds, goes to the heavenly world. अगन्म ३स्वर् 'we have gone to heaven,' (with these words) he goes to the heavenly world, (and also with the continuation) सं ज्योतिषा अभूम 'we have come together with light', for the heavenly world is light.

4. Another ritualist passage (Śatapatha-Brāhmaṇa (M) 1:1:1:4)

With the exception of a variant in the Taittirīya-Brāhmaṇa, the formula occurring in this passage, इदमहमनृतात्सत्यमुपैमि 'Here I go from untruth to truth', is limited to the White Yajurveda (and to some of the Śrauta-Sūtras). It is the closest we can come to an ancestor of the first part of the mantra in Selection IV.

द्वयं वा ऽइदं न तृतीयमस्ति । सत्यं चैवानृतं च सत्यमेव देवा अनृतं मनुष्या इदम-
हमनृतात्सत्यमुपैमीति तन्मनुष्येभ्यो देवानुपैति ॥

This (world) is of two kinds, there is no third — truth and untruth. The Gods are truth, human beings, untruth. 'Here I go from untruth to truth,' (uttering this while becoming consecrated for the sacrifice) he goes over from (the world of) human beings to (the world of) the Gods (and thus is fit to sacrifice to them).

F. Ṛg-Vedic brahmodyas (from RV 1:164)

Early Vedic brahmodyas are riddles concerned with the nature of the world, the ritual, knowledge, the origin of the world, etc. The following three examples, taken from a hymn which constitutes a collection of such brahmodyas, may suffice to illustrate the genre. The first and third passages are clearly transcendental in outlook, being concerned with the question of proper knowledge or understanding, with the nature of language, and with the transcendental unity underlying the diversity of the phenomenal world. The second selection is more ritualist in outlook. For a recent discussion of the ritual connection of this hymn as well as its philosophical concerns, see Jan Houben, 'The ritual pragmatics of a Vedic hymn', *Journal of the American Oriental Society* 120: 499-536, 2000.

द्वा सुपर्णा सयुजा सखाया समानं वृक्षं परि षस्वजाते ।
तयोरन्यः पिप्पलं स्वाद्वत्त्यनश्नन्नन्यो अभि चाकशीति ॥ २० ॥

यत्रा सुपर्णा अमृतस्य भागम् अनिमेषं विदथाभिस्वरन्ति ।
इनो विश्वस्य भुवनस्य गोपाः स मा धीरः पाकमत्रा विवेश ॥ २१ ॥
यस्मिन्वृक्षे मध्वदः सुपर्णा निविशन्ते सुवते चाधि विश्वे ।
तस्येदाहुः पिप्पलं स्वाद्वग्रे तन्नोन्नशद्यः पितरं न वेद ॥ २२ ॥

Two eagles, close friends, embrace the same tree. One of them eats the sweet berry, the other keeps looking without eating.

Where the eagles (pl.), without resting, clamor for a share, for allotments in immortality, here the mighty protector of the whole world, this wise one entered naive me.

On which tree all the sweet-eating eagles are nesting and breeding, in its top, they say, is the sweet fruit. He will not reach there who does not know the father.

[The tree is the tree of knowledge, which in turn is compared to a sweet berry. The two eagles represent two different approaches to acquiring knowledge. Only who follows the correct approach and recognizes the father, the mighty protector of the world, will reach the fruit of knowledge, a share in immortality.]

पृच्छामि त्वा परमन्तं पृथिव्याः पृच्छामि यत्र भुवनस्य नाभिः ।
पृच्छामि त्वा वृष्णो अश्वस्य रेतः पृच्छामि वाचः परमं व्योम ॥ ३४ ॥
इयं वेदिः परो अन्तः पृथिव्या अयं यज्ञो भुवनस्य नाभिः ।
अयं सोमो वृष्णो अश्वस्य रेतो ब्रह्मायं वाचः परमं व्योम ॥ ३५ ॥

I ask you for the farthest end of the earth. I ask you where (is) the navel of the world. I ask you for the seed of the male horse. I ask you for the highest pinnacle of speech.

This vedi (altar) is the farthest end of the earth. This sacrifice is the navel of the world. This soma (used in the sacrifice) is the seed of the male horse. This brahman-priest (overseer of the ritual) is the highest pinnacle of speech.

[This is the only brahmodya in the hymn that provides an explicit answer. The answer is a ritualist one.]

चत्वारि वाक्परिमिता पदानि तानि विदुर्ब्राह्मणा ये मनीषिणः ।
गुहा त्रीणि विहिता नेङ्गयन्ति तुरीयं वाचो मनुष्या वदन्ति ॥ ४५ ॥
इन्द्रं मित्रं वरुणमग्निमाहुरथो दिव्यः स सुपर्णो गरुत्मान् ।
एकं सद्विप्रा बहुधा वदन्त्यग्निं यमं मातरिश्वानमाहुः ॥ ४६ ॥

Language is measured (in) four quarters; the brahmins who are insightful do know these. Three (quarters), kept secret, they do not let circulate; human beings (only) speak a fourth of language.

They call it Indra, Mitra, Varuṇa, (and) Agni; and it is also Garutmat, the divine eagle. Being (just) **one** the wise ones call it manifold. They call it Agni, Yama, Mātariśvan.

[Later Vedic Prose texts give a variety of explanations regarding the three hidden or secret quarters of language. Unfortunately, these are mutually contradictory. Geldner is probably right in comparing the three quarters to the three immortal quarters of Puruṣa in the next selection, verse 3. The second verse touches on the issue of तदेकम्, the transcendental unity underlying the diversity of the phenomenal world, a common concern of the upaniṣads. This issue is raised more explicitly in the selections in H and I below.]

G. The Puruṣa-Sūkta (RV 10:90)

The creation of the world through a primeval sacrifice of a primordial human being (Puruṣa) by the Gods, who themselves however are created by this sacrifice. The hymn also gives the first account of the four castes (with राजन्य for the later more usual क्षत्रिय).

सहस्रशीर्षा पुरुषः सहस्राक्षः सहस्रपात् ।
स भूमिं विश्वतो वृत्वात्यतिष्ठद्दशाङ्गुलम् ॥१॥

Thousand-headed was Puruṣa, thousand-eyed, thousand-footed;
Covering the earth on all sides he extended beyond by ten fingers.

पुरुष एवेदं सर्वं यद्भूतं यच्च भव्यम् ।
उतामृतत्वस्येशानो यदन्नेनातिरोहति ॥२॥

Puruṣa is/was this whole (world), what has been and what is to be;
And he is ruler of immortality which rises beyond through food.

एतावानस्य महिमातो ज्यायांश्च पूरुषः ।
पादो ऽस्य विश्वा भूतानि त्रिपादस्यामृतं दिवि ॥३॥

Such is his greatness; and greater than that is Puruṣa;
A quarter of him are all the creatures; three fourths of him is immortality in heaven.

त्रिपादूर्ध्व उदैत्पुरुषः पादो ऽस्येहाभवत्पुनः ।
ततो विष्वङ् व्यक्रामत् साशनानशने अभि ॥४॥

By three quarters Puruṣa rose above, a quarter of him existed here in turn;
From that he went in all directions, over the eating and the non-eating (world).

तस्माद्विराळजायत　　　विराजो अधि पूरुषः ।
स जातो अत्यरिच्यत　　　पश्चाद्भूमिमथो पुरः ॥५॥

From him (masc.) was born the Virāj (a metre, feminine); from the Virāj, Puruṣa;[1]
(Just) born he extended beyond the earth in back and also in front.

यत्पुरुषेण हविषा　　　देवा यज्ञमतन्वत ।
वसन्तो अस्यासीदाज्यं　　　ग्रीष्म इध्मः शरद्धविः ॥६॥

When the Gods stretched out the sacrifice with Puruṣa as the oblation
Spring was its sacrificial butter, Summer the kindling, Autumn the oblation.

तं यज्ञं बर्हिषि प्रौक्षन्　　　पुरुषं जातमग्रतः ।
तेन देवा अयजन्त　　　साध्या ऋषयश्च ये ॥७॥

Him they sprinkled as sacrifice on the sacrificial strew, Puruṣa, born in the beginning;
Through him the Gods sacrificed, the Sādhyas, and those who are the seers.

तस्माद्यज्ञात्सर्वहुतः　　　संभृतं पृषदाज्यम् ।
पशून्तांश्चक्रे वायव्यानारण्यान्ग्राम्याश्च ये ॥८॥

From this whole-offering (= holocaust) sacrifice came about the sacrificial butter;
He made these animals, the airy ones (= the birds), the forest ones (= the wild ones), and those of the village (= the domesticated).

तस्माद्यज्ञात्सर्वहुत　　　ऋचः सामानि जज्ञिरे ।
छन्दांसि जज्ञिरे तस्माद्यजुस्तस्मादजायत ॥९॥

From this holocaust sacrifice arose the ṛces and the sāmans;
The meters arose from it; the yajus arose from it.

तस्मादश्वा अजायन्त　　　ये के चोभयादतः ।
गावो ह जज्ञिरे तस्मात्तस्माज्जाता अजावयः ॥१०॥

From it arose the horses and whatever (animals) have two rows of teeth;
The cows arose from it; from it arose the goats and sheep.

यत्पुरुषं व्यदधुः　　　कतिधा व्यकल्पयन् ।
मुखं किमस्य कौ बाहू　　　का ऊरू पादा उच्येते ॥११॥

When they divided Puruṣa how many times did they lay him apart?
What (was) his mouth (called), what the arms, what were the thighs called (and) the feet?

ब्राह्मणोऽस्य मुखमासीद् बाहू राजन्यः कृतः ।
ऊरू तदस्य यद्वैश्यः पद्भ्यां शूद्रो अजायत ॥१२॥

The brahmin was his mouth; the rājanya was made his arms;
His thighs what is the vaiśya, from the feet arose the śūdra.

चन्द्रमा मनसो जातश्चक्षोः सूर्यो अजायत ।
मुखादिन्द्रश्चाग्निश्च प्राणाद्वायुरजायत ॥१३॥

The moon arose from (his) mind, from his eye arose the sun;
From the mouth both Indra and Agni, from the breath arose Vāyu (the wind).

नाभ्या आसीदन्तरिक्षं शीर्ष्णो द्यौः समवर्तत ।
पद्भ्यां भूमिर्दिशः श्रोत्रात् तथा लोकाँ अकल्पयन् ॥१४॥

From the navel came the ether, the sky unfolded from the head;
From the feet, the earth; from the ear, the quarters; in this way they laid out the worlds.

सप्तास्यासन्परिधयस् त्रिः सप्त समिधः कृताः ।
देवा यद्यज्ञं तन्वाना अबध्नन्पुरुषं पशुम् ॥१५॥

Seven were his surrounding sticks, three times seven were the kindling sticks made,
When the Gods, stretching out the sacrifice, tied up Puruṣa as the victim.

यज्ञेन यज्ञमयजन्त देवास् तानि धर्माणि प्रथमान्यासन् ।
ते ह नाकं महिमानः सचन्त यत्र पूर्वे साध्याः सन्ति देवाः ॥१६॥

Through the sacrifice the Gods sacrificed the sacrifice; these were the first laws/ordinances/forms/norms;
These powers went to the highest heaven where the earlier Gods, the Sādhyas, are.

[1] These are the male and female principle, respectively, who engender each other mutually (see note 2 on selection H:2).

H. Being and non-being

1. The nāsadiya-sūkta (RV 10:129)

Like the puruṣa-sūkta, this hymn is a creation account, operating with paradoxes (at least, that is the usual interpretation). The hymn, especially its beginning, is widely cited in upaniṣadic literature, no doubt in part because the hymn mentions तदेकम् 'that One (ultimate entity)' (verse 2 and 4) and thus converges with one of the major interests of the upaniṣads, the question of the transcendental unity behind the diversity of the phenomenal world. The hymn ends in pessimism, but that pessimism is most powerfully expressed. Because of its significance, the hymn has given rise to a large number of translations and interpretations. The following translation has benefited from many of them, but does not attempt to follow any one of them in detail. — A recent study argues for a very different interpretation of this hymn (Joel Brereton, 'Edifying puzzlement: Ṛgveda 10.129 and the uses of enigma', *Journal of the American Oriental Society* 119: 248-260, 1999). Relying on the relatively late identification in Śatapatha-Brāhmaṇa 6 and 10 (Selection J below) of the असत् at the beginning of our hymn as referring to the ṛṣis, he questions the traditional 'cosmogonic' interpretation of the hymn and instead proposes to interpret the hymn as identifying 'the original creativity' of the poets. Brereton's proposal is highly interesting, but needs to be subjected to critical scrutiny, taking into consideration the entire range of indigenous Indian interpretations (beyond the ŚB one), ranging from allusions or direct references to our text in the Vedic literature to discussions in the commentatorial literature.

नासदासीन्नो सदासीत्तदानीं   नासीद्रजो नो व्योमा परो यत् ।
किमावरीवः कुह कस्य शर्मन्नम्भः किमासीद्गहनं गभीरम् ॥ १ ॥

There was not non-being, nor was there being then; there was no air, nor was there heaven above.
What kept on moving? Where? And under whose protection? What was the water, impenetrable, deep?

न मृत्युरासीदमृतं न तर्हि   न रात्र्या अह्न आसीत्प्रकेतः ।
आनीदवातं स्वधया तदेकं   तस्माद्धान्यन्न परः किं चनास ॥ २ ॥

There was no death, nor immortality at that time. There was no sign of night or day.
That **One** breathed windless on its own. Beyond it nothing else existed.

तम आसीत्तमसा गूळ्हमग्रे   ऽप्रकेतं सलिलं सर्वमा इदम्
तुच्छ्येनाभ्वपिहितं यदासीत्   तपसस्तन्महिनाजायतैकम् ॥ ३ ॥

Darkness there was in the beginning, hidden by darkness. All of this was a signless flood.
The force that was enclosed by emptiness, the **One**, was born by strength of (mental) heat.

कामस्तदग्रे समवर्तताधि   मनसो रेतः प्रथमं यदासीत् ।
सतो बन्धुमसति निरविन्दन्   हृदि प्रतीष्या कवयो मनीषा ॥ ४ ॥

In the beginning desire unfolded on it, which was the first seed of the mind.
The sages found the bond of being in non-being, searching in their hearts, by thinking.

तिरश्चीनो विततो रश्मिरेषाम् अधः स्विदासी३दुपरि स्विदासी३त् ।
रेतोधा आसन्महिमान आसन्त्स्वधा अवस्तात्प्रयतिः परस्तात् ॥ ५ ॥

Their measuring chord was spread athwart. Was there below by chance, was there above?
There were seed-pourers, there were powers. Desire was below, beyond was will.

को अद्धा वेद क इह प्र वोचत् कुत आजाता कुत इयं विसृष्टिः ।
अर्वाग्देवा अस्य विसर्जनेनाथा को वेद यत आबभूव ॥ ६ ॥

Who indeed knows? Who will declare here? From where did this creation come about?
The Gods are later than this (world's) creation. So, who knows whence it came about?

इयं विसृष्टिर्यत आबभूव यदि वा दधे यदि वा न ।
यो अस्याध्यक्षः परमे व्योमन्त्सो अङ्ग वेद यदि वा न वेद ॥ ७ ॥

This creation, whence it came about, whether it was created, whether not,
Who is the overseer of this (world) in highest heaven, he surely knows, unless he does not know.

2. असतः सदजायत (from RV 10:72)

In this hymn, too, the creation of the world is portrayed as something of a paradox, through images and ideas which are mutually contradictory. The hymn is included here because the असतः सदजायत of verses 2 and 3 is no doubt referred to in Selection XI.

देवानां नु वयं जाना प्र वोचाम विपन्यया ।
उक्थेषु शस्यमानेषु यः पश्यादुत्तरे युगे ॥ १ ॥

Let us now, with rejoicing, proclaim the generations of the Gods
In (well-)recited hymns, so that someone shall see them in a later age.

ब्रह्मणस्पतिरेता सं कर्मार इवाधमत् ।
देवानां पूर्व्ये युगे ऽसतः सदजायत ॥ २ ॥

Brahmaṇaspati forged them together like a blacksmith.
In the earliest age of the Gods, being was born from non-being.

देवानां युगे प्रथमे ऽसतः सदजायत ।
तदाशा अन्वजायन्त तदुत्तानपदस्परि ॥ ३ ॥

In the first age of the Gods, being was born from non-being.
The quarters (of the world) arose thereafter. It (the world) [was born] by one with spread-out legs.[1]

भूर्जज्ञ उत्तानपदो भुव आशा अजायन्त ।
अदितेर्दक्षो अजायत दक्षाद्वदितिः परि ॥ ४ ॥

The earth was born from the one with spread-out legs, and from the earth were born the quarters.
Dakṣa was born from Aditi, and from Dakṣa Aditi was born.[2]

अष्टौ पुत्रासो अदितेर्ये जातास्तन्व१स्परि ।
देवाँ उप प्रैत्सप्तभिः परा मार्ताण्डमास्यत् ॥ ८ ॥

(There are) eight sons who were born from Aditi's body.
She went forth to the Gods with seven; Mārtāṇḍa[3] she cast away.

सप्तभिः पुत्रैरदितिरुप प्रैत्पूर्व्यं युगम् ।
प्रजायै मृत्यवे त्वत् पुनर्मार्ताण्डमाभरत् ॥ ९ ॥

Aditi went forth into the first age (of the world) with seven sons;
Mārtāṇḍa, on the other hand, (him) she brought back for procreation and for death.

[1] A description of a woman in childbirth. That is, even though the world was born from non-being, there was a female principle that gave birth to it.

[2] Dakṣa (masc. lit. 'skillful') and Aditi (fem. lit. 'unbounded, infinite') are the male and female principles, respectively, that give birth to each other and thereby to the world. A parallel for this mutual creation is found in the Puruṣa-Sūkta, verse 5, where Puruṣa and Virāj engender each other in turn; see also the next selection.

[3] Mārtāṇḍa literally means 'connected with or characterized by the mortal egg'. The name is often identified as an epithet of a bird, of the sun, or of Viṣṇu. But the Taittirīya-Saṁhitā (6:5:6:1) speaks of an 'abortive egg'. The Śatapatha-Brāhmaṇa (M 3:1:3:3) reinforces this interpretation, but at the same time states that from this shapeless mass arose, among others, the sun, from which in turn the creatures of this world came about.

3. असच्च सच्च (from RV 10:5)

This hymn, dedicated to Agni, attempts to identify the one, original source of everything, but despairs of being able to do so. In the end, it identifies Agni as the first creation, born from being and non-being, from Dakṣa and Aditi (for which compare the preceding selection).

एकः समुद्रो धरुणो रयीणाम् अस्मद्धृदो भूरिजन्मा वि चष्टे ।
सिषक्त्यूधर्निण्योरुपस्थ उत्सस्य मध्ये निहितं पदं वेः ॥ १ ॥

One ocean, holder of riches, shines/speaks forth from our heart, having many births.
It looks for the udder in the lap of the two hidden ones.[1] In the middle of the source, the track of the bird is placed.[2]

असच्च सच्च परमे व्योमन् दक्षस्य जन्मन्नदितेरुपस्थे ।

अग्निर्ह नः प्रथमजा ऋतस्य पूर्व आयुनि वृषभश्च धेनुः ॥ ७ ॥

Being and non-being (are) in the highest heaven, in the birth of Dakṣa, in the lap of Aditi.

Agni is our first-born of Truth, in the first age, (he is) the bull (who also is) the cow.

[1] The two pieces of wood from which fire/Agni is drilled in the ritual.

[2] Could this be an allusion to the bird-shape of the fire altar in the agnicayana?

I. हिरण्यगर्भ and क = प्रजापति (from RV 10:121)

This hymn starts out with the speculation that in the beginning, there was a golden embryo, which arose as the **one** lord of creation. The rest of the hymn originally either was a series of brahmodyas, whose answers were later lost, or a somewhat pessimistic creation myth similar to the nāsadīya-sūkta, full of questions, but with no answers. The last verse, not analyzed in Śākalya's padapāṭha and therefore no doubt a later addition, states that Prajāpati is the creator, thereby laying the foundation for the later Vedic interpretation of the pronoun क 'who' in the questions of this hymn as an epithet of Prajāpati. The word Prajāpati, as the name of a specific God, occurs only in a few very late Ṛg-Vedic passages; the creator God Prajāpati essentially belongs to the later Vedic tradition.

हिरण्यगर्भः समवर्तताग्रे भूतस्य जातः पतिरेक आसीत् ।

स दाधार पृथिवीं द्यामुतेमां कस्मै देवाय हविषा विधेम ॥ १ ॥

In the beginning a golden embryo unfolded. It was born the **one** lord of creation.

It/he held in place the earth and this sky. Which God shall we worship with oblation?

य आत्मदा बलदा यस्य विश्वे उपासते प्रशिषं यस्य देवाः ।

यस्य च्छायामृतं यस्य मृत्युः कस्मै देवाय हविषा विधेम ॥ २ ॥

Who is the giver of self, the giver of strength, whose order do all serve, whose (order) the Gods (do serve),

Whose shadow is immortality, whose (shadow) death — Which God shall we worship with oblation?

प्रजापते न त्वदेतान्यन्यो विश्वा जातानि परि ता बभूव ।

यत्कामास्ते जुहुमस्तन्नो अस्तु वयं स्याम पतयो रयीणाम् ॥ १० ॥

Prajāpati, no one but you surrounds all these creatures (in creation).

With what desire we offer to you, let that be ours. May we be rulers over riches.

J. Ritualist passages, connected with the agnicayana, that "put it all together" (from Śatapatha-Brāhmaṇa (M) 6 and 10)

The agnicayana was the most important and complex Vedic sacrifice. Thus, about a third of the Śatapatha-Brāhmaṇa deals with the agnicayana. Given its significance and complexity, it inspired the ritualists to engage in more than the ordinary speculation on the significance of the ritual as a microcosmic replica of the world. The passages from book 6, the beginning of the Śatapatha-Brāhmaṇa's discussion of the agnicayana, draw on many of the mystical speculations of the Ṛg-Veda, add to these, and employ them to explain the agnicayana as a ritual reenactment of the primordial Puruṣa sacrifice. In the process, Puruṣa is equated, or indirectly related, to Prajāpati, a variety of other Gods, the fire altar, the world, and even immortality. Mystical speculation rises to even greater heights in the last book on the agnicayana, book 10, from which the final passage in this selection is taken. While the beginning of the present selection only indirectly refers to the nāsadīya-sūkta of the Ṛg-Veda, the final passage makes the reference explicit.

असद्वा ऽइदमग्र आसीत् । तदाहुः किं तदसदासीदित्यृषयो वाव ते ऽग्रे ऽसदासीत्तदाहुः के त ऽऋषय ऽइति प्राणा वा ऽऋषयस्ते यत्पुरा ऽस्मात्सर्व्वस्मादिदमिच्छन्तः श्रमेण तपसा ऽऽरिषंस्तस्मादृषयः ॥ ६/१/१/१ ॥

In the beginning **non-being** [see XX:H2] was here. On this they say, 'What was that non-being?' Non-being in the beginning was these ṛṣis. On this they say, 'Who are these ṛṣis?' The ṛṣis are the (vital) breaths. Since prior to all this (world) they exerted themselves (अरिषन्) by toil and austerities, desiring this (world), therefore they are ṛṣis (ऋषयः).

स योऽयं मध्ये प्राणः । एष ऽएवेन्द्रस्तानेष प्राणान्मध्यत ऽइन्द्रियेणैन्द्ध यदैन्द्ध तस्मादिन्ध ऽइन्धो ह वै तमिन्द्र ऽइत्याचक्षते परोऽक्षं परोऽक्षकामा हि देवास्त ऽइद्धाः सप्त नाना पुरुषानसृजन्त ॥ २ ॥

Now what is this vital breath in the middle, that is Indra (इन्द्र). He kindled these breaths in the middle through his power (इन्द्रिय). Because he kindled (इ(न्)ध्) therefore he is Indha (इन्ध). (Although he is) Indha, they call him Indra, mysteriously, for the Gods love the mysterious. These (breaths), kindled, created seven different **Puruṣas** [XX:G; for the number 'seven', see also verse 15 of XX:G, and verses 8 and 9 of XX:H2, as well as the common Vedic notion of सप्तर्षयः 'seven seers' = divine seers who have become the seven stars of Ursa Major].

ते ऽब्रुवन् । न वा ऽइत्थँऽ सन्तः शक्ष्यामः प्रजनयितुमिमान्त्सप्त पुरुषानेकं पुरुषं करवामेति त ऽएतान्त्सप्त पुरुषानेकं पुरुषमकुर्वन्यदूर्ध्वं नाभेस्तौ द्वौ समौब्जन् यदवाङ् नाभस्तौ द्वौ पक्षः पुरुषः पक्षः पुरुषः प्रतिष्ठैक ऽआसीत् ॥ ३ ॥

They said, 'Being thus, we will not be able to create. Let us make these seven Puruṣas into **one Puruṣa**.' They made these seven Puruṣas into one Puruṣa. They compressed these two into (what is) above the navel, these two into (what is) below the navel, a Puruṣa was a side (or wing [of the fire altar?]), a Puruṣa was (another) side, one was the support (= the feet).

अथ यैतेषाँऽ सप्तानां पुरुषाणां श्रीः । यो रसऽआसीत्तमूर्ध्वँऽ समुदौहंस्तदस्य शिरो ऽभवद्यच्छ्रियँऽ समुदौहंस्तस्माच्छिरः ··· ॥ ४ ॥

Now, what was the excellence, the essence of these seven Puruṣas, that they concentrated up above; that became his head. In that they concentrated up his excellence (श्री), therefore it is the head (शिरस्) …

स ऽएव पुरुषः प्रजापरिभवत् । स यः स पुरुषः प्रजापतिरभवदयमेव स यो ऽयमग्निश्चीयते ॥ ५ ॥

That Puruṣa became Prajāpati (lit. 'lord of creation'). Now the Puruṣa that became Prajāpati he is this Agni that is being built here (in the form of the fire altar).

स वै सप्तपुरुषो भवति । सप्तपुरुषो ह्ययं पुरुषो यच्चत्वार आत्मा त्रयः पक्षपुच्छानि ··· ॥ ६ ॥

He is (composed) of seven Puruṣas, for this Puruṣa (= Agni) is composed of seven Puruṣas, viz. the body is four, the wings and tail are three … [The most basic fire altar covers an area defined by the square of seven lengths of the sacrificer. Four equal parts of the area define the body, one each the two wings and the tail; see the diagram below. In many forms of the ritual, however, the "bird altar" is much more elaborate.]

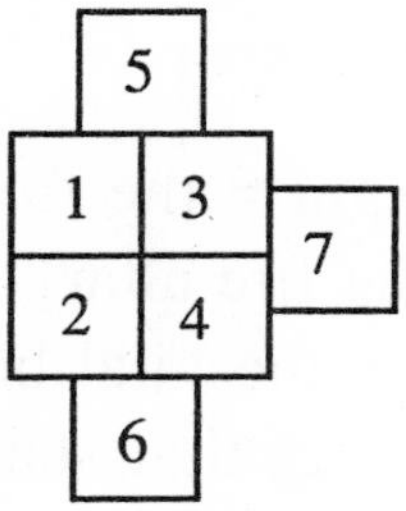

सोऽयं पुरुषः प्रजापतिरकामयत । भूयान्त्स्यां प्रजायेयेति सो ऽश्राम्यत्स तपो ऽतप्यत स श्रान्तस्तेपानो ब्रह्मैव प्रथममसृजत त्रयीमेव विद्याँऽ सैवास्मै प्रतिष्ठा ऽभवत्तस्मादाहुर्ब्रह्मास्य सर्व्वस्य प्रतिष्ठेति ··· ॥ ८ ॥

This Puruṣa, Prajāpati here desired, 'May I be greater, may I procreate.' He toiled, he practiced austerities. Having toiled, having practiced austerities, he first created Brahman (neuter), the threefold Veda. It became a support for him. Therefore they say, 'Brahman is the support of this whole (world).' …

सो ऽपो ऽसृजत । व्वाच ऽएव लोकाद्वागेवास्य ··· ॥ ९ ॥

He created the waters, from speech, from the world. Speech indeed was his …

सो ऽकामयत । आभ्यो ऽद्भ्यो ऽधि प्रजायेयेति सो ऽनया त्रय्या विद्यया सहापः प्राविशत्तत ऽआण्डꣳ समवर्तत ··· ॥ १० ॥

He desired, 'May I procreate from these waters.' He entered the waters together with this threefold Veda. From that an **egg** arose [see XX:H2, verses 8 and 9] …

अथ यो गर्भो ऽन्तरासीत् । सो ऽग्निरसृज्यत ··· ॥ ११ ॥

Now the **embryo** [see XX:I] that was inside, that was created as Agni …

सो ऽकामयत प्रजापतिः । भूय एव स्यात्प्रजायेयेति सो ऽग्निना पृथिवीं मिथुनꣳ समभवत्तत ऽआण्डꣳ समभवत् ··· ॥ ६/१/२/१ ॥

Prajāpati desired, 'May there be more; may I procreate.' By means of Agni he coupled with the earth. From that an **egg** arose …

स यो गर्भो ऽन्तरासीत् । स व्वायुरसृज्यत ··· ॥ २ ॥

Now the **embryo** that was inside, that was created as wind/air …

[Subsequent paragraphs detail how in the same manner he created the sun, the moon, the stars, this world, various Gods, etc.]

तदाहुः । कस्मै कामायाग्निश्चीयत ऽइति सुपर्णो मा भूत्वा दिवं वहादित्यु हैक ऽआहुर्न तथा विद्यादेतद्वै रूपं कृत्वा प्राणाः प्रजापतिरभवन्नेतद्रूपं कृत्वा प्रजापतिर्देवानसृजतैतद्रूपं कृत्वा देवा ऽअमृता ऽअभवंस्तद्यदेवैतेन प्राणा ऽअभवन् यत्प्रजापतिर्यद्देवास्तदेवैतेन भवति ॥ ३६ ॥

On this they say, 'For what sake is Agni = the fire altar being built?' Now some say, 'Becoming a bird [i.e., the shape of the fire altar], may he take me to the sky.' But let him not know thus. Taking that shape, the vital breaths became Prajāpati; taking that shape, Prajāpati created the Gods; taking that shape, the Gods became immortal. So, what the vital breaths became by this, what Prajāpati (became), what the Gods (became), that he becomes by this.

***

नेव वा ऽइदमग्रे ऽसदासीन्नेव सदासीत् । आसीदिव वा ऽइदमग्रे नेवासीत्तद्ध तन्मन ऽएवास ॥ १०/५/३/१ ॥

In the beginning **there was not nonbeing** here, as it were; **there was not being**, as it were. [XX:H1] In the beginning this (world), as it were, existed and did not exist. Then there was only mind.

तस्मादेतदृषिणा ऽभ्यनूक्तम् । नासदासीन्नो सदासीत्तदानीमिति नेव हि सन्मनो नेवासत् ॥ २ ॥

Therefore it was declared by the ṛṣi, **'There was not nonbeing nor was there being then'** [XX:H1], for the mind is neither being nor non-being, as it were.

तदिदं मनः सृष्टमाविरबुभूषत् । निरुक्ततरं मूर्ततरं तदात्मानमन्वैच्छत्तत्तपो ऽतप्यत तत्प्रामूर्च्छत्तत्षट्त्रिँऽशतँऽ सहस्राण्यपश्यदात्मनो ऽग्नीनर्कान्मनोमयान्मनश्चितस् ते मनसैवाधीयन्त मनसा ऽचीयन्त मनसैषु ग्रहा ऽगृह्यन्त मनसा ऽस्तुवत मनसा ऽशँऽसन् यत्किञ्च यज्ञे कर्म क्रियते यत्किञ्च यज्ञियं कर्म मनसैव तेषु तन्मनोमयेषु मनश्चित्सु मनोमयमक्रियत तद्यत्किञ्चेमानि भूतानि मनसा संकल्पयन्ति तेषामेव सा कृतिस्तानेवादधति तांश्चिन्वन्ति तेषु ग्रहान्गृह्णन्ति तेषु स्तुवते तेषु शँऽसन्त्येतावती वै मनसो व्विभूतिरेतावती व्विसृष्टिरेतावन्मनः षट्त्रिँऽशत् सहस्राण्यग्नयो ऽर्कास्तेषामेकैक ऽएव तावान्यावानसौ पूर्व्वः ॥ ३ ॥

Created, this mind wanted to become visible, more defined, more solid. It sought after a self/body. It practiced austerities. It became solid. It saw thirty-six thousand arka fires[1] of its self, consisting of mind, piled in mind. They were set by mind, they were piled by mind [i.e. mentally only, not physically]. Mentally the (soma) cups were drawn near them; mentally (the udgātṛs) chanted (the stoma chant), mentally (the hotṛs) recited the śastra. Whatever action is performed in the sacrifice, whatever sacrificial action, that, consisting of mind, was performed mentally at these (fires) consisting of mind, piled in mind. So, whatever these beings conceive of by mind, that is their performance; these (fires) they put on, these they pile, near them they draw the (soma) cups, near them they chant, near them they recite the śastra. So great is the growth of mind, so great is the creation of mind, so great is mind — thirty-six thousand arka fires. Of these each one is as great as the preceding one.

ते हैते व्विद्याचित ऽएव । तान्हैतानेवंविदे सर्व्वदा सर्व्वाणि भूतानि चिन्वन्त्यपि स्वपते व्विद्यया हैवैत ऽएवंविदश्चिता भवन्ति ॥ १२ ॥

These fires are piled in knowledge. All beings always pile them for one who knows thus, even when sleeping. By knowledge (alone) these fires are piled for (or by) one who knows thus.

[1] That is, a fire for each day of a person living 100 years of 360 days each.

K. A late upaniṣadic passage that "puts it all together"
(from Subāla Upaniṣad 1 - 3)

This upaniṣad, traditionally associated with the White Yajur-Veda, attempts to provide an integrated explanation of the origin of the whole world and of its underlying, transcendental unity. It does so by quoting, or alluding to, the most famous relevant passages in the Ṛg-Veda as well as other texts, including the earlier upaniṣads, and even post-Vedic philosophical systems such as sāṁkhya and mīmāṁsā, and by stringing these together into a more coherent "story". Some of these earlier sources are highlighted in the translation, with references to relevant selections in this Reader. The upaniṣad's most direct inspiration probably was the preceding ritualist selection (XX:J), of which so many ideas reappear here that cross-reference would be redundant. — The upaniṣad is traditionally characterized as a dialogue between the seer Subāla and Brahman (masc.), the post-Vedic creator God. It starts somewhat abruptly, with a statement, apparently by Subāla, but phrased as a question by some unnamed persons.

तदाहुः ' किं तदासीत् ' तस्मै स होवाच ' न सन्नासन्न सदसदिति ' तस्मात्तमः संजायते ' तमसो भूतादिः ' भूतादेराकाशम् ' आकाशाद्वायुः ' वायोरग्निः ' अग्नेरापः ' अद्भ्यः पृथिवी ' तदण्डं समभवत् ' तत्संवत्सरमात्रमुषित्वा द्विधाकरोत् ' अधस्ताद्भूमिम् ' उपरिष्टादाकाशम् ' मध्ये पुरुषो दिव्यः ' सहस्रशीर्षा पुरुषः सहस्राक्षः सहस्रपात्सहस्रबाहुरिति ' सो ऽग्रे भूतानां मृत्युमसृजत् त्र्यक्षं त्रिशिरस्कं त्रिपादं खण्डपरशुम् ' तस्य ब्रह्माभिधेति ' स ब्रह्माणमेव विवेश ' स मानसान्सप्त पुत्रानसृजत् ' ते ह विराजः सत्यमानसानसृजन् ' ते ह प्रजापतयः '

ब्राह्मणो ऽस्य मुखमासीद्बाहू राजन्यः कृतः ।
ऊरू तदस्य यद्वैश्यः पद्भ्यां शूद्रो अजायत ॥
चन्द्रमा मनसो जातश्चक्षोः सूर्यो अजायत ।
श्रोत्राद्वायुश्च प्राणश्च हृदयात्सर्वमिदं जायते ॥ १/१ ॥

'They say, "What was this (in the beginning)?"' He (Brahman [masc.]) said to him: '"(There was) **not being, nor nonbeing** [see Selection XX:H1], nor **being-and-non-being** [XX:H3]." From that, darkness was born, from darkness the subtle elements [these and the following terms come from sāṁkhya philosophy], from the subtle elements ether, from ether wind/air, from the air the waters, from the waters the earth. That became an **egg** [compare XX:H2, verses 8 and 9, and XX:I]. Having dwelled for a year (= after incubation), that (egg) made (itself) split in two, with the earth below, the sky above [see XX:H1, verse 5]. In the middle there was a divine **Puruṣa** ['divine' to distinguish this being from ordinary, human puruṣas], "**thousand-headed, thousand-eyed, thousand-footed, thousand-armed** [XX:G]".[1] He first created death of/for the beings, three-eyed (i.e. Śiva ?), three-headed, three-footed Khaṇḍaparaśu ['cutting his enemies to pieces with his ax', an epithet of Śiva and Viṣṇu]. His name is Brahman (neut.?).[2] It/he did indeed enter into Brahman (masc.). He created seven mind-born sons. They created **Virājes** [see XX:G, verse 5], mind-born truth-sons; they are the Prajāpatis. "**The brahmin was his mouth; the rājanya was made his arms; His thighs what is the vaiśya, from the feet arose the śūdra. The moon arose from (his) mind, from his eye arose the sun; From the ear both wind and breath, from the heart arises all this (world).**" [Compare XX:G].'[1]

अपानान्निषादयक्षराक्षसगन्धर्वाः ··· तस्यैतस्य महतो भूतस्य निःश्वसितमेवैतद्यदृग्वेदो यजुर्वेदः सामवेदो ऽथर्ववेदः शिक्षा कल्पो व्याकरणं ··· सो ऽन्ते वैश्वानरो भूत्वा संदग्ध्वा सर्वाणि भूतानि पृथिव्यप्सु प्रलीयते । आपस्तेजसि प्रलीयन्ते ··· अव्यक्तमक्षरे विलीयते । अक्षरं तमसि विलीयते । तमः परे देव एकीभवति । परस्तान्न सन्नासन्न सदसदित्येतन्निर्वाणानुशासनमिति वेदानुशासनमिति वेदानुशासनम् ॥ २/१ ॥

From the down-breathing (arose) the Niṣādas ("tribals" living in the jungle), Yakṣas, Rākṣasas, Gandharvas (i.e. all kinds of human and superhuman beings) ... **Of this Great Being this is (just) an outbreathing, viz. the Ṛg-Veda, Yajur-Veda, Sāma-Veda, Atharva-Veda,**[3] [see Selection VI §10], phonetics, ritual (sūtras), grammar ... In the end, he having become (Agni) Vaiśvānara, having burned up all beings, (as) the earth (he) dissolves in the waters; the waters dissolve in brilliance/fire ... the non-manifest dissolves in the imperishable, the imperishable dissolves in darkness, darkness becomes one in = with the transcendental God.[4] Beyond (there) is no "**being nor nonbeing nor being-and-nonbeing**", this is the instruction on the blowing out (the ultimate release), this is the instruction in/of the Veda (i.e. Vedānta), the instruction in/of the Veda.'[5]

असद्वा इदमग्र आसीत् । अजातमभूतमप्रतिष्ठितमशब्दमस्पर्शम् ··· ब्रह्मैव सन् ब्रह्माप्येति य एवं वेद ॥ ३/१ ॥

This (world) in the beginning was **nonbeing** [see XX:H2], **unborn, non-becoming, without support, without sound, without touch** ... [see e.g. IX §8] ... Being Brahman he goes to/becomes Brahman who knows thus.

[1] The citations from the puruṣa-sūkta do not always agree with the version in XX:G. Partly this is because they come from a slightly different version in the Vājasaneyi-Saṁhitā (VS (K) 35:1); but some differences cannot be thus explained and may reflect later changes in the tradition. For instance, the second verse cited at the end of this paragraph runs as follows in VS (K) 35:1:12

च॒न्द्रमा म॒न॑सो जा॒तश्चक्षो॒स्सूर्यो॑ अजायत ।
श्रोत्रा॑द्वा॒युश्च॑ प्रा॒णश्च॒ मुखा॑द॒ग्निर॑जायत ॥१२॥

'The moon arose from (his) mind, from his eye arose the sun; from the ear both breath and wind, **from his mouth Agni arose.**'

While last part of the VS version (highlighted in the translation) clearly fits the gāyatrī meter of the rest of the verse (and of almost the entire hymn), the version presented in our upaniṣad does not conform and would have to be considered irregular in any meter.

[2] Both Radhakrishnan and Śāstrī have तस्य ब्रह्माभिधेति, lit. 'his/its appellation or name is Brahman'; but Radhakrishnan translates 'Of him Brahmā [i.e. masc.] became afraid', as if the text read तस्माद् ब्रह्मा बिभेति. The translation given here tries to take the transmitted text seriously, while at the same time attempting to make sense of it, as referring to Brahman (neut.) which then enters Brahman (masc.).

[3] The early upaniṣadic version in Selection VI §10, has the older Vedic expression अथर्वाङ्गिरसः 'Atharva-Aṅgirases'. The use of the later expression अथर्ववेद is just another indication of the lateness of the present text.

[4] As Radhakrishnan points out, 'The order of dissolution is the reverse of the order of evolution and the account is based on the Sāṁkhya theory.'

[5] Repetition of the last part of a paragraph commonly indicates the conclusion of a discussion.

Notes

Notes

General Notes: For the convenience of students not familiar with Vedic texts, the selections in I - XIX are generally presented in a commonly employed type of 'upaniṣadic' edition, with Classical Sanskrit sandhi and without accent notation, as well as with division of sentences etc. within paragraphs[1] by means of a reduced daṇḍa [']. The only exception is Selection I, which also appears in a "Vedic" version with various peculiarities of sandhi and phonetics, accent marking (characteristic of the Śatapatha-Brāhmaṇa and Bṛhad-Āraṇyaka-Upaniṣad), and without separation of sentences etc. within paragraphs. Non-upaniṣadic selections (in XIII) and the selections in XX are presented in the manner in which they are found in the consulted editions, with minor adjustments for typographic reasons. These texts tend to ignore sentence boundaries within paragraphs; they exhibit various aspects of Vedic sandhi and phonetics; and depending on the text tradition, they may show various types of accent marking (or be unaccented). The peculiarities of Vedic accent marking, sandhi, and phonetics are treated briefly at the beginning of the notes to Selection XX.

1. Like most publications of its genre, this reader is organized such that the notes to the early selections contain the richest information on grammar, usage, and religious, philosophical, and cultural background. Users who would like to start with a later selection might want to glance through the notes for the early selections in order to be familiar with this information and so as to know where to find it, if needed.

The reader is intended for students who have a firm foundation in Classical Sanskrit (i.e., who have read the selections from Nala and Damayanti, the Hitopadeśa, the Kathāsaritsāgara, and Manu in Lanman's *Reader*, or comparable texts). Students should therefore be familiar with the general inflectional patterns of the present system (present and imperfect), of the perfect, and of the future, covered in parts IX, X, and XII of Whitney's *Grammar*, as well as with the system of participles, gerunds, gerundives, and infinitives (Part XIII of Whitney's *Grammar*). They should also be familiar with the general patterns of noun, adjective, and pronoun inflection, dealt with in Parts V and VII, including the pronouns इदम् (nom. sg. masc. अयम्) and अदस् (nom. sg. masc. असौ).

---

1 The term "paragraph" is used to refer to numbered subsections of Vedic Prose texts, such as the part in Selection II that ends with ॥ १ ॥.

At this point, users of the Reader are advised to further familiarize themselves with certain general aspects of Vedic grammar. Many of these are dealt with in Whitney's *Grammar*. These are given below, with references to Whitney. Items marked by a preceding "bullet" (•) are especially important. Terms in CAPS are different from the ones employed by Whitney.

Phonetics:

Pluti/pluta, or tri-moric prolongation of final vowels and its functions: §78

Inflection:

Peculiarities in noun and pronoun inflection:

ablative/genitive singular of feminine vowel stems: §§390h, 363c, 365d
a-stems: §§328b, 329a-d
i- and *u*-stems: §338a plus §343d on पति
पुंस्: §§183a, 394
neuter *r*-stems: §375
a(ñ)c-stems: §408-410
n-stems: §425
ma(n)t/va(n)t- stems: §454
perfect participle (which occurs more commonly than in Classical Sanskrit): §458
• enclitic personal pronouns: §500 with §502a (see also below)

Peculiarities in verb inflection:

• Tense (including aorist): §532 plus Part XI (with §§928-930 on the functions of the aorist)
See also §778c on पुरा and/or स्म with present = habitual past
• Subjunctive mood (absent in Classical Skt.): §§553, 557-563, 574
• Negative imperative or prohibitive: §579
Augmentless imperfects and aorists ("INJUNCTIVES"): §587
The type स्तौति, pl. स्तुवन्ति: §626
• Reduplicated presents, especially the type जुहोति: §§647-657
Long-vowel reduplication syllables in the perfect: §786
Inflection of अह् 'speak, say': §801a
• Separation of verbal prefixes from the verb ("TMESIS"): §1081

Other:

• Various particles and conjunctions whose use differs from that of Classical Sanskrit or which are not normally used in Classical Sanskrit: §§1122ab, 1122j, 1131-1133

Many of the particles enumerated in Whitney's §§1122ab, 1122j, and 1131-1133 are difficult to translate. This is especially true for वै (alternative form वाव) and ह/अह. At the same time, as will be seen in §3 below, these particles can be useful in reading texts without sentence separation.

2. Whitney's discussion regarding enclitic third person pronouns (§500 with §502a) needs to be supplemented by observing that the forms of the stem एन and the enclitic forms of the pronoun अयम्/इदम् together form a paradigm of the following type, in which only the nominative forms are missing. (There are no enclitic nominative forms; structures without any overt pronoun may be considered to take their place.)

	Singular			Dual		Plural		
	m.	n.	f.	m.	n. f.	m.	n.	f.
Accusative	एनम्	एनत्	एनाम्	एनौ	एने	एनान्	एनानि	एनास्
Instrumental	अनेन/एनेन		अ/एनया	आभ्याम्		एभिस्		आभिस्
Dative	अस्मै		अस्यै	आभ्याम्		एभ्यस्		आभ्यस्
Ablative	अस्मात्		अस्यास्	आभ्याम्		एभ्यस्		आभ्यस्
Genitive	अस्य		अस्यास्	अयोस्/एनयोस्		एषाम्		आसाम्
Locative	अस्मिन्		अस्याम्	अयोस्/एनयोस्		एषु		आसु

3. Anyone reading Vedic Prose texts, including those of the upaniṣads, cannot help being struck by the overwhelming presence of a syntactic or rhetorical feature absent from the classical texts: Sentences tend to begin with complex "initial strings" consisting of the following elements.

- An initial element, commonly a single word, which in accented texts always bears accent [abbreviation: X́];
- Enclitic pronouns, both of the third person (see above) and of the first and second persons [E];
- Accented [= Ṕ] and unaccented particles [= P];
- Accented pronouns of the type तद्/एतद् (demonstrative), क/किम् (interrogative), and य- (relative) [= D́].

In many cases, initial strings are fairly simple, consisting of only a few of these elements. But occasionally the strings may become quite complex, containing one or more representatives of every one of the above categories. In such cases, a clear structure is discernible, with five distinct positions, which accommodate the different categories as follows:

Position	1	2	3	4	5		
	X́	P	Ṕ	E	D́	—	Rest of the sentence

The following examples may illustrate the pattern. The first one represents one of the relatively rare cases where every position in the string has been filled. The first and last examples show that, as a consequence of being placed into initial strings, elements may be separated from words with which they syntactically belong. Thus, in the last passage the pronouns एताम् and एष are separated from विक्रान्तिं and विष्णुः respectively. (Where necessary, sandhi has been undone for better alignment of the examples.)

1	2	3	4	5		
दैवीं	च	वाव	अस्मै	एतद्	—	विशं मानुषीं चानुवर्त्मानौ करोति

'He now makes both the divine and the human folk subservient to him'

यथा	ह	वै	---	---	—	पदेनानुविन्देत्

'as one might find (something) by means of the foot (trace)'

भगवान्	---	तु एव	मे	तद्	—	ब्रवीतु

'but may your lordship tell me this'

एताम्$_1$	उ	एव	---	एष$_2$ एतस्मै	—	विष्णुः$_2$ … विक्रान्तिं$_1$ विचक्रमे

'and this Viṣṇu … stepped this stepping for him'

While discontinuities of this sort may cause some difficulties, initial strings have a certain advantage in texts without sentence separation, in that they can be interpreted as something like punctuation marks. The presence of initial strings, and especially of position 2 and 3 elements (above all वै / वाव and ह / अह), usually signals that the preceding word begins a new sentence or sub-clause within a sentence.

4. A slight complication results from the fact the entire initial string may optionally be preceded by an adverbial sentence linker, as in the following examples. The most common linkers of this type are तद् 'so, then' and अथ / अथो 'now'; sometimes स is used in this way, too, and may then be translated as 'so, then, now'. Note that in this function, स shows no agreement with the subject of the sentence, as in the third example below, where the subject is in the dual, but स in the singular.

	1	2	3	4	5		
अथ	यो	ह	वा	---	---	—	अस्माल्लोकात्… प्रैति

'Now, who departs from this world …'

तद्	इन्द्रो	ह	वा	---	एतद्	—	देवतानाम्

'Now, Indra (is) that one of the deities …'

स	यद्	---	एव	अस्य	एतौ	—	हविर्भवतः

'So, if these two are his oblation …'

5. Other aspects of word order:

In Vedic Prose, the predicate commonly precedes the subject, as in उषा वा अश्वस्य मेध्यस्य शिरः 'The head of the sacrificial horse is Dawn' (Selection I, line 13.) This is a consequence of a general tendency in these texts to place what is new and more significant into the most prominent, initial position of the clause.

6. Agreement:

A very common pattern in Vedic is that demonstrative pronoun subjects agree with their predicates in gender, as in तद्यदपां शर आसीत्तत्समहन्यत । सा पृथिव्यभवत् 'Now what was the foam of the waters that (neuter) congealed. **That/it** (feminine) became the earth (feminine).' (Selection II, line 5)

7. Use of the aorist:

The aorist (as in अभूत् Selection II, line 3) occurs frequently in our texts. Its most basic function is to indicate an action anterior to another action which may either be explicitly mentioned or may be implicit in the context. In many cases it can be translated as a present perfect or pluperfect, depending on the context. But occasionally such a translation is not idiomatic in English. In such cases the aorist indicates an earlier action that still has relevance to the speaker. (See Whitney, Part XI, with §§928-930.)

8. Relative-correlative structures:

a. Sanskrit relative clauses usually exhibit the structure below. Either the relative clause precedes and the main clause follows, or vice versa; but ordinarily, relative clauses are not inserted into main clauses as they are in English. The relative clause contains a RELATIVE pronoun (RP) or relative adverb; the main clause may contain a corresponding CORRELATIVE pronoun (CP) or adverb. Structures of this sort may take some initial adjustment on the part of the western reader; sometimes an initial literal translation may be useful, to be then converted into a more idiomatic English version.

य एवासावादित्ये पुरुष एतम् एवाहं ब्रह्मोपासे (Selection V, line 4)
RP CP

'I worship as Brahman the man/puruṣa yonder that (is) in the sun.'
(Lit. "Which man yonder (is) in the sun, that I worship as Brahman.")

b. Relative clauses may be "stacked up", one on top of the other, as in the following example:

ओषति ह वै स तं यो ऽस्मात्पूर्वो बुभूषति य एवं वेद (Selection IV, line 5)

'Who knows thus burns (up) the one who wants to be before = better than him.'
(Lit. "He_1 burns up him_2 who_2 wants to be before him_1 who_1 knows thus.")

c. A common use of relative clauses is found in quasi-elliptical constructions such as the following. Here the relative clause (यं कामं कामयेत 'what desire he might desire') is followed by a "truncated" correlative (तम् 'that', to be construed as तं वृणीत 'that (one) he should choose').

> तस्माद् तेषु वरं वृणीत यं कामं कामयेत तम् (Selection III, lines 12-13)
>
> 'And therefore he should choose a boon among them, what he might desire, that he should choose.'
>
> (Lit. "And therefore he should choose a boon among them, what desire he might desire, that.")

d. The "invariable *yad*" construction. See for instance Selection IV, lines 40-41: तदेतत्पदनीयमस्य सर्वस्य यदयमात्मा, to be translated as 'This is the foot-trace of this entire (world), namely ātman.' The syntactic construction may appear somewhat unusual, but it is common enough in Vedic Prose to bear special comment. What is unusual about the structure can be illustrated more effectively by sentences of the following type: स एव यज्ञो यदयमग्निः, lit. 'That (masc.) is the sacrifice (masc.), what (neut.) is this Agni (masc.)'. As can be seen, the form of the relative pronoun here is invariably neuter (यद्) and does not agree in gender either with the antecedent (स यज्ञः) or with the noun phrase in its own clause (अयमग्निः). Structures of this type are best translated along the lines suggested above; hence स एव यज्ञो यदयमग्निः = 'That is the sacrifice, namely this Agni.'

9. Other:

The verb चर् or other verbs of going, standing, sitting plus present participle or gerund may be used to indicate continuous action (Whitney §1075), as for example सोऽर्चन्नचरत् 'he kept praising' (Selection II, line 2) .

Selection I

This passage is quite ritualist in outlook, dedicated to explaining the aśvamedha as part of the larger ritual of the agnicayana (for which see e.g. Selection XX:J; see also §2 of the Introduction to this Reader). Nevertheless, by equating the sacrificial horse with in effect the entire universe it represents a stage of ritualist thinking that comes closer to what we would consider typical of upaniṣadic thought. That stage must go back at least to the time of the Taittirīya-Saṁhitā, one of the earliest Vedic-Prose texts, which offers substantially the same passage, with the same "global" interpretation of the sacrificial horse (TS 7:4:15). Note, however, that the latter text constitutes the last section of the Taittirīya-Saṁhitā and therefore may be a relatively late addition. (The Gian edition of the Śatapatha-Brāhmaṇa does not include this passage in the Bṛhad-Āraṇyaka-Upaniṣad portion.) — The notes below refer to the upaniṣadic version of the text (lines 13-23).

Summary: The first part equates the different parts of the sacrificial horse's body with different parts or aspects of the phenomenal world. For instance, the head is equated with the dawn (whose significance can be inferred to lie in the fact that it initiates the daily return of the life-giving sun). Lines 18-19 equate activities of the sacrificial horse with natural phenomena. Thus, opening its mouth is equated with the lightning. The final part refers to the ceremony in which the horse is sacrificed and where two vessels named "greatness" are used, one placed in front of the horse, the other behind. The placement in front is equated with the eastern direction and eastern ocean, and the placement in back with the western direction and western ocean, based on the fact that the words for 'east' and 'west' are identical to words for 'in front' and 'in back'. Inserted into this final part of the text is a brief passage giving different names for the sacrificial horse, as vehicle of the Gods, the Gandharvas, the Asuras, and humans.

13: In Vedic texts, प्राण usually refers to 'breath' or 'life-breath', or to a particular type of breathing (see e.g. the note on Selection VII, line 43-44); it does not normally have the meaning 'life' which it has in the classical language. — व्यात्तमग्निर्वैश्वानरः Here the order switches from "predicate before subject" to the more basic "subject before predicate". Such switches are not uncommon in longer enumerations such as the present one.

14: आत्मा here 'body'; the word, however, can also mean 'self', or can be used to designate the transcendental principle behind the diversity of the phenomenal world. — द्यौष्पृष्ठम् Note the Vedic sandhi.

14/15: Note the equation of the back of the horse (= the top) and the hoof (the lowest part) with sky/heaven and earth, respectively, and of the belly with the intermediate area, the visible air/sky between the earth and the heaven; a useful English translation for the latter is 'ether' or 'air'.

16: अहोरात्र dvandva (Whitney §1256e, see the Glossary under अहस्, रात्र. — प्रतिष्ठा, lit. 'support', here 'the feet'.

18: उद्यन्, निम्लोचन् pres. participles (√इ + उद्, √म्लुच् + नि) supply 'the sun'. — विजृम्भते 'opens the mouth' in order to yawn according to one commentary (or to whinny?). Śaṅkarācārya interprets the verb as meaning गात्राणि विनामयति विक्षिपति 'bends, throws about (its) limbs'.

19-21: पश्चात् and पुरस्तात् are adverbs.

20: महिमा lit. 'greatness', here the name of a golden vessel. In the horse sacrifice, a golden vessel is placed in front of the sacrificial horse, and another one, made of silver, behind it, to hold the sacrificial libations. The places in which they are located are called their योनि 'womb, nest, home'.

22-23: The horse is assigned different names depending on its association with the Gods, the Gandharvas, the Asuras, and human beings. The precise differences between these names are not always clear.

Selection II

This passage, too, is quite typical of ritualist speculation and is representative of a common attempt at explaining the world and the sacrifice as a series of creations by a primordial deity or principle. The passage is somewhat unusual in that the primordial principle is identified as Death. Moreover, by declaring that there was nothing in the beginning, the passage establishes a certain link with early Ṛg-Vedic speculations on the origin of the world from non-being, or from a state when there was neither being nor non-being (see the selections in XX:H). (The Gian edition of the Śatapatha-Brāhmaṇa does not include this passage in the Bṛhad-Āraṇyaka-Upaniṣad portion.)

Summary: In paragraphs 1-4, the world is said to be created by Death (equated with hunger) who engages in worshiping, practicing austerities, and intercourse with Speech. As in the rest of this passage, there are several attempts at etymological explanations, such as that of the "arka-hood of the arka" through derivation from the root √ऋच्. He who knows these explanations (य एवं वेद) will enjoy well-being. The remaining part of the selection shifts gear. "He", i.e. presumably Death, sets out to eat his creation, becomes weak, and his body begins to swell. The word for 'swell' is taken as the etymological source of the word for 'horse', which then provides an explanation of the aśvamedha, the horse sacrifice.

2: मनो ऽकुरुत an idiom similar to Engl. 'It/he made up its/his mind.' — सो ऽर्चन्नचरत् see §9 of the General Notes above. — तस्यार्चतः could be a genitive absolute construction (Whitney §305b); but the negative connotations usually associated with that construction are not present here. The structure more likely is a simple genitive. This case form is commonly used in our texts to indicate the source from which something or somebody is born.

3: Supply 'He thought'. — कम् (indecl.) normally in Vedic means 'good, well, wellbeing'. Śaṅkarācārya glosses it as meaning 'water', an interpretation repeated in later translations. His interpretation is probably influenced by the next paragraph in this selection, which talks about the waters. — 'That is the arka-hood of the arka': one of many etymologies offered in our texts to convey a deeper or more significant meaning. अर्क 'ray, fire; hymn, singer' is considered derived from the root √ऋच् 'praise, worship' which underlies the preceding forms of अर्चत्.

5: तत् see §4 of the General Notes above. — सा पृथिव्यभवत् see §6 of the General Notes above.

6: तप्त the root तप् commonly is used intransitively, as in (तपस्) तप्यते or in our case, तप्त, in the meaning 'practice austerities'. — अग्निः is used appositively with तेजो रसः; translate 'of him ... the splendor, essence evolved, namely Agni.'

7: आत्मानम् here 'himself'; see also the note on Selection I, line 2. — The third part into which he divides himself, of course, is he himself.

8-10: The implicit comparison here is to the fire altar, in the shape of a bird, but also equated with the primordial Puruṣa of RV 10:90 (= Selection XX:G, see also XX:J). As usual, the altar is oriented toward the east ('forward'); then the different parts of the bird/Puruṣa are equated with the various cardinal points or 'quarters', including the intermediate quarters which are referred to simply as असौ चासौ 'yonder and yonder (direction)'. Such a use of demonstrative pronouns without overt reference reflects the oral nature of our texts. The reciter would indicate by gestures which direction each instance of असौ refers to.

10: इयम् supply पृथिवी. — स एषः duplication of demonstrative pronouns, both of the type स एषः and of the type स सः, serves to focus precisely on what is designated or modified by the pronouns. In many cases, such structures can be translated as 'this very ...', 'that very ...'. Note that unlike other duplications, such as यो यः, these structures do not act like compounds and may therefore be separated by "initial-string" material (for which see §3 of the General Notes above).

11: Forms of एवं + √विद् occur frequently in our texts to refer to one who has a proper understanding of the ritual or of esoteric knowledge.

12: मिथुनम् plus √भू (+ सम्) 'have intercourse with' acts like a simple verb and takes a direct object, in this case वाचम्.

13: अशनाया, मृत्यूः are appositives.

14: अबिभर् from √भृ.

15: भाण् is quasi-onomatopoetic; it may have been influenced by √भाष् 'speak' and √भन् 'speak' (in post-Vedic also √भण्).

16: √मन् + अभि (fut.) lit. 'think against' = 'turn against' etc.

18: स see §4 of the General Notes above. — The intransitive present of √धृ has the special meaning 'to set out to' when accompanied by the infinitive (here अत्तुम्).

19: Another example of an etymology: अदिति, lit. 'the unbounded', is considered related to √अद् 'to eat'.

23: श्वयितुम् from √श्वा. — तस्य शरीरे etc.: The fact that 'his mind (still) was in his body' (which had swollen, being dead) created a problem.

24. आत्मन्वी from आत्मन्विन्.

25: Another etymology: अश्वत् (aor. of √श्वा) = अश्व and मेध्य = मेध. (From the historical perspective, the latter equation is fine; but the former one is another case of a "folk etymology", not unlike what we find in the Greek and Roman traditions.)

Selection III

This selection has been chosen mainly because of its beautiful triple formula: 'From untruth lead me to truth, from darkness lead me to light, from death lead me to immortality.' Forerunners of parts of this famous formula appear in the Ṛg-Veda and other earlier texts; see the selections in XX:E. For the rest, the selection deals with aspects of the ritual, specifically the use of particular sāmans and their benefits.

Summary: The passage starts with different views on what is the (underlying) support for a particular sāman (chant) and then transits to a ritual called the "ascent" of the sāman. In this context, the sacrificer is asked to recite the three famous short formulas, which are explained in subsequent paragraphs. The passage then returns to other, more general aspects of the ritual and the benefits they offer to the priest and the sacrificer.

1: The sāman referred to here is the udgītha (for which see Selection XIII). — तस्य ... एतस्य. — प्रति ह तिष्ठति "tmesis"; see the General Notes and Whitney §1081. Note too the play on words प्रतिष्ठा ... प्रति तिष्ठति.

2: खलु. — एतत् here 'now'. — अन्ने. — For उ see Whitney §1122a. The functions of the particle range from 'and' to 'but' and 'on the other hand'. — एके 'some (people)', a common reference to persons who have a different opinion, especially one which the composer of the text disapproves of.

3: अभ्यारोह, lit. 'ascent' is a special ritual through which the sacrificer rises to the world of the Gods. — The prastotṛ is an assistant of the udgātṛ priest.— यत्र here 'when'; the correlative (next line) is तद्.

4: जपेत् the जप is a special form of recitation at a sub-audible or barely audible level, often glossed as 'muttering'. The person who should perform this recitation at this point is the "sacrificer".

5: मा clitic sg. acc., first person singular pronoun.

7: यद् here 'in so far as'.

10: As in many other cases, इव does not refer to any particular part of the sentence, but to the sentence as a whole, and is best translated as 'as it were'.

12: आत्मने ऽन्नमागायेत् 'he should "sing up" food for himself.'

14: तद् ह एतद् लोकजित् — अलोक्यता lit. 'worldlessness', i.e. not having a world to live in or to go to after death. — आशा here 'prospect, fear'.

15: Supply तस्य 'of/for him' as antecedent for the relative clause.

Selection IV

This selection offers several attempts to identify the source of this world as the Self (आत्मन्) or as Brahman (neuter). There are strong echoes here of the Ṛg-Vedic puruṣa-sūkta (Selection XX:G), especially in §§2, 7-9, and 23-25. In addition, §§28-29 are significant because they assert the superiority of esoteric knowledge to mere ritual performance; and §22 suggests that the Gods are not happy that human beings know that they and the Gods ultimately are the same (namely Brahman).

Summary: This passage contains several creation stories intended to explain the nature of the world. The first of these singles out आत्मन्, the Self, as the creator of the world. His first creation is himself, to this is added a woman, and from union with her the various beings arise. This is followed by a short passage on the creation of fire and of its use in the sacrifice, and the interesting assertion that the creator, being mortal, created the immortals. The next passage focuses on the creation of the world through differentiation, and on the Self as the underlying unity behind this differentiation. Two passages follow in which ब्रह्मन् is considered the source of creation. The first of these introduces the extraordinary idea that knowing one's identity with Brahman makes a person identical — and superior — to the Gods, and that the Gods do not like this fact, since human beings therefore no longer need to sacrifice to the Gods, thus depriving them of their sustenance. The second passage deals more specifically with the creation of the castes, both human and divine, and extols especially the brahmin caste. The final story returns to focus on the Self, who creates mind, speech, breath, eye, and ear — which, being five, are identified as the five-fold sacrifice, the five-fold cattle, the five-fold human being — everything is five-fold. Each of the creation stories tends to conclude with a statement that knowledge conveyed by the story brings great benefits to the knower. In addition, there are several attempts at etymological explanations.

1: इदम् is in principle ambiguous; it may either refer to 'this (world)' or simply mean 'here'. The latter reading is supported by the parallel इह in §1 of Selection III. Note similarly आप एवेदमग्र आसुः (BAU (K) 5:5:1) 'the waters were here in the beginning', where the plural आसुः shows that the subject is the plural आपः 'the waters', not the singular इदम्. — √ईक्ष् + अनु + वि. — आत्मनः may either refer to the ultimate आत्मन् 'Self' or be simply the reflexive pronoun.

1-2: सो ऽहम् On the use of demonstrative pronouns with personal pronouns, see Whitney §§498, 499c. (The same use is found with अयम्/इदम् and असौ/अदस्.) The demonstratives in structures like this have a strongly locational force: 'I here', 'you there', etc.

4: पाप्मनः here accusative plural. — Another etymology: पुरुष (RV also पूरुष) from पूर्व 'before, prior' + √उष् 'burn'.

5: बुभूषति desiderative of √भू 'wants to be'.

6: स ... अयम् This type of structure is similar both to the type स (...) सः (see the note on Selection II, line 10) and the type सो ऽहम् above. A close English match would be 'that one here', 'he here'. — ईक्षां चक्रे periphrastic perfect (Whitney §1070 with 1034 [√ईक्ष् is desiderative in origin]).

7: कस्मात् नु — अभेष्यत् conditional of √भी. — वि इयाय (√इ).

9: रेमे perf. mid. of √रम्.

11: अपातयत् causative of √पत् 'fall'.

12: तस्मादर्धबृगलं स्वः 'Therefore one's self (स्वः) here is (only) a half-morsel.' — The combination of इति ह plus a verb of speaking commonly indicates a statement by a person of authority (who may be mentioned after the verb of speaking, as in the present case). — See Whitney §778c on the use of स्म and/or पुरा 'before' or a form of पूर्व 'earlier, former' with present indicative to refer to a habitual action in the past. — तस्मादयमाकाशः स्त्रिया पूर्यत एव translate as 'Therefore this (empty half-)space is filled by a woman/wife.'

14: सा + उ, ह + इयम् — मा enclitic 1st person pron. acc.

15: असानि sg. 1 subj./impve. of √अस् 'be'.

16: समेवाभवत् "tmesis".

20: अजावयः a dvandva, अज + अवि. (Compare Selection XX:G, verse 10.) — मिथुनम् here 'paired'. — आ पिपीलिकाभ्यः 'up to, all the way down to the ants'.

22: असृक्षि *s*-aorist of √सृज्

23: √भू here means 'prosper'. This usage is common in Vedic Prose, especially in combinations like भवत्यात्मना परास्य द्विषन्भ्रातृव्यो (भवति) 'he prospers by himself, his hateful enemy is defeated (परा √भू with "tmesis")'; see e.g. Selection XX:B.2.

24: इति here has its literal meaning 'thus'. The reciter of the orally transmitted text would clarify the precise reference of इति by an appropriate gesture. — योनेः is appositive to मुखात् ('from his mouth as the womb'). योनि here and in the next line evidently must be read both as 'source' and as 'womb, vagina'. To our mind, this might be a play on words; but to the minds of the composer and audience of our text there was no doubt a single word योनि whose semantic range included all of these meanings, and others as well.

26: तद् यद् 'Now, in so far as'. — एकैकं देवम् represents one of the two objects of the verb of speaking (the person talked about), the other one being the quotation अमुं यजामुं यज = अमुं यज अमुं यज, transl. 'Now, in so far as they say here about each God "sacrifice to him, sacrifice to him" ...' — एतस्य refers back to the आत्मन् who created everything.

29: Soma is a deified, hallucinatory substance. He/it is often equated with the moon, the source of the rain which impregnates the earth. He/it also is the food of the Gods. (See e.g. Selection XVII:A below.)

30: The accented text shows that ब्रह्मन् here is neuter and thus no doubt refers to Brahman, the transcendental principle (an alternative to आत्मन्).

31: अतिसृष्टि in so far as the creatures created by this act are higher in status than their creator.

32: तद् ह इदम्.

32-33: असौनाम 'having such-and-such a name'. This is a special occurrence of the common use of असौ/अदस् as a kind of "variable" or "place holder", with the details to be filled in according to the actual situation (in this case, by a particular name). Manu (2:122) offers a specific parallel in the context of discussing how one should announce one's name. इदंरूप 'having this-kind-of form'; the construction is parallel to the preceding असौनाम. Transl. 'This one (i.e. he) has this name, this shape.' — इति marks the end of the formula.

35: आ plus ablative 'up to'.

38: While एव usually is simply an emphasizing particle, which may be left untranslated in English, here it is better rendered as 'merely', qualifying the preceding word. — एकैक here 'individual(ly)'. — √आस् + उप The most appropriate translation in the present context is 'meditate'. (Compare उपनिषद् which also contains उप, plus √सद्, a root semantically closely related to √आस्.)

39: अतः here 'of these'.

40: आत्मेति 'as ātman'.

44: अन्यमात्मनः प्रियम् is the object of ब्रुवाणम् which in turn is the object of ब्रूयात्. — रोत्स्यति future of √रुध्, here 'perish'. — ईश्वर plus optative (or a special form of the infinitive) is used in the meaning 'be liable to'. — Translate as 'Now, if somebody might say that something is dearer than the self (and) if somebody might say to that person "What is dear to you will perish," that is likely to happen.'

47: √मन् plus nominative form of a middle voice participle (or gerund, or predicate noun or adjective) is construed reflexively: 'they believe (themselves as) becoming (fut. participle)' = 'they believe they will become'; similar constructions are found with verbs of speaking. — Transl. 'In so far as humans believe they will become everything through the knowledge of Brahman, what is it then that Brahman knew (as the source) from which everything came about?'

53-54: तस्य ह न देवाश्चनाभूत्या ईशते 'Even the Gods do not have power of = over him.'

54-55: 'That one is different, I am different' = 'we are not the same Self'.

55: भुञ्ज्युः pl. 3 opt. of √भुज्. — पशु may mean 'animal', as well as 'sacrificial victim'.

56: एकस्मिन्नेव पशावादीयमाने locative absolute; √दा + आ here 'take away', पशु here must mean 'sacrificial victim'.

57: किमु ... to be interpreted along the lines of 'what, then, would be the case if there are many?'. — तस्माद् ... That is, the Gods are not happy that human beings have the esoteric knowledge that they are (identical to) the Self of the Gods and therefore need not sacrifice victims to them.

58-59: अति here should be rendered fairly literally, as 'in addition'; no separate account is given for the creation of the brahmin caste, but it clearly coexists with the other three castes.

59ff.: Here क्षत्र and ब्रह्मन् are used to refer to the kṣatriya and brahmin castes, qua institutions; at the same time, brahmin caste and Brahman, the transcendental principle, are also identified with each other.

60: A special use of इति after enumerations, more or less meaning 'here's the end of the list'.

61: क्षत्रे — तद् here 'at that time'.

62-64: This is an example of the recurring need felt by brahmins to enjoin kṣatriyas from injuring or killing them.

65: स Evidently we are returning from ब्रह्मन् (neuter) in §23 to the आत्मन् (masc.) of the earlier discussion. — विश् lit. 'clan, people, common people' is used like क्षत्र and ब्रह्मन् as a designation of a caste (the वैश्य).

65-66: The Vasus, Rudras, Ādityas, All-Gods, and Maruts are **groups** of Gods.

67: It is not quite clear why Pūṣan, the God of herdsmen and farmers is introduced here. The vaiśyas are more prominently identified as herdsmen and farmers than are the śūdras. But some subgroups of the śūdras do serve as pastoral and agricultural laborers.

67-68: Another etymology: पूषन् from पुष्.

70: अथ + उ 'moreover'. — आशंसते supply 'to defeat'.

73: Construe as 'This very Brahman/brahmin (is also) kṣatra, viś, and śūdra.'

76-77: √इ + प्र lit. 'go forth' = 'depart; die'. — अननूक्त neg. ta-participle of √वच् + अनु lit. 'say after, repeat' = 'study' or 'recite'. — कर्मन् here probably refers to a 'sacrificial action', i.e. a sacrifice. — Transl. 'Now, if one dies without seeing his own world [which is Brahman, as explained further below], this — not being known to him — does not support him, like either an unrecited Veda ...'

77: अनेवंविद् 'one who does not know thus'.

82: √ब्रू + अनु see the note on l. 76-77 regarding √वच् + अनु.

82-83: यत्पितृभ्यो निपृणाति refers to the offering of piṇḍas (flour dumplings) to the pitṛs at the śrāddha ceremony (a ritual performed at certain intervals after one's ancestors' death to assure that they reach the पितृलोक and do not roam the earth as ghosts).

83: वासयते causative of वस् 'dwell' = 'give shelter'.

85: वयांसि — आ पिपीलिकाभ्यः see the note on line 35 above.

87: विदितं मीमांसितम् ta-participles of √विद् 'know' and of the quasi-root √मीमांस् (desiderative of मन्)

89-90: न इच्छन् चन अतस् भूयस् विन्देत्.

91-92: अकृत्स्नः ...मन्यते See the note on l. 47-48.

92: तस्य + उ. — What the कृत्स्नता consists of is detailed in the next paragraph.

94: दैवम् supply वित्तम्.

95: 'five-fold' by having mind, speech, breath, eye, and ear.

Selection V

This is one of several passages in which a brahmin admits defeat to a kṣatriya in a spiritual argument and then asks to become his pupil. The esoteric knowledge imparted in this selection is that the identity of the individual self and the primordial Self can in this world be experienced only in deep sleep.

Summary: A discussion about Brahman between Bālāki Gārgya, a brahmin, and king Ajātaśatru of Kāśi. Gārgya proposes a series of definitions of Brahman, each of which Ajātaśatru refutes. When Gārgya runs out of suggestions, he asks Ajātaśatru to teach him. Ajātaśatru responds that it is not normal for a kṣatriya to teach a brahmin but that he will teach him anyway. Taking him to a sleeping man, whom he awakes, Ajātaśatru asks him where the man had been when he was asleep. Gārgya does not know, and Ajātaśatru explains that he was lying in a space within the heart, "taking the intelligence of these breaths with him." When he is sleeping that way, breath is restrained, speech is restrained, the eye is restrained, the ear is restrained, the mind is restrained. He has his own world in which he is a great king or a great brahmin, or he enters a state of "up-and-down"; he moves around in his own body, taking his senses with him, just as a great king moves around in his country, taking his people with him. In deep sleep the man is not aware of anything. Taking (one of) the 72,000 channels extending from the heart to the pericardium, he creeps towards the pericardium and lies there in greatest bliss. The passage concludes with the suggestion that just as a spider moves up by its thread, as small sparks emanate from a fire, so from the Self emanate all the breaths, all the worlds, all the Gods, all beings, all the individual selves. The esoteric meaning of this is "the truth of truth"; the breaths are truth; the Self is truth.

1: दृप्तबालाकि The parallel version in the Kauṣītaki-Upaniṣad (4:1) simply has गार्ग्यो बालाकिः, suggesting that दृप्त here should be interpreted as an epithet, 'proud' or 'arrogant', a reading which is quite natural, given the context.

2: सहस्रम् supply 'cows'. — दद्मः The "royal we"; but the use of the first person plural by individual persons is not limited to people of nobility or power. (See e.g. Selection XVII:A, §5, where Śvetaketu, worsted by King Jaivali, uses a first plural pronoun in talking to his father, a person of greater authority and status than himself.)

2-3: जनको जनक इति This is evidently what he claims the people say about him; he thus compares himself with Janaka, another learned king and a great patron of brahmins (see e.g. Selection VII).

5: मा prohibitive neg. (+ aorist injunctive) followed by मा enclitic pronoun. — संवदिष्ठाः from √वद् + सम्.

12: एतावत् नू३ A question: 'Is that all now?' Note the use of pluti (Whitney §78). — एतावत् हि, with idiomatic use of हि in answer to a question ('indeed, yes').

12-13: न ... विदितं भवति 'is not known' = 'there is no (real) knowledge'.

13: उप (tmesis) + त्वा + अयानि (subj. or impve.), lit. 'may I go to you', the traditional formula with which a person asks a teacher to take him on as a pupil. The parallel version in the Kauṣītaki-Upaniṣad (4:19) runs as follows:

> तं होवाचाजातशत्रुः 'एतावन्नु बालाका(३) इति 'एतावदिति होवाच बालाकिः 'तं होवाचाजातशत्रुः 'मृषा वै खलु मा संवादयिष्ठाः 'ब्रह्म ते ब्रवाणीति 'यो वै बालाक एतेषां पुरुषाणां कर्ता यस्य वै तत्कर्म स वै वेदितव्य इति 'तत उ ह बालाकिः समित्पाणिः प्रतिचक्रमे 'उपायानीति 'तं होवाचाजातशत्रुः 'प्रतिलोमरूपमेव तन्मन्ये यत्क्षत्रियो ब्राह्मणमुपनयेत 'एहि व्येव त्वा ज्ञपयिष्यामि ...
>
> 'To him Ajātaśatru said, 'So much now? = Is that all?' Bālāki said, 'So much.' Ajātaśatru said to him, 'In vain/falsely did you make me converse [caus. imperf. injunctive] (with you, by saying:) "Let me tell you about Brahman." Who, O Bālāki, is the creator of these persons [talked about earlier], of whom this is the creation, he is to be known.' Then Bālāki, kindling in his hands (i.e. with a gesture of obedience to the teacher) went toward (him, saying:) 'Let me come to (you as your pupil).' Ajātaśatru said to him, 'I consider it against the grain that a kṣatriya should lead up a brahmin (= accept him as pupil, invest him with the sacred cord). Come, I will make you understand.'

15: व्येव ... ज्ञपयिष्यामि tmesis (see Whitney §1089 and the note on Selection II, line 1).

17: आपेषम् present gerund (Whitney §995) of √पिष् + आ. — आमन्त्रयां चक्रे periphrastic perfect.

18: Here we have a case where aorists are difficult to translate as an English present perfect or pluperfect; see General Notes, point 7. — तदा + अभूत्. — यत्र ... यः ... एषः Complex relative-correlative structure: 'When he was just asleep, (the person) who is this person consisting of intelligence, where was he then?'

19: आ + अगात्

20-21: Complex relative-correlative construction: 'Where = when he has been asleep, then this person consisting of intelligence, taking by his intelligence the intelligence of these (vital) breaths (or senses), sleeps in that space that is within the heart.'

21: प्राणानाम् The commentary suggests interpreting this as referring to the 'senses'. This is a plausible interpretation, both here and in §20. — य एषो ऽन्तर्हृदय आकाशः The commentary ultimately identifies this 'space' with the परमात्मन्, the highest, transcendental Self.

22: शेते

23: तानि 'these (senses)'. The change in gender reflects the fact that the following enumeration of these senses, 'breath, speech, etc.', contains words of mixed gender, and, since the words do not refer to animate or human beings, the proper gender to refer to these conjointly is neuter. — नाम (particle) see Glossary — गृहीत here 'restrained'.

25-26: तद् उत इव. The series of correlated उतs conveys something like 'either ... or ... or'. As in many other cases, the इव following each of the उतs is to be translated as 'as it were'. — That is, he is no longer tied down by the "real" world.

29-30: हिता नाम नाड्यो द्वासप्ततिः सहस्राणि हृदयात्पुरीततमभिप्रतिष्ठन्ते This is an inserted, quasi-parenthetical statement; the two preceding relative clauses, introduced by यदा, are answered by the correlative clause starting with ताभिः प्रत्यवसृप्य. (हिता is the name (नाम) of these arteries.) — पुरीतत् The commentary is no doubt correct in identifying this with the अन्तर्हृदय आकाश of paragraph 17.

32: शयीत opt. of √शी 'lie'.

33: Supply '[having become the Self]'.

34: यथा ऊर्णवाभिः

35-36: Note the distinction between the ultimate Self and the individual selves.

37: एषः (masc.) no doubt refers to आत्मन् 'the Self'.

Selection VI

While Manu's perspective on women is highly restrictive, a large amount of evidence suggests that he represents only one view, that of the brahmin law giver. In the post-Vedic period, the story of Nala and Damayantī offers one of many examples of strong women who know how to take care of their own interests and who have no fear about confronting men, or even the Gods. In Vedic literature, too, we get occasional glimpses of women who can hold their own around men. Several hymns of the Ṛg-Veda are attributed to women seers (e.g. RV 10:39-41), and in a passage of the Jaiminīya-Brāhmaṇa (2:219), the women of the Atri clan are referred to as मन्त्रकृतः 'mantra-makers', i.e. seers. In ritualist literature, however, such references to scholarly women are exceedingly rare. It is therefore worthy of note that the Bṛhad-Āraṇyaka-Upaniṣad mentions two women as being interested in esoteric knowledge or even as being scholars in this field. (On the status of women see also Rajeshwari Pandharipande, 'Spiritual dimensions of fertility cult and the power of women', *Dharma* 3: 248-266, 1988.)

The present passage deals with Maitreyī, one of the two wives of the seer Yājña-valkya. Maitreyī is quite different from his other wife, Kātyāyanī who, as stated explicitly in BAU (K) 4:5, is not spiritually inclined. Yājñavalkya clearly considers Maitreyī capable and worthy of spiritual instruction, and he is obviously delighted by her interest; but he consistently uses the term अरे (which can be glossed as 'my dear') in addressing her, a word usually employed with persons of somewhat inferior social status. She, in turn, frequently uses forms of the honorific quasi-pronoun भगवत्, such as भगोः in §2 and भगवान् in §3. While we may deplore this uneven social relationship, we are here probably getting a realistic glimpse of the social situation in (late) Vedic times. Even in modern northern India, a man may freely use the word अरे in addressing his wife, while such a use by his wife would be frowned upon. Moreover, although Maitreyī is interested in spiritual matters, she clearly is no scholar. In Selection IX, by contrast, Yājñavalkya is boldly confronted by a woman scholar; and here he does not use the term अरे. This, too, no doubt reflects some element of social reality.

Beyond its interest as a mirror on the late Vedic social relationship between men and women, the conclusion of the present selection offers a very famous early argument in favor of the later monistic philosophy of अद्वैत, lit. '(doctrine) of non-duality'. (A slightly elaborated version of the same story concludes the "Yājñavalkya Cycle"; see Introduction, §3.5.)

<u>Summary</u>: Yājñavalkya is about to depart from the householder stage of his life and proposes to make a settlement between Maitreyī and his other wife, Kātyāyanī. Maitreyī responds that she prefers to know what would make her immortal. Delighted with the response, Yājñavalkya sets out to explain. He begins with a series of statements that drive home the message that the Self is or should be dearer than anything else in the world. By understanding the Self one understands everything there is to be known; for the Self is (in reality) everything in this world. A series of comparisons with real-world phenomena serves to demonstrate that knowledge of the Self is not possible through focusing on its external manifestations. Just as sparks emanate from a fire, so the phenomena of this world are just "outbreathings" of the Self. Another series of comparisons

serves to illustrate a deeper unity underlying and subsuming the phenomena of the world; for instance, the skin is the "single goal" into which all touch sensations merge. As a lump of salt thrown into water dissolves in the water and cannot be grasped, but still pervades all of the water, so the Self, 'this great being ... pure knowledge ... rising from these beings vanishes with them. Having died there is no consciousness.' At this point, Maitreyī professes confusion. Yājñavalkya responds with a final series of statements explaining that the duality of this world, where one sees the other, smells the other, and so on, comes to an end at death, when everything in this world becomes the Self [i.e., when one merges with the Self]. At that point, there is no difference between the seer and the seen, the smeller and the smelled, and so on. 'By means of what would one know the one through whom one knows this whole world; by what, my dear, would one know the knower?'

1: उद्यास्यन् ... अस्मात्स्थानात् 'about to depart (fut. pple.) from this place/state', i.e., no doubt from the householder state (गृहस्थ) to the stage of the ascetic forest-dweller (वानप्रस्थ).

2: अनया from इदम् — अन्त a final (settlement).

3: यद् मे. — Here as elsewhere note that vocatives can go anywhere within the sentence. Here, भगोः is inserted into the noun phrase इयं सर्वा पृथिवी.

6-7: Note the switch from honorific, third-person भगवान्वेद to informal, second-person ब्रूहि. As in the post-Vedic language (e.g. the story of Nala and Damayantī), there is no need to use honorific forms consistently; all that matters is that such forms are used some of the time. (The issue of verbal politeness, with emphasis on Sanskrit, is dealt with by Lieve Van de Walle, *Pragmatics and Classical Sanskrit*, Amsterdam, Benjamins, 1993.)

8: बत अरे. — The "royal we" again, but followed by the singular pronoun 'I' in the next line. — सती sg. nom. fem. of सत्, pres. act. pple of √अस्. — एहि (आ इहि) आस्स्व.

9: व्याचक्षाण pres. mid. pple. of √चक्ष् + वि + आ. — निदिध्यासस्व sg. 2 impve. mid. desid. from √ध्या + नि, lit. 'try to think' = 'pay attention'.

11: कामाय here 'for the sake of'.

12: आत्मन् here refers to the ultimate Self. — जायायै on the use of the dative in -आयै for the genitive/ablative in -आयाः see Whitney §§307h, 363c, 365d.

16-18: ब्रह्मन् and क्षत्र here refer to the priestly and royal power.

26: √दा + परा; either aorist 'has abandoned' or injunctive 'may/should abandon'; the commentary adopts the latter interpretation.

28-29: For the यद्-construction see §8.d of the General Notes above.

30: Here begins a multi-paragraph series of arguments, each one introduced by स यथा 'now, as ...'; the resolution is found in §10 (एवम्, line 36). — The construction of √शक् with the dative of a verbal noun, rather than the infinitive, is unusual. Translate as 'would be able to grasp'. — The idea here is this: You can hear the external sounds (बाह्याञ्छब्दान्), but you cannot grasp or feel them, it is only by touching (ग्रहण) of the instrument or the player that you can feel the sound …

30: हन्यमान pres. pass. pple.

32: वीणायै see the note on line 12 above. The viṇā is a stringed musical instrument. — वाद्यमानायै pres. pass. pple. of √वादय.

36: आर्द्र + एध + अग्नि. — √धा + अभि + आ.

36-37: अस्य महतो भूतस्य no doubt refers to the Self or Brahman.

37: अथर्वाङ्गिरसः the old Vedic name for the Atharva-Veda, reflecting its dual nature as a collection of spells and speculative hymns, but perhaps also, by the absence of the element वेद, the fact that it has not yet been fully accepted as the fourth Veda.

37-38: इतिहासः … The differences between the texts designated by these terms are not always clear. Later on, इतिहास comes to mean 'history'; here it probably refers to something like legends or stories of the past. पुराणम् later comes to refer to a particular type of literature, related to the epics; here it might refer to epics in general. विद्या here probably does not refer to the त्रयी विद्या of the Ṛg-, Yajur-, and Sāma-Veda, since these already have been mentioned. Perhaps what is meant are forerunners of the later शास्त्र texts. श्लोकाः may be gnomic verses or gāthas that are occasionally found in Vedic-Prose literature. सूत्राणि no doubt refers to such texts as the śrauta- and gṛhya-sūtras. अनुव्याख्यानानि and व्याख्यानानि seem to be commentaries on the mantras and the ritual. (The commentary on our text is no help here, since it tries to explain all of the terms very narrowly from a ritualist Vedic perspective.)

40: एकायनम् the sole goal or locus.

45: उपस्थ the lap as the seat of the sexual organs.

47-48: न हास्योद्ग्रहणायेव स्यात् '(and) would not be for one's grasping as it were' = 'and could not be grasped'.

48: यतस् यतस् तु. — आददीत sg. 3 mid. opt. of √दा + आ. — लवणमेव supply 'there is' and compare Selection XII, paragraph 13/2.

49: एतेभ्यो भूतेभ्यः समुत्थाय तान्येवानुविनश्यति Compare Manu 12:20-22 on the body's dissolution after death into the five elements, as well as the expression पञ्चत्वं √गम् lit. 'go to the fivehood (of elements)' = 'die', commonly used in the fables. The idea is that we arise from the combination of the five elements, and when these dissolve, we dissolve too. — For the sandhi in समुत्थाय see Whitney §233c. — अनुविनश्यति 'dies along with'.

49-50: न प्रेत्य संज्ञा अस्ति इति अरे; construe न with संज्ञास्ति; प्रेत्य 'having gone forth = having died, after death'. The idea is this: After death, when we have dissolved into the five elements, there is nothing left of us through which we could have (worldly) consciousness or awareness; or (at a deeper level) we merge with the ultimate principle and hence there is no duality of observer and observed etc.

51: अमूमुहत् reduplicated aorist (causative) of √मुह् (Whitney §§824, 856-873).

52-53: अलम् with dative, 'enough for'. The following इदम् may perhaps refer to the content of the next two paragraphs, which represent the conclusion of the discussion.

56: यत्र तु अस्य सर्वम् एव आत्मा अभूत्

59: तम् refers to आत्मन्, through whom one knows all of this world.

Selection VII

This is the first of a long series of disputations held by the sage Yājñavalkya with various learned opponents at the court of King Janaka. Yājñavalkya is the most important sage in the Bṛhad-Āraṇyaka-Upaniṣad; and Janaka not only is patron of extended disputations between different sages, but also has a strong and very active interest in spiritual matters. — The present text has been selected because of its humorous interlude in §4.

Summary: Janaka, king of the Videhas, sets out a prize of a thousand cows, with gold pieces attached to their horns, to be awarded to the most learned brahmin. When Yājña-valkya tells his pupil to drive the cows away, the other assembled brahmins become angry, and one of them, Aśvala, begins to test him by questioning him. His questions concern the manner in which the sacrificer can free himself from the control of death, day and night, and so on; how the sacrificer can ascend to heaven; how the priests will conduct the sacrifice; and what the benefit of the sacrifice will be. In each case, Yājña-valkya provides an answer that is appropriate not just superficially, but also at a deeper level. Aśvala, evidently defeated, falls silent.

1: बहुदक्षिण 'having many dakṣiṇās (rewards, remunerations to the priests)'. — ईजे perf. mid. of √यज्. — The Kurus and Pañcālas are the most important peoples of the brāhmaṇa period. Their location appears to have been in the मध्यदेश ('central area'), in present-day Haryana and most of Uttar Pradesh. The Videhas are "Easterners", located in eastern Uttar Pradesh and Bihar, close to Kāśī, present-day Banaras (or Varanasi). The premise of this text, that brahmins from the central area have come to the court of the king of the Videhas, probably mirrors the historical fact that such brahmins were called to the east by kings eager to have them perform Vedic rituals for them and thereby to enhance and legitimize their status as rulers. (The Jaiminīya-Brāhmaṇa (1:245) relates the story of how King Janaka, being challenged by a certain Sucitta Śailana, asked that priests should be called to his court; and तस्मै ह कुरुपञ्चालानृत्विज ऊहुः 'they brought him Kuru and Pañcāla priests'. For more details on the locations and migrations of peoples and brahmin schools during the Vedic period, see Michael Witzel, 'On the localisation of Vedic texts and schools', *India and the Ancient World: History,*

Trade, and Culture before A.D. 650, ed. by G. Pollet [Orientalia Lovaniensia, Analecta 25], Leuven, 1987.)

2: See glossary under स्विद्.

4: दशदश 'ten each'. — पादाः here 'gold pieces'.

5: उदजताम् fut. impve. 'shall drive away'

7: सौम्य + उदज. — सामश्रवा३स् vocative form with pluti.

8: √कृ + उद् + आ.

8-9: Verbs of speaking in the middle voice can be used reflexively 'declare oneself (to be X)', where X agrees in case with that of the speaker.

10: Yājñavalkya is an adhvaryu belonging to the Yajur-Vedic tradition. Perhaps it is no accident that his first opponent is a hotṛ, associated with a different, and perhaps rival tradition, that of the Ṛg-Veda. (On the different types of priests in the Vedic ritual see section 5 of the Introduction.)

11: ब्रह्मिष्ठाय for effect, supply 'whoever that may be' — a flippant reply by Yājña-valkya.

12: गोकामाः a bahuvrīhi compound. — For effect render एव as 'simply'.

13: आप्त here, 'controlled' or 'pervaded'. — √वद् + अभि.

14: होत्रा ऋत्विजा अग्निना, that is 'with the hotṛ as priest, with Agni, with speech.' — This begins a series of interchanges which focus on the hotṛ, the adhvaryu, the brahman, and the udgātṛ.

15: तद् here 'now'. — या इयम्. — अतिमुक्ति picks up on earlier अतिमुच्यते.

16: अहोरात्र (du. n.) dvandva (Whitney §1256e).

20: पूर्वपक्षापरपक्ष a dvandva compound referring to the first or "light" (i.e. waxing) and the second or "dark" (i.e. waning) fortnight of the lunar month. (See also Selection XVII:A, §18.)

27: अतिमोक्षाः refers to what precedes; अथ संपदः introduces the following discussion.

28: कतिभिस् अयम् अद्य ऋग्भिस् होता अस्मिन् . . . — √कृ here 'conduct the sacrifice'. — तिस्रः (from त्रि, Whitney §482f.)

29: The पुरोनुवाक्या is the introductory verse, the याज्या is recited during the sacrifice, and the शस्या is recited in the śastra, which accompanies the grahas ('ladlings') of Soma mixed with milk. The common name for these verses is स्तोत्रिया.

33: या हुताः . . . Note the use of relative clauses without corresponding correlative clauses. — The oblations consist, respectively, of wood and oil (which flare up), of the meat etc. of the victim (which burns up with a great noise), and of milk and Soma (which being watery, just sink down into the ground). These oblations correspond, respectively, to the puronuvākyā, yājyā, and śasyā.

34: अधिशेरते Vedic third plural pres. middle form (Whitney §613).

36: The commentary plausibly suggests to read अतीव as अति 'excessively (noisy)' plus इव 'as it were'.

37: अधस्

38: कतिभिः ... This passage refers to the fact that in the ritual of taking Agni to the fire altar, the brahman priest, representing the God Bṛhaspati, mutters the apratiratha hymn, in a reenactment of his and Indra's defense of the sacrifice from the Asuras who came from the south (दक्षिणतः) and tried to prevent the Gods from performing the sacrifice (ŚB (M) 9:2:3:ff.).

39: सा एका.

40: विश्वे देवाः 'the All-Gods', a special class of Gods.

43: अधिदेवतम् and अध्यात्मम् '[merely] in reference to the deities' vs. 'in reference to the Self/the transcendental principle' — a common distinction in late Vedic texts.

43-44: प्राण — अपान — व्यान Terms in a sometimes very elaborate theory of breathings found throughout the Vedic Prose texts (see e.g. Selection X, §27). The terms may be rendered as 'up-breathing', 'down-breathing', and 'diffused breathing' (which is diffused through the body).

Selection VIII

In this short selection Yājñavalkya eventually winds up talking about the issue of पुनर्मृत्यु 're-death'. On this matter see also §3.5 of the Introduction.

> Summary: Bhujyu Lāhyāyani takes his turn questioning Yājñavalkya. His question repeats a question he and fellow wandering pupils had once asked a Gandharva: 'What became of the Pārikṣitas?' Yājñavalkya correctly tells him the answer that the Gandharva had given and then gives a more elaborate, esoteric reply: The Pārikṣitas were given by Indra to Vāyu (the wind), through an infinitesimally small opening between the earth and the surrounding ocean. Vāyu then placed them in their final destination. Yājñavalkya concludes by praising the wind as, in effect, the ultimate principle. 'He defeats re-death, he reaches a complete life-time, who knows thus.' Bhujyu Lāhyāyani falls silent.

1: The Madras were a people of the northwest, beyond मध्यदेश. — चरकाः 'as wandering (pupils/scholars)'.

2: ते refers to the implicit first plural subject of ऐम; see the note on Selection IV, lines 1-2 regarding this use of demonstrative pronouns. — गृह commonly is construed as masculine plural in Vedic Prose. — गन्धर्वगृहीत There are many parallels for women being possessed by Gandharvas. We are not told of any adverse effects on the women.

3: तम् This refers to the Gandharva of the compound गन्धर्वगृहीत. (See Whitney §1316 on the sometimes very loose construction of compounds, which makes it possible to refer to the first member of a compound as if it were its head.)

4: The Pārikṣitas are a royal family who performed the aśvamedha. A great king of this lineage, Janamejaya, is mentioned in the Aitareya-Brāhmaṇa as having performed the aśvamedha and conquered the whole world (AB 8:21:1). — अभवन् here, 'came to be'; or translate क्व ... अभवन् as 'What became of ...'

6: The second सः refers to the Gandharva.

7-9: द्वात्रिंशतं ... According to the commentary, these are still the words of the Gandharva. Construe as 'This world (is of the extent of) thirty-two day-trips (अह्नानि) of the divine chariot (देवरथ, i.e. the chariot of the sun). The earth surrounds that complete world on all sides (in an area) twice that extent. The ocean surrounds that earth (in an area) twice that extent.'

9: तावानन्तरेणाकाशः 'of such an extent (there is) a space between these two'.

10: तान् ... Supply 'Through that space ...'. तान् refers back to the Pārikṣitas of the preceding paragraph. (Vāyu placed them within himself and went there ...)

11: सः apparently still refers to the Gandharva.

12: अप ... जयति tmesis.

Selection IX

In this selection a woman who evidently is an established scholar, Vācaknavī Gārgī, challenges the great sage Yājñavalkya to answer two questions and thereby either to prove his superiority over all the brahmin challengers present at King Janaka's court or to run the risk that 'his head will fly apart' — apparently not an idle threat, for as we see in the next selection, this dire fate can in fact befall someone who is too presumptuous and then is defeated in a brahmodya, a disputation on Brahman. (On the topic of the "bursting head", see Stanley Insler, 'The shattered head split and the Epic tale of Śakuntalā', *Bulletin d'études indiennes* 7-8: 97-139, 1989-1990.)

Unlike Maitreyī, Gārgī uses very bold language; and Yājñavalkya clearly does not treat her patronizingly (he does not use the अरे which he employed throughout his discussion with Maitreyī). Eventually he defeats Gārgī by successfully answering her questions; but he does the same to all of his opponents.

Summary: Vācaknavī Gārgī, with permission by the assembled brahmins, questions Yājñavalkya in bold language. Her question is 'What is above the heaven, Yājñavalkya, what is below the earth, what is between these two, heaven and earth, what they call "past, present, and future", wherein is all of that woven back and woven forth?' In the first round, Yājñavalkya gives a fairly simple, straightforward answer — 'in space'. He gives the same answer when she repeats the question, insisting on a deeper, more meaningful reply. It is only after her follow-up question, 'In what now is space really woven back and forth?' that Yājñavalkya gives the desired deeper reply. Space is woven back and forth in the "Imperishable", which can only be negatively defined. At its command, the elements of the visible world are distinguished, and human beings, Gods, and pitṛs behave the way they do. A person who dies without knowing this Imperishable is pitiful; but who dies knowing it, he is a knower of Brahman. Although invisible, inaudible, unthinkable, unknowable, this Imperishable is the seer, hearer, thinker, knower. It is in this Imperishable that space is woven back and forth. Defeated, Gārgī informs the other brahmins, 'Not one of you will defeat this one in a disputation on Brahman.' Then she falls silent.

2: चेद्. — जेता periphrastic future (Whitney §§532, 931, 942-949). Note that √जि takes two direct objects, one of the person defeated, the other of the object won.

4-6: This sentence would in traditional western grammar be called an anacoluthon: Gārgī begins with अहं वै त्वा, something like a false start; right after that she almost gets lost in a long comparison of herself with a bold warrior; and eventually she starts more or less all over again by saying अहं त्वा द्वाभ्यां प्रश्नाभ्यामुपोदस्थाम्. Such false starts occasionally occur elsewhere in our texts, and in this case the effect is to give a certain colloquial flavor to Gārgī's speech, just like Yājñavalkya's अरे when talking to Maitreyī or his quip in Selection VII that he is merely interested in the cows. (Another "anacoluthon" of this type is found in Selection XVII:A, §19.) — √स्था + उप + उद्.

8: अवाक् from अवाच्. — द्यावापृथिवी nom./acc. du. dvandva; see Whitney §1255ab.

9: ओतं ... प्रोतं The root is √वा. Render the two participles as 'woven back and forth', with comparison to the warp and weft (or woof) which hold together a weaving.

13: वि अवोचस् (from √वच् 'speak'). — अपरस्मै Whitney §§522-526. — धारयस्व Note the special reflexive flavor of the middle voice causative.

16: The presence of एव in this virtual repetition of the question adds an element of insistence: '... what **really** is this woven back and forth in?' This use of एव recurs in subsequent selections. (See the earlier comments on Selection IV, line 38, and VIII, line 12.)

20: The same idea is expressed here by नु 'now' (कस्मिन् नु अकाशः). — This line is spoken by Gārgī.

21-24: अक्षर here has its literal meaning, 'imperishable', and is used as an epithet for the transcendental principle, which can only be negatively defined. Look up the meanings for the following long series of negatives (beginning with अस्थूलम्) under the corresponding positives. Toward the end of line 21, the word अनणु is hidden; the middle of line 22 contains अवायु; line 22-23 अचक्षुष्क and line 23 अतेजस्क show extensions of *s*-stems by the suffix क; अनाम and अगोत्र refer to the fact that human beings are socially defined in terms of their name and their affiliation with a गोत्र (or clan).

24-25: अश्नोति normally is to be translated as 'reaches, acquires', but the two roots √अश् have a tendency to be confused in their inflection; and the commentary supports the reading 'eats'. Note that तद् in one sentence is subject, in the other object.

29-30: अन्य ... अन्य translate as 'some ... others'. This refers to the flowing of the rivers from the Himalayas either east to the Gangetic system, or west toward the Sindhu.

31: ददतम् sg. acc. pres. act. pple. of √दा; see Whitney §§667-668 and §444 with 646.

36-37: Observe the rare use of neuter gender for agent nouns in *-tṛ-*; and note that negated *ta*-participles tend to have an "impossibility" reading, so that 'unseen' can mean 'invisible'.

39: अस्मात्

39-40: मुच्याध्वै subjunctive; translate the verb intransitively (rather than as a passive).

Selection X

This selection, an elaboration of an earlier, shorter disputation in Śatapatha-Brāhmaṇa (M) 11:6:3, is the dramatic conclusion of Yājñavalkya's disputations at the assembly of King Janaka. The passage goes back and forth between ब्रह्मन् and आत्मन् in referring to the transcendental principle, without making a clear distinction. The negative definition of the transcendental principle, which we already saw in the last selection, is carried even farther, especially in Yājñavalkya's characterization of आत्मन् 'the Self', as नेति नेति "not", "not", i.e., as not definable in any way. The expression नेति नेति is, to the present day, one of the favorite upaniṣadic citations in Hindu religious philosophy.

What adds to the drama is that Yājñavalkya gets increasingly angry at his opponent, Śākalya; and when the latter eventually loses, he suffers a fate threatened in several other passages (including the preceding selection) — his head flies apart. Whatever must have been meant by the claim that somebody's head may fall apart or actually does so, the present selection shows that this phenomenon was considered a genuine physical event, not surprisingly ending in the death of the one who met this dire fate. The earlier version of ŚB (M) 11:6:3:11 simply tells us that Yājñavalkya threatens Śākalya that he will die 'before such and such a day'; and Śākalya did.

Yājñavalkya concludes with a set of brahmodya ślokas which can be interpreted as suggesting either that he rejects the doctrine of karman and reincarnation (or does not approve of it) or that he does approve of it. The latter interpretation is prevalent in the commentaries (such as that of Śaṅkarācārya); the former interpretation has been adopted by many western interpreters. Whatever the proper understanding of this passage may be, it is clear that Yājñavalkya later on in the Yājñavalkya Cycle accepts the doctrine (see section 3.6 of the Introduction).

Summary: Vidagdha Śākalya takes his turn questioning Yājñavalkya. He begins by asking about the number of Gods. Yājñavalkya progressively reduces that number from "303 and 3003" to just one, namely 'Brahman, this'. [A number of similar questions and answers follow. These have been omitted in the interest of keeping the selection within limits.] Our selection resumes with an angry and often ironic exchange between Yājñavalkya and Śākalya. Yājñavalkya asks Śākalya whether the other brahmins have made them their "fire extinguisher". Śākalya accuses Yājñavalkya of "out-talking" the brahmins and asks him to tell what he knows as Brahman. Yājñavalkya responds that he knows the directions, together with their Gods, together with their support. [Again, parts of the continuing verbal battle are skipped, including one episode that leads to the answer that there are 'eight abodes, eight worlds, eight persons'.] The selection resumes with Śākalya asking Yājñavalkya 'In what, now, is the heart established?' Yājñavalkya calls him a fool for thinking it to be anywhere else but within ourselves. Śākalya follows up, 'In what now, are you and the Self established?' In the ensuing verbal exchange, Yājñavalkya rehearses the प्राण theory and ends with a negative definition of the Self as नेति नेति 'not, not' — ungraspable, indestructible, unattached, unfettered. 'These are the eight abodes, the eight worlds, the eight persons.' Yājñavalkya concludes the debate by asking Śākalya about the "upaniṣadic person" who takes apart these persons, puts them together, and goes beyond them. 'If you do not explain him to me, your head will fly apart.' Śākalya cannot think of him, and his head flies apart. Robbers take away his bones. In the dramatic conclusion, Yājñavalkya challenges the remaining brahmins with several ślokas (for which see the detailed notes below).

1: विदग्ध The literal meaning is 'clever', and given the context it is tempting to see this as an ironic epithet, comparable to the दृप्त 'proud' of Selection V; the commentary simply takes विदग्ध as a name.

4: This line is found in earlier Vedic literature (Kāṭhaka-Saṁhitā 35:6). It contains several examples of early Vedic nominative/accusative neuter plural forms (त्री, शता, and सहस्रा); see Whitney §§329c and 338a. For the interpretation of त्रयश्च त्री च शता and त्रयश्च त्री च सहस्रा see Whitney § 477d, and note that त्री is construed as an adjective modifying the following शता and सहस्रा (hence: three hundred, three thousand).

5: ओम् here is simply 'yes'.

6: एव see the comment on Selection IX, line 16.

12: त्रयस्त्रिंशत् तु एव

14: त्रयस्त्रिंश Ordinal numerals may be used to indicate what completes a series; in this case, 'the two thirty-third ones' are the ones that make the series of thirty-three complete.

16: Another etymology: वसवः because they वासयन्ते.

18: The त्रयो लोकाः of course are earth, ether, and heaven/sky.

19-20: यो ऽयं पवते, lit. 'who purifies here', is a standard epithet of the wind.

21: तद् आहुः 'On this (issue), they say ...'

21-22: Another etymology: अध्यर्ध from √ऋध् + अधि.

22: The exact interpretation of त्यद् in this context is not quite clear, but there is a Ṛg-Vedic demonstrative स्य/त्यद्. The commentary suggests that it is a mysterious name for Brahman, but gives no further reason for this interpretation.

23-24: The first, ironic outburst of Yājñavalkya. अङ्गारावक्षयण literally means an instrument for extinguishing coals; perhaps what is meant is the hot coals or fire of Yājñavalkya's performance. — अक्रता३ pl. 3 aor. mid of √कृ plus pluti.

25: अत्यवादीः sg. 2 aor.

26: किं ब्रह्म विद्वान् 'what Brahman do you know (lit. are you a knower)' or 'what do you know as Brahman'. विद्वस् here is used in its original sense, as a perfect active participle. — वेद sg. 1 perf. of √विद्. — सदेवाः सप्रतिष्ठाः construe as coordinated adjectives, modifying दिशः.

28-29: Yājñavalkya's second, more angry outburst. Such outbursts of irony or anger are not unusual in these disputations and are not limited to Yājñavalkya. For instance, in BAU (M) 3:5:1, an opponent of Yājñavalkya complains about an answer he has just received:

> यथा वै ब्रूयादसौ गौरसावश्व इत्येवमेवैतद् व्यपदिष्टं भवति यदेव साक्षादपरोक्षाद् ब्रह्म य आत्मा सर्वान्तरस्तं मे व्याचक्ष्वेति
>
> 'This has been explained (by you) is as if one were to say, "That is a cow, that is a horse" [i.e., it is mere description, not an explanation]. What is clearly, not mysteriously Brahman, what is the Self (which is) inside everything, that explain to me.'

And in BAU (M) 3:7:4-5 another opponent who is angry with Yājñavalkya for having attempted to drive off the brahmodya-cows, engages in the following dialogue with him:

> तदहं वेद तच्चेत्त्वं याज्ञवल्क्याविद्वांस्तं चान्तर्यामिणं ब्रह्मगवीरुदजसे मूर्धा ते विपतिष्यतीति ॥ ४ ॥

वेद वा अहं गौतम तत्सूत्रं तं चान्तर्यामिणमिति । यो वा इदं कश्च ब्रूयात् ˈवेद वेदेति ˈयथा वेत्थ तथा ब्रूहीति ॥ ५ ॥

'I know it. If you, Y., not knowing this (thread) and this inner controller, drive out these brahman-cows for yourself, your head will fly apart.'

'I know, Gautama, this thread and this inner controller.' 'Anyone (यः . . . कश्च) might say here "I know, I know." Tell (me exactly) how you know.'

यत्र here 'if'. — अन्यत्र अस्मत् (abl. of first plural pronoun). — मन्यासै subjunctive. — श्वानः 'dogs'; वा एतद् अद्युः (pl. 3 opt. act. of √अद्). — वयांसि (fr. वयस्) वा एनद् विमथ्नीरन् pl. 3 opt. of √मथ् + वि.

30: स्थः. — प्राणे.

30-32: This passage enumerates the five breaths of traditional theory. प्राण here is best translated as 'up-breath' (lit. 'forward breath'); अपान as 'down-breath'; व्यान is a breath that is diffused (वि) in the body; the उदान is defined by the commentary as a breath directed to (or from?) the navel; and the commentary explains समान (lit. 'common or equalizing breath') as one that prevents the other breaths from flying apart and ultimately identifies it as Brahman.

34: नेति नेति See the introduction to this Selection.

35: इति may be inserted because there is a pause in Yājñavalkya's disquisition, or it may be a sign that an enumeration has come to an end.

35-36: The eight abodes, eight worlds, eight persons were discussed in paragraphs 11-18, which were omitted to reduce the length of this selection.

36: वि उद् and प्रति + उह्य (gerund of √वह्). — अति + अक्रामीत् (aor. of √क्रम्; translate as 'has gone beyond').

37: चेद् मे.

38: तस्य . . . अस्थीनि (from अस्थि). According to the commentary, the robbery took place when Śākalya's pupils were taking his bones home to perform the agnihotra ritual for him. In his translation of ŚB (M) 11:6:3:11, Eggeling cites references to suggest that after cremation, the bones of the deceased were collected to be placed in an earthen vessel and buried.

40-41: 'Who of you should desire (to do so), let him question me; or all (of you) question (impve.) me.'

44: वृक्ण from √व्रश्च्.

46: रेतसः is an answer which Yājñavalkya does not want them to give. वोचत pl. 2 aor. injunctive of √वच्. — जीवतः gen./abl. pres. pple. 'from somebody or something living' (i.e. not from a dead person or thing).

47: जात एव न जायते को न्वेनं जनयेत्पुनः This passage has given rise to different interpretations which, in turn, would favor different interpretations of Yājñavalkya's attitude toward the doctrine of reincarnation. According to many western interpreters and also some Indian ones (e.g. Radhakrishnan), the passage is to be translated as '(Once) born, he is not born again', followed by the rhetorical question 'Who now would cause him to be born again?' which is repeated more elaborately in the following śloka. In short, according to this interpretation Yājñavalkya here questions the possibility of rebirth. Traditional Indian commentaries, by contrast, interpret the passage as meaning 'He is born (already); he is not **being** born; so who (= what human being) could cause him to be born (when he already is born)?'. As a consequence they believe that Yājñavalkya merely rejects the cyclical view of reincarnation through one's son and that the real answer lies in the final passage which, according to this view, informs us that ब्रह्मन्, the ultimate principle, is the source for human rebirth. (Western interpreters tend to consider this final passage a later addition to the text, added by somebody who was not satisfied with Yājñavalkya's earlier "nihilistic" answer.)

The traditional Indian interpretation may be considered supported by the fact that later on in the "Yājñavalkya Cycle", Yājñavalkya does in fact accept the doctrine of karman and reincarnation. At the same time, its analysis of जात एव न जायते is a bit forced.

A possible resolution of the different interpretations might be as follows. As noted in the introductory notes on this selection, an earlier, simpler version of our selection is found at ŚB (M) 11:6:3:11. This suggests that our present selection is a later elaboration; part of that elaboration consists of the final ślokas, whose original purpose may have been to serve as a conclusion to the cycle of Yājñavalkya's disputations at King Janaka's court. At this point in the development of our text, the passage in question may indeed have expressed skepticism on Yājñavalkya's part regarding the new doctrine of karman and reincarnation. At a later point, the cycle of Yājñavalkya's disputations was incorporated into the larger Yājñavalkya Cycle, at whose conclusion Yājñavalkya clearly accepts the doctrine (while at the same time arguing that release from karman and reincarnation can come only from an advaita realization of the ultimate unity of the self with the transcendental principle; see Introduction, §3.5). At that point, the "nihilistic" interpretation of our passage could no longer be maintained. As a consequence, the passage was reinterpreted to conform to the prevailing Indian analysis, and the final passage referring to Brahman was added.

48: अन्यतः here to be construed as ablative 'from another one' — प्रेत्य (gerund) is often used as an adverb, 'after death'.

49: उद्वृहेयुः from √वृह् + उद्.

51: विज्ञानमानन्दं ब्रह्म रातेर्दातुः परायणम् Note that रातेः modifies दातुः which in turn modifies परायणम्. — तिष्ठमानस्य तद्विदः refers to the one who has विज्ञानमानन्दं

etc. — The commentary suggests the following interpretation: A voice (or holy tradition) declares what is the root of the world … what Yājñavalkya has queried the brahmins about: Knowledge, bliss, Brahman (neuter), the highest goal of the giver of gifts (i.e. of the yajamāna, the sacrificer), (and also) of the one standing firm and knowing Brahman (even if he may not be engaged in ritual action). What is curious is that Brahman here is said to be the source for rebirth, whereas in Yājñavalkya's later argument, merger with Brahman stops the cycle of rebirths.

Selection XI

This selection initiates an extended chapter in which Śvetaketu is instructed by his father in esoteric wisdom. The present selection in effect tells us that such wisdom goes beyond traditional, ritualist Veda study. It also picks up on one of the favorite topics of the upaniṣads, which had already been raised in the Ṛg-Veda, namely the idea that in the beginning there was non-being, or no difference between being and non-being (see the selections in XX:H).

<u>Summary</u>: Śvetaketu Āruṇeya is told by his father to go study the Veda. Having gone at age 12, he returns at 24, conceited and arrogant. His father asks him whether he had inquired about 'that instruction through which the inaudible becomes heard; the unthinkable, thought; the unknown, known?' Śvetaketu asks for a clarification. His father replies with a set of comparisons that serve to indicate that the instruction he is concerned with is about the underlying, essential nature of things. Śvetaketu admits that he has not gained that instruction and asks his father to impart it to him. His father begins with the statement that Being 'was here in the beginning, alone, without a second. It reflected, "May I be many, may I procreate."' It created heat, which in turn created the waters. 'Therefore wherever a man grieves or sweats, water is born from his heat.'

1. ह आरुणेयः

2: सोम्य, more correct सौम्य, lit. 'connected with Soma or the Soma ritual', appears to have come to be used as a term of mutual collegial address among priests involved in the ritual, whence the meaning 'my friend, my dear', used in addressing brahmins. (According to Manu 2:125, the term is obligatory when addressing brahmins.) — अननूच्य neg. gerund of वच् + अनु 'not having studied'

3: Having set out at age 12 and returned at age 24, he must have studied 12 years. (For a brahmin boy, he started rather late: Manu 2:36 states that a brahmin should start his studies at age 8.) — उपेत्य gerund of √इ + उप (see Glossary). — अधीत्य gerund of √इ + अधि.

4: आ इयाय.

5: असि उत — अप्राक्षीः s-aor. of प्रछ्.

5-6: The sentence continues across the paragraph boundary.

6: For the "impossibility" reading of negated *ta*-participles, see Selection IX, line 36-37. — भगवः Vedic vocative of भगवत् (Whitney §454.b)

8: Here begins a long series of comparisons यथा ... यथा ... यथा ... एवम्, stretching from line 8 through line 14.

8-9: Render as 'the differentiation [being merely a matter of] a name (based on) conventions of speech'.

9: मृत्तिका इति एव सत्यम् 'The truth is that it is clay.'

15: भगवन्तः refers to his former teachers. — यद हि एतद् — अवेदिष्यन् ... अवक्ष्यन् conditionals of विद् 'know' and वच् 'speak, say'. — इति In its usual quotative use, the particle may follow every sentence in a longer utterance.

17: सत् एव 'Being indeed' — तद् ह एके आहुः 'On this count some say ...' This expression is frequently used to refer to opinions considered less acceptable by the speaker (or the author of the text). — असत् एव.

17-18: This is, in fact, the position of RV 10:72:2d, 3d; see Selection XX:H.2.

18: जायत sg. 3 imperf. injunctive.

19-20: All of the consulted translations attribute the entire passage in this paragraph to the father. On the multiple occurrence of इति see the note on line 15. — The rejection of the position of RV 10:72:2d and 3d is curious, especially since the position is accepted elsewhere in the Chāndogya-Upaniṣad (3:19:1): . . . असदेवेदमग्र आसीत् तत्सदासीत् ... 'In the beginning there was non-being here; that was (= became) being.'

21: ऐक्षत from √ईक्ष्. — बहु स्यां प्रजायेय lit. 'May I be much, may I be procreated'. — तेजस् here 'heat'.

22: अपः acc. pl. — यत्र क्व च शोचति स्वेदते वा पुरुषः 'wherever (Whitney §507) man toils or sweats'.

23: तदधि 'as a consequence of that'.

Selection XII

The two passages in this selection are part of an extended dialogue in which Śvetaketu's father attempts to convince him of the transcendental unity of the entire phenomenal world. The two parables in the present selection, which he employs to express what in effect is beyond human expression, are justly famous. (The second one has a precedent in Selection VI, §12.) The refrain तत्त्वमसि श्वेतकेतो 'you are (identical with all of) that, Śvetaketu' is even more famous and became one of the major maxims of the monistic philosophy of advaita. The style is quite colloquial. As common in colloquial language, sentences tend to be highly abbreviated, with everything left out that can be inferred from the context.

Summary: Śvetaketu's father asks him to bring a fruit from a fig tree, to break it, to see the tiny seeds inside, to break one of them, and to see what is inside it. Śvetaketu does not see anything inside, and his father tells him, 'The subtle essence or atom, my friend, which you do not perceive, from that atom thus this great fig tree stands. Believe, my friend. Now, this entire world is of the nature of this atom. That is truth; that is the Self. That you are, Śvetaketu.' — Śvetaketu asks for more. His father tells him to place salt in a vessel with water and to return in the morning. The salt no longer is visible, but whatever part of the water Śvetaketu drinks, it tastes salty. 'Here indeed, my friend, you do not perceive true Being ... This entire world is of the nature of this atom. That is truth; that is the Self. That you are, Śvetaketu.' Śvetaketu asks for more instruction, and his father agrees.

1: The first sentence is a request by the father. — Technically, न्यग्रोध refers to the banyan tree; but the usual translation is 'fig tree'. — अतः 'from it (the tree)' — भगवः Ved. voc. sg. of भगवत् (Whitney §454.b) — भिन्द्धि sg. 2 impve. of √भिद्.

2: अण्व्यः Nom. pl. fem. of अणु. — Here it will be important to review the inflection of the pronoun इदम्. — अङ्ग is a favorite particle in this passage.

4: अणिमानम्.

4-5: Construe as एतस्य अणिम्नः + एवं महान् न्यग्रोधः

5: श्रद्धत्स्व sg. 2 mid. imperative of श्रद् + √धा.

6: एतदात्म्य see the Glossary. — आत्मन् here 'transcendental principle'. — All editions agree in not changing the final ओ of श्वेतकेतो to अ; this is an occasional phenomenon in Vedic sandhi which Whitney failed to observe in his §134.

8: उपसीदथाः injunctive used as imperative. (The imperative would be उपसीदस्व.)

9: दोषा see the Glossary. — अवाधाः sg. 2 aor. of √धा + अव. — तद् ह अवमृश्य.

10: This is a very abbreviated version of the construction with relative clause plus reduced correlative clause discussed in the General Notes, point 8c.

11-12: अङ्ग अस्य अन्तात् आचाम. — Śvetaketu evidently does what his father tells him, and then his father asks him कथम् 'How (is it)?'

12: अभिप्रास्य can be both sg. 2 act. impve. and gerund.

13: तच्छश्वत्संवर्तते (तद् शश्वत्) This apparently is said by Śvetaketu, as a general observation.

14: सत् here: 'truth; the true nature, essence'. — अत्रैव किल is commonly interpreted as meaning 'Here indeed (it is)'; but it could just as well be considered a simple elaboration of what precedes: '... here indeed'.

Selection XIII

The particle ओम् (with a variant ओ) has a wide range of uses in the Vedic language. We find it attested in two distinct uses from the time of the early Saṁhitās of the Black

Yajur-Veda. One is as a particle more or less corresponding to English *Oh*, used with imperatives, vocatives, and other forms of address (see e.g. XX:C1a, first two selections); the other is as a change in pronunciation of *a*-vowels in certain modes of recitation (e.g. XX:C1a, third selection, and XX:C2) and in other types of ritual recitation (e.g. XX:C1c). In late Vedic Prose it also begins to be used in the meaning 'yes' (e.g. Selection X, line 10).

As a ritual particle it coexists with a number of other particles, such as हिम् (Selection XVI), हो and वा (e.g. XX:C2), some of which likewise can be used in non-ritualist, "ordinary" contexts (such as the हो in Selection XV, §11). Like other implements or expressions used in the ritual, these particles tend to be given mystical interpretations (e.g. XX:C3 and 4).

Among all of these particles, ओम् came to acquire the greatest significance. This is no doubt because it is used by the priests of all the **three** branches of the Veda and, although constituting a single syllable, it is analyzable into **three** elements, अ उ म्. As a consequence of this "triune" character it could be drawn on as indicating the unity underlying the diversity of the three branches of the Veda and then, by extension, the diversity of the entire phenomenal world. (Note in this regard the concept of the **three** worlds — heaven, ether, and earth.)

The historical significance of ओम् may perhaps extend even farther. As noted in §3.7 of the Introduction, '(t)he transcendental significance assigned to a "mere particle" has striking counterparts in the Tantric tradition ... where ओम् / ॐ and similar "bīja mantras" serve ... to direct attention to the underlying identity between oneself and the ultimate principle.'

The mystical significance of ओम् is further supported by its connection with the sacred Gāyatrī mantra (see Selections XV and XX:D) which every practicing Hindu has to recite at morning and evening twilight, and which must be preceded and followed by ओम् (see e.g. Manu 2:76).

(For more detailed discussion and references to earlier literature, see Hans Henrich Hock, 'On the origin and early development of the sacred Sanskrit syllable *om*.' *Perspectives on Indo-European Language, Culture, and Religion: Studies in Honor of Edgar C. Polomé* 1: 89-110 [*Journal of Indo-European Studies Monographs*, 7] 1991.)

Note that the non-upaniṣadic passages in this Selection are presented in the way they appear in the consulted editions, without systematic indication of sentence breaks.

1.

A Sāma-Vedic perspective. ओम् is identified as the udgītha, the essence of the Sāma-Veda, and ultimately of the entire three Vedas.

Summary: ओम् is the essence of the udgītha, for one chants with ओम्. The explanation is that ओम् is the essence of essences. (The essence of creatures is the earth; the essence of the earth is the waters … the essence of human beings is speech; the essence of speech is the ṛc; the essence of the ṛc is the sāman; the essence of the sāman is the udgītha — the quintessence of essences.) The ṛc is defined as speech; the sāman as breath; the udgītha as 'this akṣara' ओम्. Speech and breath, ṛc and sāman are a couple, joined together in ओम्. They fulfill each other's desire. Who knows thus and meditates on this syllable as the udgītha has his desires fulfilled. ओम् is also a syllable of agreement, of accomplishment. Who knows thus and meditates on this syllable as the udgītha accomplishes his desires. The threefold Veda unfolds through ओम्. The syllable is used in calling for the śrauṣaṭ, in the śastra recitation, in Sāma-Vedic chant. The syllable is employed both by those who "know thus" and those who do not; but performing with knowledge, faith, and esoteric understanding is more powerful.

1: उद्गीथ is variously glossed as Sāma-Vedic chant in general; the office of the उद्गातृ, the main priest associated with Sāma-Vedic chant; the second part of the Sāma Veda; or even, no doubt inspired by passages like this, the syllable ओम् / ॐ. — तस्योपव्याख्यानम् supply 'is the following'.

5: अष्टमः the eighth (of the essences enumerated in the preceding paragraph, and therefore the ultimate).

6: कतमा ऋक्. — विमृष्टं भवति supply 'the following'.

8-9: The notion of coupling or sexual union between ritual concepts or implements is widespread in Vedic Prose, with the idea that such a union produces powerful results (see e.g. the selections in XX:B and the discussion by Rajeshwari Pandharipande, 'Metaphor as ritualistic symbol', *Anthropological Linguistics* 29: 3: 297-318, 1987). In the present case, the coupling of ṛc and sāman has a very specific and probably significant parallel in a mantra of the wedding ritual; see e.g. XX:A.1-2. In upaniṣadic literature the mantra appears in a fairly literal sense in BAU (M) 6:4:19, a passage concerned, in quite explicit language, with begetting a learned son. More significantly, various upaniṣadic texts contain echoes or even direct citations of the mantra in reference to mystical unions; see e.g. XX:A.3. A curious attestation, illustrating the popularity of the mantra, is found in the next to last chapter of the Aitareya-Brāhmaṇa, close to the end of the rājasūya 'royal consecration', where a variant of the formula is used to reaffirm the bond between purohita and king — both males.

10: मिथुनौ the two members of a couple.

10-11: आपयतः caus. of √आप्.

12: आपयितृ.

13: अनुज्ञा refers to the use of ओम् in the meaning 'yes'. — एषा + उ.

16: आश्रावयति refers to the call by the **adhvaryu** to the agnīdhra, a Ṛg-Vedic priest, to make the śrauṣaṭ call, through which he invites the deities to hear the prayers

(XX:C1a). — शंसति in this context refers to the śastra recitation by the **hotṛ**. — उद्गायति refers to the activity of the third group of priests, the **udgātṛ** and his assistants.

17: एतस्यैवाक्षरस्यापचित्यै महिम्ना रसेन 'for the veneration of that akṣara, with its greatness (and) its essence'

18: कुरुतः no doubt refers not just to any action, but to performing the sacrifice.

2.

This selection from the Jaiminiya-Brāhmaṇa has been shortened and simplified by omission of a number of passages that are not of primary concern in the present context.

> Summary: Prajāpati, being alone, desired to procreate. ... (Among the creatures that he created) was the Gāyatrī [consisting of eight syllables] with the praṇava [ओम्] as the ninth syllable ... He asked her to cast out this ninth syllable. ... She did so, and it became the praṇava, which is the adhvaryu's response, the udgītha, the call for the śrauṣaṭ. Therefore one makes the "droning sound" with ओम्, responds with ओम्, chants with ओम्, calls for the śrauṣaṭ with ओम्.

2: In the first omitted passage, Prajāpati engages in various acts of creation. — प्रणवनवमा The Gāyatrī now has eight syllables; but according to our selection, Prajāpati originally created her with an additional ninth syllable, the praṇava = ओम्. — At the end of the line: ते 'of you'.

3: √ऊह् + उद्.

5: प्रतिगरस्स Vedic sandhi. — The प्रतिगर is the "response" of the **adhvaryu** to the hotṛ, encouraging him to recite the śastra; the उद्गीथ is the chant of the **udgātṛ**; the आश्रावण is the call for the śrauṣaṭ by the adhvaryu, to the agnīdhra, assistant to the Ṛg-Vedic **hotṛ**.

3.

Another Sāma-Vedic perspective, this time from the Jaiminiya-Upaniṣad-Brāhmaṇa.

> Summary: Prajāpati conquered this world with the threefold Veda. He was concerned that the other Gods would do the same; so he took away the essence of the threefold Veda. With भूर् he took the essence of the Ṛg-Veda, which became the earth, whose essence is Agni. With भुवस् he took the essence of the Yajur-Veda, which became the ether, whose essence is the wind. With स्वर् he took the essence of the Sāma-Veda, which became the sky, whose essence is the sun. He could not take the essence of ओम्. That became speech, whose essence is breath ... This syllable is the support of the threefold Veda. The hotṛ, the adhvaryu, the udgātṛ are all supported by ओम्, the threefold acme of the Vedas. The priests place the sacrificer in this syllable and depart for the heavenly world. Therefore one should follow up with ओम्.

1: यदस्येदं जितं तत् A reduced relative-correlative structure (see General Notes, point 8.c) which further characterizes what Prajāpati won.

2: Another instance of a reduced relative-correlative structure. — यक्ष्यन्ते (sandhi across the daṇḍa !)

4: आददै (√दा + आ).

4-9: भूर्भुवः स्वः are three other ritual particles. One of their important uses is as an introductory formula for the Gāyatrī, preceded by ओम् (see e.g. Manu 2:76).

5: √नेद् + प्र.

12: त्रय्यै विद्यायै For the case form see Whitney §§309h, 363c, 365d.

12-13: Here we find explicit references to the three main priests in the ritual, the **hotṛ**, the **adhvaryu**, and the **udgātṛ**.

4.

An early account from the Ṛg-Vedic tradition.

Summary: Prajāpati desired to procreate. He performed austerities and thereby created the worlds — the earth, the ether, the sky. He performed austerities on these worlds and created three lights — Agni from the earth, Wind from the ether, the Sun from the sky. He performed austerities on these lights and created the three Vedas — the Ṛg-Veda from Agni, the Yajur-Veda from Wind, the Sāma-Veda from the Sun. He performed austerities on the three Vedas and created three essences — भूर् from the Ṛg-Veda, भुवस् from the Yajur-Veda, स्वर् from the Sāma-Veda. He performed austerities on these essences and created three sounds — अ उ म. He brought them together into one. That is ओ३म्. Therefore one makes the praṇava with ओम्. It is the heavenly world, the sun.

8-9: The first explicit "triune" phonetic analysis of ओम् as consisting of अ उ म्.

8: वर्णाः 'sounds'.

10: असौ यो ऽसौ तपति A circumlocution for the sun, similar to the one for the wind in Selection X, §9.

5.

A parallel from the Yajur-Veda.

Rough translation: ओम् is Brahman, the entire world. (The call for the śrauṣaṭ) is ओम्-like (ओ श्रावय); with ओम् they chant the chants; with ओं शोम्, they recite the śastras; with ओम् the adhvaryu gives the response; with ओम् the brahman-priest impels the other priests; with ओम् he acknowledges the agnihotra; with ओम् the brahmin declares, 'Let me obtain Brahman.' He obtains Brahman.

1: For the variant ओ श्रावय see Selection XX:C1a and the introductory remarks to Selection XIII.

2: For ओं शोम् see Selection XX:C1b.

3: प्रसौति supply 'the other priests to perform their respective duties'.

4: प्रवक्ष्यन् आह. — ब्रह्म followed by a form of √आप् + उप.

Selection XIV

The initial verse of the first of the two brief passages in this Selection recurs in several later upaniṣads (e.g., as the introduction to the Īśa-Upaniṣad) and to the present day is held in high esteem and interpreted in various, philosophically and theologically highly significant ways. At an overt or superficial level, the verse is a praise of "fullness", which in effect is characterized as inexhaustible. But from the beginning it must have had a deeper meaning. The commentary's interpretation can be summarized as follows: 'Transcendental, mysterious (परोऽक्षम्) Brahman, manifest Brahman (which is merely a manifestation of the ultimate Self, the परमात्मन्). From the causal Self, characterized by ignorance, the Self emerges. What has been made manifest, made into or by ignorance etc., of that, having removed its appearance through knowledge, the infinite, true Self remains.'

The second passage no doubt is a myth told in order to teach students of sacred lore, or according to the commentary, all present-day human beings, the qualities of self-control, giving, and compassion. The passage has been imbued with a certain degree of mysticism in the last lines of T. S. Eliot's *Wasteland*: Datta. Dayadhvam. Damyata. Shantih shantih shantih. (Note, however, that Eliot's order, *datta, dayadhvam, damyata*, is different from the one in our text.)

Fairly literal translation of part 1: ओम् Fullness in yonder world, fullness in this world; from fullness, fullness is produced. Taking away the fullness of fullness, fullness indeed remains.

Summary of part 2: The son of Kauravyāyaṇī declared that Brahman is the ether, the "Ancient" is the ether, ether is air-like. This Veda is known by the brahmins and through it one knows what is to be known. — Prajāpati's three-fold descendants, the Gods, human beings, and Asuras, dwelled with him to study Brahman. At the end of their studentship, the Gods asked him for instruction. He responded with one syllable, द and asked if they understood. They said they did and that he told them 'Be controlled.' He informed them that they understood right. The human beings made the same request, and he gave the same reply, which they correctly understood as telling them 'Give.' The Asuras made the same request and received the same answer, which they correctly understood as telling them 'Be compassionate.' The repetition द द द is the sound of thunder — 'Be controlled, give, be compassionate.' This triad — control, giving, compassion — is what one should learn.

1: On ॐ, see Selection XIII. — पूर्णम् is interpreted as ब्रह्मन्. — अदः in yonder (world), i.e. heaven; इदम् in this (world), on earth.

3: 'Om, Brahman is the ether' (or: 'Brahman is Om, the ether'). — स्म see Whitney §778c.

5 ब्रह्मचर्यम् + √वस् to live with someone as a Veda student.

6: द इति the syllable द.

7: व्यज्ञासिष्ट *(i)ṣ*-aorist with pluti (Whitney §78). — आत्थ sg. 2 perf. of √अह्.

9: एव see Selection IX, line 16.

15: शिक्षेत् supply 'to practice'. In Classical Sanskrit the pseudo-root √शिक्ष् normally is inflected in the middle voice; but the Vedic language (and also the Epic) often follows its own rules, different from those laid down by the grammarians, since its tradition began centuries before the latter appeared on the scene.

Selection XV

The topic of this passage is the mystical significance of the Gāyatrī, also known as Sāvitrī, for which see the Appendix, Selection XX:D. This mantra is composed in the gāyatrī meter, with three lines of eight syllables each, usually ending in a cadence ˘ - ˘ ⏓. In the first three paragraphs of this selection, this "eight-hood" of syllables is mystically identified with the world or with other important phenomena, the words for which likewise consist of eight syllables. The selection concludes with two paragraphs making the point that understanding the mystical significance of the Gāyatrī saves even a sinner. The notion that esoteric knowledge is more powerful than correct performance of the ritual begins to be expressed in late ritualist texts and becomes one of the major topics of the upaniṣads (see also Selection XVII:B, §10:1-7).

Summary: The Gāyatrī consists of eight syllables. The text takes three Gāyatrī lines with three words each and, on the basis of the meanings of these words — 'earth, ether, sky', 'ṛcs, yajuses, sāmans', 'up-breath, down-breath, and diffused-breath' — argues that knowledge of these lines provides victory over the three worlds, the threefold Veda, and the animate world. — After some omitted passages the praise of the Gāyatrī continues with a story of Janaka of Videha and Buḍila Āśvatarāśvi. In response to Janaka's question why Buḍila has become an elephant and is carrying (Janaka), Buḍila replies that this happened because he did not know the mouth of the Gāyatrī. The mouth of the Gāyatrī is Agni/fire. Who knows thus is purified and becomes ageless, immortal, even if he commits much evil.

1: द्यौः here is to be read as two syllables दियौः. In the earlier mantra literature, sequences of consonant plus य् frequently have to be read as consonant plus इ(य्). — After इति supply 'this expression'.

1-2: एतदु हास्या एतत् 'and (उ) this is this of her/it'; i.e., her eight-syllable-hood is or consists of this.

2: पदम् supply 'of the Gāyatrī'.

7: For अपान and व्यान see Selection X, lines 30-32. On the trisyllabic reading of व्यान see the note on line 1 above. Note further that to come up with eight syllables, we have to assume a Vedic sandhi प्राणो अपानो with retained अ- in the second word.

9: एतद् 'on this point', i.e., the discussion of the mystical significance of the Gāyatrī. — See the Glossary under हो. — गायत्रीविद् अब्रूथाः On the nominative with middle voice forms of verbs of saying or thinking, see the note on Selection VII, line 8-9.

10: 'How have you become an elephant and carry (me)?' The precise import of this passage is not clear. Radhakrishnan, trying to clarify its meaning, cites an interpretation of Madhvācārya: 'Why then being a fool like an elephant dost thou carry (the burden of sin of accepting gifts)?' — सम्राट् from सम्राज्, here vocative. — विदां चकर periphrastic perfect of √विद् 'know', presumably to distinguish this as past tense from the present-tense value of the ordinary perfect वेद. For चकर sg. 1, see Whitney §793cd.

12: According to the commentary, this paragraph is a statement of King Janaka (एवं वदंतं प्रति राजा मुखमुपदिशति 'to (him) thus speaking, the king explains the mouth'). — बहु इव.

13: एवम् ह एवंविद् यद्यपि — √प्सा + सम्.

Selection XVI

Radhakrishnan plausibly characterizes this selection as 'a satirical protest against the externalism of the sacrificial creed [i.e. ritualism], in the interests of an inward spiritual life.' A more traditionalist, philosophical interpretation goes back to Śaṅkarācārya: Pleased by Baka's study, a deity or sage, or even the chief breath appears to him in the guise of a dog so as to help him.

> Rough translation: The canine udgītha. When Baka Dālbhya, a.k.a. Glāva Maitreya, went for Veda study, a white dog appeared. Other dogs came and asked it to "sing up" food for them. It told them to return the next day, and Baka Dālbhya kept watch. Just like human priests "creep" along when about to chant the bahiṣpavamāna, so they crept. Sitting down they made the sound हिम् and chanted 'ओम्, let us eat, ओम्, let us drink. ओम्, may God Varuṇa, Prajāpati, Savitṛ bring food hither. Lord of food, bring food hither, bring hither, ओम्.'

1: उद्गीथ see Selection XIII:1. — The passage बको दाल्भ्यो ग्लावो वा मैत्रेयः is traditionally considered to refer to one and the same person. He is said to have been born Baka, the son of Dalbha, but then to have been adopted by Mitrā and given the new name Glāva.

5: उपसमीयात from √इ + उप + सम्. The long ई is unusual before the optative suffix -या- and may reflect a tendency in late Vedic texts (as well as in the Epics) to use forms that are not as rigidly correct as demanded by later normative grammar. For other examples in ChU, note the अप्राक्ष्यः of Selection XI (footnote 2), or the augmentless past tense form जायत 'was born' in paragraph 2:1 of the same selection. The latter may well represent an archaism, a continuation of the earlier Vedic "injunctive" (Whitney §587), echoes of which are found as late as the Epics. A similar archaism is found in आहरत्

(see the note on line 10 below), which looks like an injunctive used as an imperative. Note also the form सोम्य instead of सौम्य, found in Selection XI and elsewhere in ChU.

7: सर्पन्ति This refers to a particular stage in the Soma ritual when the various priests involved take each other by the hand and "creep", i.e. move in a crouching position, in a row, to a pit dug out to provide earth for the northern altar. — इति may perhaps have been used in its literal meaning 'thus', reinforcing the following एवम्.

8: हिम् is a particle which is commonly used at the beginning of Sāma-Vedic chant.

10: अदामों Note that the vowel of ओम् follows special sandhi rules, contracting to ओ with a preceding *a*-vowel, rather than to औ. — सविता अन्नम् — आहरत् an archaic use of the injunctive as imperative. — The numerals appearing above the text indicate aspects of the melody of Sāma-Vedic chant. Among the consulted editions, only the Kumbakonam one has a reasonable-looking version of these numerals; the other nāgarī editions use ३ and २ inserted in the text, but do not always agree with each other; Radhakrishnan's version does not include any such marks.

Selection XVII:A

For the philosophical and religious significance of this and the following selection, see section 3 of the Introduction and the references provided there. As noted there, given that the Vedic tradition has been handed down by brahmins (and, one might add, for brahmins), it is extraordinary that these two selections credit kṣatriyas with introducing the knowledge of karman and reincarnation. In fact, the commentator on the present selection had some difficulties with the idea that a brahmin might ask a kṣatriya to be his teacher and stated that brahmins can become students of kṣatriyas or vaiśyas only in an emergency and in that case do not undergo the upanayana (investiture with the sacred thread, performed by the teacher) and do not perform gestures of obedience (such as bringing kindling wood or touching the teacher's feet — for the latter practice see e.g. Manu 2:72).

In a number of Vedic-Prose parallels, however, kṣatriyas are the teachers of brahmins or at least have greater insight; see e.g. Selections V and XV, as well as JB 1:22-25, 2:276, ChU 1:8:1 and 5:11:4, ŚB (M) 10:6:1:2. Some passages explicitly depict brahmins as making gestures of obedience to the teacher (see the citation from the Kauṣītaki-Upaniṣad in the comments on Selection V, line 13). There are also passages in which kṣatriyas, vaiśyas, and even slaves or śūdras become ṛṣis by 'seeing a hymn' or performing other ṛṣi-deeds; e.g. JB 1:222 (kṣatriya), 3:125 (vaiśya), AB 2:19:1 (दास्याः पुत्र ... अब्राह्मण 'son of a slave woman ... non-brahmin'). A number of Vedic hymns are attributed to such non-brahminical seers as Kakṣīvat (descendant of a female slave, RV 1:18:1), Dasyave Vṛka (a prince, RV 8:55 and 8:56), or Viśvāmitra (to whom is attributed the entire third book of the Ṛg-Veda and who from the time of the Aitareya-

Brāhmaṇa is considered to have been of royal ancestry). There is evidence, too, of women being learned (Selections VI and IX), or even 'mantra-makers' (JB 2:219).

Altogether, then, we have good reason to believe that even as late as the time of the upaniṣads, the caste system and society as a whole had not become as rigid as later brahmin commentators depict it. At the same time, Selection V, §15 and the passage cited in the notes on line 13 of that selection show that, in some cases at least, kṣatriyas felt uncomfortable about accepting a brahmin as pupil.

The doctrine of karman and reincarnation is propounded toward the end of our two selections. Its formulation is still quite rudimentary and somewhat incomplete, but the two different versions complement each other sufficiently to make it possible to arrive at a more complete picture. (See also §§3.4 - 3.7 of the Introduction.)

An additional interest of our selections lies in the different nature of the introductions to the two versions. In the BAU version, Śvetaketu is portrayed as overly proud and perhaps even irascible (in this regard, compare the beginning of Selection XI), while King Jaivala is portrayed as kind and considerate; the roles are pretty much reversed in the ChU version, where King Jaivala comes through as brusque, and Śvetaketu as polite and deferential (note his frequent use of the honorific vocative भगवः). On this issue and its possible motivations, see Patrick Olivelle, 'Young Śvetaketu: A literary study of an upaniṣadic story,' *Journal of the American Oriental Society* 119: 46-70, 1999.

Summary: Śvetaketu Āruṇeya meets King Jaivala Pravāhaṇa, who asks him whether he has been properly taught by his father. When Śvetaketu answers in the positive, King Jaivala asks him a series of five questions concerning where creatures go after death and related topics. Śvetaketu does not know the answers. The king offers him to stay, but he runs home to complain to his father. His father does not know the answers either and asks to become King Jaivala's pupil. The king informs him that the answers to the five questions were previously known only to kṣatriyas, but that he will instruct him. He proceeds to lay out the cyclical doctrine of the पञ्चाग्निविद्या. Each stage of the cycle is marked by a different fire, starting with yonder world (the sky), and proceeding to Parjanya (God of rain), this world (the earth), Man, and Woman. Each fire has its appropriate kindling wood etc. (for instance, yonder world has the sun as kindling wood). And each fire gives rise to what is offered in the next one (for instance, the fire of Man gives rise to semen which is offered in the next fire, that of Woman). The last of the five fires gives rise to a new man, who lives and dies, and then is consigned to a sixth fire, in which Fire is the fire, Kindling Wood is the kindling wood, etc. Those who know thus or meditate in the forest, rise to the flame, from there to the day, to the light half of the month, to the period between winter and summer solstice (when the sun gets stronger), to the world of the Gods, to the sun, to the region of lightning, from where a spiritual man takes them to the worlds of Brahman. There they will stay, not turning back. Those who sacrifice, are charitable, and perform austerities, rise to the smoke, from there to the night, to the dark half of the month, to the period between summer and winter solstice, to the world of the pitṛs, to the moon. There they become food, like King Soma (the food of the Gods). When their time is up, they return to space, from there to the wind, to the rain, to the earth, to which they return as food. Those who do not know either of these two paths return as insects and other biting creatures.

2: परिचारयमाण middle-voice = reflexive causative (see Glossary).

4: वेत्थ sg. 2 perf. of √विद् — प्रयत्यः nom. pl. f. pres. pple. of √इ + प्र. — विप्रतिपद्यान्तै subjunctive.

5: On एव see the comments on Selection IX, line 16.

6: प्रयद्भिः instr. pl. m./n. pres. pple. of √इ + प्र.

7: आहुत्याम् The Ch.U. version has आहुतौ; for the variation in case endings see Whitney §336.g with §339. — समुत्थाय gerund of √स्था + सम् + उद्.

8: वेत्थ उ. — वा ... वा 'either of the path leading to the Gods or (of that) leading to the pitṛs'.

10: नः 'by us'.

11-12: This verse recurs with some variations (mainly सुती for सृती) in RV 10:88: 15, MS 2:3:8a, and VS (M) 19:47. — To make sense, the genitives in the first line have to be construed differently: the first two referring to the goals of the two courses or roads (see also §3 of our selection, and §§18-19 below), the third one, to the persons who take the road. — The commentary confirms that the 'father' and the 'mother' of the second line are to be read as 'sky/heaven' and 'earth' respectively. Rough translation:

> I have heard of two courses of the mortals, that of the pitṛs, and also that of the Gods.
>
> By these two all of this here that moves comes together, what is between the father and the mother.

13: अतः here 'of these'.

14: The "visit" is the customary hospitality that is expected to be offered, especially by kings, and especially to brahmins. — अनादृत्य neg. gerund from √दृ + आ.

15: The first इति has its literal meaning 'thus'. — नः a quite "unroyal" *we*. — अवोचः redupl. aor. of √वच्. Note the switch from third-person honorific भवान् to second-person verb — not quite correct according to the rules of number agreement, but a possible construction in more "relaxed" Sanskrit. — पुरा अनुशिष्टान् (acc. pl. agreeing with नः).

16: सुमेधः (voc.) Perhaps an attempt by the father to assure Śvetaketu that he is, indeed, well educated. — For बन्धु (with negative connotations) at the end of a compound see the Glossary.

17: √हृ + उद् + आ.

18: जानीथाः sg. 2 opt. mid of √ज्ञा.

19: प्रतीत्य gerund of √इ + प्रति. — वत्स्यावः fut. of √वस्. — Evidently, Śvetaketu doesn't want to go back with his father.

21: प्रवाहणस्य जैवलेः supply 'abode' or 'assembly'. — आहार्य caus. gerund of √हृ + आ.

22: The "honor" consists in the traditional hospitality treatment.

23: प्रतिज्ञातो म एष वरः is usually interpreted as 'This boon has been promised to me' = 'You have promised me this boon.' But given the semantic range of √ज्ञा + प्रति, an alternative is possible: 'This (following) boon is or has been accepted by me', i.e., 'I accept your offer in the following way.'

25: दैवेषु वै गौतम तद्वरेषु 'This (wish of yours), Gautama, is in (the category) of divine boons.'

26: The glossary definition अपात्त (n.) 'abundance', based on the commentary, is the one most commonly accepted. But under this interpretation, the form अपात्त is opaque. An alternative, implicit in Böhtlingk's translation, derives the form from √दा + अप + आ and interprets it as meaning '(has been) taken away'. (Essentially the same meaning could be derived from √दा 2 'cut off' + अप + आ.) In this case, Gautama would be saying that he has been deprived of earthly possessions in the past and that the king should not now deprive him of divine possessions as well.

27: भूत् injunctive with negative मा.

28: इच्छासै subjunctive.

28-29: पूर्वे with स्म and present: Whitney §778c. (From now on, this usage will no longer be commented on.)

29: The Kāṇva recension (6:2:6) adds स होपयानकीर्त्योवास 'having made the announcement of coming (to be his pupil), he stayed (as a pupil).'

30: उपयानकीर्तौ Vedic sandhi, especially before *u*-vowels (Whitney §134c). — अपराधाः irregular *a*-aorist injunctive of √राध् + अप.

30-31: तथा ... यथा ... lit. 'so ... as ...'; translate as '... about the fact that ...'

31: विद्या इतः (adv.).

32: त्वा enclitic pronoun.

33: Here and in the following, the sacrificial fire is meant. Altogether, five different types of fire were traditionally enumerated; hence the name पञ्चाग्निविद्या 'the doctrine of the five fires'. But as noted in the Introduction, both the BAU and the ChU versions add a sixth fire, the fire of cremation which sets the stage for the question of what happens to the deceased after death. — असौ ... लोकः 'yonder world' = heaven/sky. — समित् fr. समिध्.

35: जुह्वति pl. 3 pres. act. — आहुतेः (abl.) — सोम is sacrificed in liquid form; hence the transition to the "watery" paragraph that follows.

36: संवत्सर because the rainy season plays a major role in the yearly cycle; compare वर्ष 'rain, rainy season; year'.

39: अयं ... लोकः 'this world' = the earth.

45-48: According to tradition, this part indirectly answers the earlier question (in § 3) concerning the "how-manieth" oblation in which the waters become a human voice and speak. To get this interpretation we need to equate (i) the fifth fire discussed in this paragraph with the fifth oblation, (ii) the semen offered by the Gods with the waters, and (iii) the human being that is born with the human voice. (The parallel Chāndogya-Upaniṣad version provides a more explicit answer; see XVII:B, §9:1.)

48: अग्नये here the cremation fire.

49-51: This part gives details about the cremation fire. (As remarked earlier, this is technically a sixth fire.)

51: Here begins the discussion of the doctrine of karman and reincarnation. Note the पुरुष of brilliant color, possibly a reference to the primordial पुरुष in Selection XX:G. (Or is it an echo of the guardian or gate keeper in Selection XVIII and its Jaiminīya-Brāhmaṇa antecedents? See also the पुरुष मानस in §18.)

52: च अमी. For अमी see Whitney §503. — अरण्ये, the वानप्रस्थ stage of life (see Manu 6:1-32), or the forest or wilderness outside the village, where the esoteric doctrines of the āraṇyakas and upaniṣads are imparted.

53: आपूर्यमाणपक्ष See the note on Selection VII, line 20.

53-54: यान्षण्मासानुदङ्ङादित्य एति 'The six months (षड् मासान्) (during) which the sun (आदित्य) goes northward (उदङ् एति)', i.e. the period between the winter and summer solstices, when the sun rises further north each day and the days get longer.

55: एत्य gerund of √इ + आ.

57: Sacrifice, giving (of alms), and austerities thus are not considered of equal value as esoteric knowledge and devotion to faith and truth.

59: The moon (= Soma) is the food of the Gods.

60-61: Another example (beside Selection IX, line 4-6) of a "false-start" construction. In the यथा clause supply 'they eat', which is overtly contained in the "restart" after आप्यायस्व अपक्षीयस्व. The latter expression is perhaps what the Gods say to the moon = Soma. But it could also be comparable to the जायस्व म्रियस्व of Selection XVII:B, line 56 (see the comment on that passage).

61: √इ + परि + अव. — The ChU version is more explicit concerning what determines the amount of time after which this (period) passes or comes to an end; see Selection XVII:B, line 46.

Selection XVII:B

Summary: In its general outline, this selection is remarkably similar to the preceding one. The major difference lies in the conclusion, where the present selection is much more explicit about several issues. One of these is that return to this earth as food gives rise to reincarnation, as the offspring of the person who eats the food. More important, our selection distinguishes between different types of incarnation — those who are of pleasant conduct reach a pleasant (brahmin, kṣatriya, or vaiśya) womb, while those who are of evil conduct reach an evil womb (of a dog, a pig, or a caṇḍāla). Finally, our selection also provides an explicit answer to one of the king's questions, namely why yonder world does not become full with all the creatures that pass away. Creatures that merely live by the maxim 'be born and die' do not follow either the path to Brahman or back to this world; they occupy a third state, against which one should be on one's guard. The selection ends with a śloka decrying five different ways of evil conduct and contrasting these with knowledge of the Five Fire doctrine. Those who know this doctrine do not get stained by evil, even when consorting with evil people.

2: कुमार अनु त्वा अशिषत् (with tmesis of prefix and verb). — अनु हि supply अशिषत्. Note the use of the particle हि in answering a question to indicate a positive reply. — भगवः Ved. voc. sg. of भगवत् (Whitney §454.b)

3: इतो ऽधि lit. 'beyond from here' = 'after their departure from here'. Also note the double meaning of √इ + प्र (compare English 'depart').

4-5: व्यावर्तने acc. du. n. with pluti (Whitney §78)

6: संपूर्याते subj. mid + pluti.

8: अथा archaic variant of अथ + नु. (A different interpretation in Patrick Olivelle's 'Young Śvetaketu: A literary study of an upaniṣadic story,' *Journal of the American Oriental Society* 119: 46-70, 1999: अथ + अनु, with tmesis duplication of the prefix अनु contained in the following अनुशिष्ट, for emphasis. While such duplication is common in the extant Avestan texts, it is extremely rare in Vedic, if it occurs at all.)

9: ह आयस्तः (√यस् + आ).

12-13: Two occurrences of conditional verb forms.

14: सभागः.

17: कृच्छ्रीबभूव For the form see Whitney §§1093-1094. The interpretation is problematic; perhaps the following is on the right track. He became perplexed because the knowledge for which he is asked has been a property of kṣatriyas and should therefore not be imparted to brahmins; moreover, for a kṣatriya to teach a brahmin would be rather unusual.

18: The speaker of the first two sentences is the same person (Jaivala Pravāhaṇa). There may have been a slight interval between the two statements, in which Jaivala Pravāhaṇa thought things over (or was again entreated by Gautama).

18-20: The syntax of this passage causes some difficulties: The double यथा, found in all the consulted editions, should be followed by a correlative एवम् or तथा which would "resolve" or complete the structure; the तस्मादु that follows does not do so, since it is not a correlative of यथा either in meaning or in form. Further, note the उ in तस्मादु, which suggests coordination with what precedes. The whole issue can be resolved if we assume an error in transmission and read यथा मा त्वं गौतमावदस् तथेयं न प्राक्त्वत्तः पुरा विद्या ब्राह्मणान्गच्छति तस्मादु सर्वेषु लोकेषु क्षत्रस्यैव प्रशासनमभूदिति. In that case there is a resolution of the first यथा by तथा, and the clause introduced by तथा is coordinate with the clause introduced by तस्मादु. The translation would be: 'As you, Gautama, expressed it to me, so this knowledge before you never used to go to brahmins (= the knowledge of which you, Gautama, spoke to me never used to go to the brahmins before you), and therefore in all the worlds it has become the domain of the kṣatriyas.' This interpretation is supported by the parallel passage in the BAU which indeed offers a correlative structure with तथा ... यथा, albeit in reverse order; see Selection XVII:A, §11. (Note a similar problem in §3.5, where Radhakrishnan's reading यथा ... तथा has here been accepted instead of the यथा ... यथा of the other consulted editions.)

19: प्राक् + त्वत्तः (for the latter see Whitney §§494 and 1098).

24: Paragraphs 5:1 - 6:2 of this version essentially duplicate what is found in the parallel BAU version and have been omitted.

31: इति In this context the form can be interpreted either in its original sense 'so, thus', or as a special, transferred quotative use: 'with this thought' → 'therefore'; Śaṅkarācārya's commentary gives the gloss एवम् 'thus, so'. What follows gives an explicit answer to the question regarding the oblation at which the waters become human-voiced.

32: यावद्वा A special usage: 'or whatever/however long' (lit. 'or of what extent').

33: दिष्टम् Śaṅkarācārya plausibly explains this as कर्मणा निर्दिष्टं परलोकम् 'to the yonder world ordained by karman (previous actions in life)'. — इतः adv. 'from here', probably to be connected with प्रेतम्. — यतः adv. 'from where', i.e., the fire from which he was previously born (see §8.1 ff.). — इतः (second occurrence): ta-pple. of √इ.

35: श्रद्धा तप इति This expression functions as the object of उपासते; the nominatives are due to the इति. — अर्चिषम् One would expect अर्चिर्, since the word is neuter.

36-37: यान् षट् उदङ् एति मासान् See the note on lines 53-54 of the preceding Selection. On the reduced correlative clause construction see the note on Selection III, line 13. The BAU version (§18 of the preceding selection) lacks the correlative structure.

41: इष्टपूर्ते nom. du. neut. dvandva — दत्त ta-pple., here used as a noun, 'giving'.

46: यावत्संपातम् adv. 'as long as (their) residue', i.e. according to the length of time determined by the residue of their actions in their previous life. — उषित्वा gerund of √वस्. — यथेतम् adv. 'as (they had) gone'. — आकाशम् supply 'namely'.

47: Note the shift in verb number, determined by the fact that wind/air is singular.

48-49: A series of dvandva compounds.

49-50: अतः here literally 'from here'. As Śaṅkarācārya explains it, the idea is this: In order to move up from the state of being a plant, they must become the food of an animate or human male that impregnates a female, so that they can be born in his shape or image. This, of course, requires a certain amount of serendipity; hence the expression दुर्निष्प्रपतरम्. (The form दुर्निष्प्रपतर creates problems. One would either expect दुर्निष्प्रपत्तर [a comparative] or दुर्निष्प्रपतन [a noun, meaning 'a difficult escaping']).

50: 'That (food and/or semen of his) becomes better (भूयः).'

51: The usual interpretation of अभ्याशो, going back to Śaṅkarācārya, is that it means क्षिप्रम् 'quick(ly)', but this would not explain the following यद्-clause with its optative verb.

53: चण्डाल refers to a person of the lowest layer of society. — Śaṅkarācārya suggests that the choice between these different good and bad reincarnations is determined 'according to their karman'.

55: 'By neither of these two paths'.

56: जायस्व म्रियस्व This is the "maxim" by which these creatures live. — Our selection fails to explicitly state where these creatures come from, but the end of the last paragraph of the parallel BAU version does. Accordingly, in his commentary on the present selection, Śaṅkarācārya states that the third state is reached by those who do not concern themselves with (sacred) knowledge at all. — तेनासौ लोको न संपूर्यते This is the answer (missing in the BAU version) to the question why yonder world does not become full with those who are departing, i.e., dying here. (See §2 of the BAU version.)

57: तस्मात् either causal 'therefore' or referring to this 'third state' against which one should be on one's guard (desid. of √गुप्).

59: गुरोस्तल्पमावसन् defiling his teacher's bed by sleeping in it (i.e. with his wife). — See Glossary under ब्रह्महन्.

61: आचरन् nom. sg. m. pres. act. pple.

62: पञ्चाग्नीन् see the note on line 39 of the preceding selection. — तैः refers back to the five people mentioned in the preceding śloka.

63: य एवं वेद य एवं वेद Repetition of the last few words of a paragraph is used in a number of Vedic Prose texts to indicate that the discussion has come to an end.

Selection XVIII

This is the third early Vedic passage which propounds the new doctrine of karman and reincarnation. As in the preceding two selections, the doctrine is proclaimed by a kṣatriya to a brahmin who comes to him as his pupil. Unlike the other two passages, it does not discuss the "Five-Fire doctrine". Rather, it introduces a guardian or gate keeper who questions the deceased and, depending on his answer, either permits him to go on to the world of Brahman or forces him to be born again. The passage states clearly that the manner in which a person is born again depends on karman and knowledge, but in contrast to the preceding two selections it does not distinguish between the different types of incarnations that are in store for those who have been concerned with knowledge vs. those who have not been so concerned.

Although quite cryptic and disjoint in many places, this passage does add something to our understanding of the earliest form of the doctrine of karman and reincarnation. Even more significant is the fact that according to this passage, those who are permitted to go to immortality, go to the world of a personal God, Brahman (masc.). In this regard, and also by using the formula (यस्त्वमसि) सो ऽहमस्मि (§6), it agrees with Selection XIX; see the introductory note to that selection. (The longer form of the formula can be traced to the Jaiminīya-Brāhmaṇa (1:18), like many other ideas in this selection and in the two preceding ones. On this general relation to the Jaiminīya-Brāhmaṇa see §§3.6 and 3.7 of the Introduction. See also Hendrik Wilhelm Bodewitz, *Jaiminīya-Brāhmaṇa I, 1-65: Translation and Commentary with a Study: Agnihotra and Prāṇāgnihotra*, Leiden: Brill, 1973, as well as Patrick Olivelle, 'Young Śvetaketu: A literary study of an upaniṣadic story,' *Journal of the American Oriental Society* 119: 46-70, 1999. The most recent, detailed discussion is found in Henk Bodewitz's *Kauṣītaki Upaniṣad: Translation and Commentary, with an Appendix: Śāṅkhāyana Āraṇyaka IX-XI*, Groningen: Egbert Forsten, 2002.)

The text of the KU has been handed down with a fair amount of variation (see the notes on the text). Some variants found in the different extant manuscripts and incorporated in Śāstrī's edition, are clearly inferior readings and suggest corruption in the transmission. Especially problematic are the verses in paragraph 2. Here H. W. Bodewitz's translation and commentary on the parallel passages in the Jaiminīya-Brāhmaṇa are most helpful; see also Henk Bodewitz's publication of 2002.

Summary: Citra Gāṅgyāyani chooses Āruṇi as priest for his sacrifice. The latter sends his son Śvetaketu instead. The king asks him whether he would place him in a hidden place in the world. Śvetaketu does not know how to answer, nor does his father, who therefore decides to become Citra's pupil. Citra then explains to him that a person who departs from this world goes to the moon, which is the gate of the heavenly world. [A gate keeper puts a question to him.] If he answers the question [correctly] he is permitted to go on, if not, he becomes rain and is born again as various types of animals or as a human being 'according to karman, according to knowledge'. Now follows the question that the gate keeper asks the deceased, namely 'Who are you?' The answer he should give is a set of verses of difficult interpretation (see the detailed notes). Apparently the deceased is again asked 'Who are you?', to which he should answer 'I am you.' That permits him to proceed on the way to the Gods. He comes to the world of Agni, of Vāyu, of Varuṇa, of Indra, of Prajāpati, and finally of Brahman. In that world there is a lake and a river "Unaging"; and the gate keepers are Indra and Prajāpati ... One who "knows thus" comes to him. Brahman (masc.) runs up saying 'Through my fame he has reached the river Unaging. He will not age.' ... The selection ends with 'Who you are, that am I.'

1: चित्र गाङ्ग्यायनि evidently is a kṣatriya. He is about (fut. pple.) to 'sacrifice for himself' (i.e. be a यजमान) and for this purpose chooses (वव्रे) a priest, आरुणि, father of श्वतकेतु (the latter is characterized in Selections XVII:A and B as आरुणेय, descendant of आरुणि). — प्रजिघाय from √हि + प्र.

2: See Glossary for the semantics of याजय. — गौतमस्य पुत्र (voc.) + अस्ति which begins a question 'Is there a hidden place in the world in which you will place me?'

3: वा + अध्वा. — तस्य We might expect यस्य.

4: पृच्छानि could be imperative or subjunctive. — आसाद्य caus. gerund. — इतीति 'thus and thus'.

6: अधीत्य gerund of √इ + अधि. — हरामहे indicative for imperative (a common feature in "relaxed" Sanskrit), and also the "royal we". — यन्नः परे ददति 'the alms which others give to us = me (as a student)', or 'what others, i.e. the kṣatriyas, give to us'. Bodewitz (2002) translates this passage differently, interpreting सदसि as 'in a [sacrificial] session' — 'After having finished our studies it is only in a session that we obtain what others give us.' — एहि = आ इहि (sg. impve. of √इ).

6-7: समित्पाणि 'having kindling wood (समिध्) in his hand(s) (पाणि)'.

7: उपायानि see the note on Selection V, line 13

8: यो न मानमुपागाः translate as 'because you did not become conceited (lit. did not go to conceit)'

10: आप्यायते from √प्या + आ.

11: प्रत्याह i.e. gives the correct answer (namely the verses which follow a little later).

13: तेषु तेषु 'in these and these ...' = 'in various ...'.

14-15: Here we find out what the प्रत्याह in line 11 refers to: The moon, as guardian or gate keeper of the heaven, asks the deceased person to identify himself, and the latter should first answer by means of the following verses.

16-21: These verses are notoriously difficult to interpret, and no two scholars fully agree with each other. The following translation owes much to H. W. Bodewitz's interpretation of the related Jaiminīya-Brāhmaṇa verses and to Bodewitz's (2002) translation of the KB text; but much remains unclear. (In the Jaiminīya-Brāhmaṇa, the gate keeper is one of the seasons, which accounts for the recurrent references to "seasons" in these verses.)

> From the brilliant one (the moon), O seasons, the semen was brought forth, from the fifteenth pressing,[1] from the land (or the person) connected with the pitṛs.
>
> Then me, [O seasons,] you sent (आ ईरयध्वम्) into a man as (your) agent; through that man, (your) agent, you poured me forth into (my) mother.
>
> I here am born (जाये) as an addition, being produced as an addition (as) the thirteenth additional month of the twelve,[2]
>
> Through the "twelve-thirteen" father.[2] That I know fully, that I recognize.
>
> So, O seasons, bring me forth[3] to immortality.
>
> By that truth, by that austerity I am a season, I am of the seasons.[4]

1 The Soma pressing on the fifteenth day, at the end of the first fortnight. As Bodewitz shows, the parallel version in JB 1:18 has प्रसुतात्; moreover, 'The three roots *su-* "to press", *sū-* "to impel", and *sū-* "to procreate" often coincide in the mind of the Vedic thinkers.' Henk Bodewitz (2002) interprets सुतात् as meaning 'from the one born'.

2 I.e. the year, which consists of 12 months plus a 13th intercalary month.

3 Or: you brought me forth (imperfect tense).

4 That is, I am one with the immortal gate keepers.

22: को ऽसि त्वमस्मीति This constitutes a second exchange between the gate keeper and the deceased, with the answer त्वमस्मि explicitly restating the idea that was more indirectly expressed in the last line of the verses. The exact nature of who says what in this exchange may become clearer if we examine the parallel JB version. Here the sun accepts the deceased who has uttered the verses and thereby established his worthiness, by saying यस्त्वमसि सो ऽहमस्मि यो ऽहमस्मि स त्वमसि ' एहि 'who you are, that I am; who I am that you are. Come.' Part of this formula occurs as यस्त्वमसि सो ऽहमस्मि in §6 of the present selection; but the context in which it occurs there is different. (Henk Bodewitz accepts the alternative reading को ऽस्मि, interpreting it as meaning 'I am Ka (i.e. Prajāpati).')

24. ब्रह्मलोक here probably refers to the world of Brahman (masculine); see note on line 26.

25: आरः.

26: ब्रह्मा Brahman (masculine), i.e. a personal deity, not the usual neuter, impersonal Brahman of the early upaniṣads. — अभिधावत probably sg. 3 middle voice injunctive, used as present 'comes up to, meets'.

26-27: मम यशसा विजरां वा अयं नदीं प्रापत् These are the words of Brahman. The passage is something like a false start construction: मम यशसा — विजरां वा अयं नदीं प्रापत् (the particle वा = वै normally appears in second position).

Selection XIX

The early upaniṣads generally search for the underlying unity in an abstract entity like ब्रह्मन् (neuter), आत्मन्, ॐ, or even नेति नेति (Selection X). The present selection differs by identifying the individual self with a personal God, a view much more common in the later upaniṣads, which are often called "sectarian" because they profess allegiance to one or another deity.

This personal identification finds linguistic expression in the statement सो (masculine) (अ)हमस्मि, in contrast to the तत् (neuter) त्वमसि of Selection XII. Both expressions, सो ऽहमस्मि and तत्त्वमसि, have acquired great significance, even sanctity, in the later tradition.

The expression सो ऽहमस्मि is similar to the longer formula यस्त्वमसि सो ऽहमस्मि of Selection XVIII and its even longer antecedent in the Jaiminīya-Brāhmaṇa. But in addition to being shorter, it looks more clearly like a "personal" counterpart to the "impersonal" तत्त्वमसि. This is no doubt the reason for its popularity.

Concerning the identification with a personal God, it may be relevant that the relevant passage in the present selection appears to be relatively late. Our text clearly constitutes an addition to the Bṛhad-Āraṇyaka-Upaniṣad in its Kāṇva recension; it is absent in the Mādhyandina recension. Moreover, it recurs in a late, "sectarian" text, the Vājasaneyi- or Īśa-Upaniṣad, appended as the last book to the Kāṇva recension of the Vājasaneyi-Saṁhitā. At the same time, the idea of a personal deity is also found in the Kauṣītaki-Upaniṣad passage of Selection XVIII. Perhaps it was borrowed from that text.

According to Müller and Radhakrishnan, our text is the prayer of a dying man, addressed to Āditya, the sun.

The claim that the text is addressed to the sun is quite probable, for the 'golden disk' referred to in §1 must refer to the sun and would, moreover, relate the passage to the pravargya, a ritual connected with the sun, which immediately precedes the major part of the Bṛhad-Āraṇyaka-Upaniṣad (see §2 of the Introduction).

A fair amount of evidence also supports the interpretation of this selection as a funeral hymn or prayer. The Kauṣītaki-Upaniṣad passage in Selection XVIII, with which our text shares the notion of a personal deity as well as part of the formula यस्त्वमसि सो ऽहमस्मि, deals with the fate of somebody who has died. One of the two related Jaiminīya-Brāhmaṇa passages (JB 1:45-46 and 49-50) contains, inserted into it, a passage dealing with funeral rites (JB 1:46-49). In the two selections of XVII, the declaration of the doctrine of karman and reincarnation begins after a paragraph that talks about cremation as the concluding stage in the cycle of existence. Radhakrishnan (p. 577-578) further notes that the verses are used to the present day in Hindu cremation rites. Finally, paragraph 3 of this selection seems to provide explicit support for this interpretation.

However, while death and cremation are a good occasion for thinking of transcendental issues, this does not mean that such issues are relevant only at that time. They are of universal significance. In fact, except for JB 1:45-50, which is clearly connected with cremation rites, none of the other related passages occurs in a context which suggests that they were composed for use at the time of cremation. Here as elsewhere we have to distinguish between the theological and transcendental significance of a given text and its use within the ritual.

In fact, reading paragraph 3 of this selection as being specifically connected with a cremation rite requires taking some liberties in interpreting the passage, which can be avoided if we understand it as stating a general truth about the mortality of human beings and their need to overcome this mortality; see the comments on line 5 below. Moreover, in his commentary on the VS (K) version of our text, Sāyaṇa simply states that the mantras explain by which way one may attain immortality; he does not state the mantras to be the prayer of a dying man.

Some of the difficulties in interpreting this passage may stem from the fact that it appears to be a composite of different elements.

The last verse is identical to RV 1:189:1, which occurs in a hymn addressed to Agni. It asks for protection from evil, danger, enemies, etc. and, as the present verse states it, requests Agni to 'lead us to wealth' (नय ... राये अस्मान्). One suspects that this rather "mundane" purpose was the original one.

More than that, the combination of this last verse with the verse that precedes it has a near-parallel in BAU (M) 5:3:1:

वायुरनिलममृतम् ' भस्मान्तं शरीरम् ।
ॐ३ क्रतो स्मर । क्लिबे स्मर '
अग्ने नय सुपथा राये अस्मान्   विश्वानि देव वयुनानि विद्वान् ।
युयोध्यस्मज्जुहुराणमेनो   भूयिष्ठां ते नमउक्तिं विधेम ' इति ॥ १ ॥

Most of the differences between this version and that of the Kāṇva recension are minor. But it may be significant that where the latter has कृतम्, which may be read as synonymous with कर्मन्, the Mādhyandina passage has क्लिबे, which is generally interpreted as having the much more mundane meaning 'for prosperity, success' and thus agrees well with the राये of the last verse.

Given these facts, it is possible to speculate that the present selection came about as follows.

The core of the selection is paragraph 4, which goes back to Ṛg-Vedic times.

Paragraph 3 was added before the Kāṇva and Mādhyandina recensions of BAU diverged. This addition lent a more esoteric interpretation to paragraph 4, especially when the Kāṇva recension substituted कृतम् for the more mundane क्लिबे. What may have supported this development is the appearance of जुहुराणमेनः in the Ṛg-Vedic verse, which could be interpreted as referring not to guilt that may be an obstacle to acquiring wealth, but to guilt that may stand in the way of proper esoteric knowledge and release from mortality.

Finally the Kāṇva recension added the first two paragraphs, with the expression सो ऽहमस्मि perhaps borrowed from the Kauṣītaki-Upaniṣad, but reshaped and redefined so as to clearly identify the transcendental principle as a personal God, in contrast to the impersonal principle of तत्त्वमसि.

(In its next to last verse this selection also offers an instance of ओम्, apparently in its early use as a particle used in addresses; see the introduction to Selection XIII.)

Rough translation: The face is covered by a golden disk. Pūṣan, open it up for the one who has truth as his dharma so as to see. Pūṣan, single seer, controller, Sun, descendant of Prajāpati, spread out your rays, bring together your brilliance. I see your most auspicious form. The person yonder, that am I. The wind, not resting, is immortal. Then there is this body, ending in ashes. ओम्, inspiration, remember; remember what I have done. Inspiration, remember; remember what I have done. Agni, lead us to wealth on a good path, O God, knowing all the sign-posts. Repel from us crooked evil. May we offer you the greatest expression of praise.

1: मुखम् 'face'; Śaṅkarācārya gives a more esoteric interpretation of this word, as referring to मुख्यम् 'the principal nature'. In his commentary, Sāyaṇa plausibly identifies this as Āditya, the sun. In BAU (M, K) 5:5, a passage almost immediately preceding the present one, the latter is identified as सत्यम्, as well as एष एतस्मिन्मण्डले पुरुषः 'this person/puruṣa in this disk' — two of the key ideas of this paragraph.

2: सत्यधर्माय a bahuvrīhi compound, probably referring to the speaker; the first part of the compound also may pick up on the सत्यम् of BAU 5:5 (see the preceding note). The person designated by this word is the implicit agent of the following verbal noun, inflected for dative because he is the beneficiary of the verb अपावृणु. — दृष्टये is a purpose dative of the verbal noun दृष्टि.

3: यम Sāyaṇa plausibly interprets this word literally, as the controller, 'because (the sun) controls the reins (of its chariot) … '. — Sāyaṇa construes the sentence as going across the daṇḍa (|), to include तेजस्.

4: असावसौ intensive duplication, comparable to that of तत्तत्, तदेतत् (see Selection II, line 10). — For पुरुष see the comment on line 1 above.

5: Construe as: 'Wind/air, (what is) not resting (is) immortal. Then (there is) this body, ending in ashes [when being cremated, i.e. mortal].' Commentaries such as Sāyaṇa's do not give a gloss, but merely an interpretation of the passage as indicating that 'वायु, identified as प्राण, the vital breath of one who dies, should reach the immortal [sun]'. To make this interpretation work they supply a third-person imperative form of a verb of 'going'. Accordingly, Müller translates 'Breath to air and to the immortal! Then this my body ends in ashes' and Radhakrishnan offers 'May this life enter into the immortal breath; then may this body end in ashes.' Similar interpretations are found in Griffith's translation of VS and in Böhtlingk's German translation of the BAU (M) version of this passage. Interpretations of this sort, however, are rather forced and are motivated by identifying this selection as the prayer of a dying man.

7: राये dat. sg. of "रै" 'wealth', see Whitney §361b for inflection; but note that the Vedic nominative and accusative singular are रयिः, रयिम्. — वयुनानि The earlier Vedic meaning is 'sign-posts'; Sāyaṇa and other commentators interpret it as referring to 'actions, deeds', i.e. karman.

8: युयोधि from √यु. — नमस् + उक्ति (a compound). — विधेम aorist optative of √धा + वि (Whitney §850).

Selection XX

The format of this Appendix is very different from that of the selections that precede it. Many of the texts come from the Ṛg-Veda and represent a much earlier stage of the language and a very different literary style. (The mantras in Selection XIX may provide some idea as to how different the language and style really are.)

For the benefit of those not up to exploring this earlier language and literature, or the technical and ritualist literature of the Brāhmaṇas, the passages in this Appendix are accompanied by translations which, in effect, contain a fair amount of the type of information that is contained in the notes to the preceding selections. Those who are interested in learning to read earlier texts on their own may want to try their hand at Lanman's Vedic selections. (For his Selections XXXVI and LXII they may cross-check their interpretations with the translations of the corresponding passages in Selections XX:D and XX:I of this Reader.)

Most of the selections in this Appendix are given in the format in which they appear in the manuscripts and in printed editions, with a few typographically motivated adjustments. Those who want to understand how these texts "work" should therefore familiarize themselves with aspects of Vedic sandhi and accentuation that were glossed over in the earlier Selections. To accomplish this goal, they may find it useful to go over the following passages in Whitney's *Grammar*.

Phonetics:

ळ, ळ्ह: §54

ऽँ and ँ : §73

Sandhi: §§134c, 125c, 138bc, 172, 207, 209

Consonant doubling (marked mainly in ŚB texts): §228

Inflection:

रयि 'wealth': §360b (Whitney's account will suffice for practical purposes, but it is in need of considerable improvement)

Vedic endingless locative singular of *n*-stems: §425c

In addition, readers need to become familiar with Vedic accent, which is treated by Whitney in §§80-97, but not entirely successfully. The following discussion is intended as a supplement to his account, for the benefit of those who are interested in this rather complicated matter.

First, it should be noted that not all Vedic texts have been handed down in accented form. Since unaccented texts generally are later than the accented texts of the respective branch of the Veda, one possible explanation is that they represent a later stage of the language, closer to that of the epics or Classical Sanskrit, where the old accent system had been lost. But some of the unaccented texts are relatively early. Moreover, these include all of the extant brāhmaṇas of the Ṛg- and Sāma-Vedic traditions. The latter fact suggests an alternative explanation. We know that in the ritual recitation of the Ṛg-Veda, the accentuation of the mantras is usually suppressed, and the texts are recited at a "monotone" (एकश्रुति, see ĀŚS 1:2:8-9). At the same time, ritual recitation may impose accents of its own, which constitute an integral element of the performance. (The nyūṅkha recitation in Selection XX:C1c, for instance, is accompanied by such imposed accents; see ĀŚS 7:11:3-4, 12, 16.) The Sāma-Vedic tradition likewise imposes its own accentual or tonal elements in the chant; see e.g. the end of Selection XVI. It may be suspected that outside their mantra collections, these two branches of the Veda placed the greatest emphasis on these "recitational" accentuations and that this is the reason for the suppression of the ordinary accent system in their brāhmaṇas. In fact, the Sāma-Veda ignores "ordinary" accent even in its Saṁhitā, which instead gives the melodies of the chants, which in written versions of the texts are marked by the same convention of superscript numerals as the melodic line in Selection XVI.

We thus have to distinguish between a "recitational" accent system and the accent system found in "ordinary" Vedic. In the following, let us take a closer look at this "ordinary" system of accentuation.

Most lexical items have an "inherently" accented syllable; some compounds may have more than one. On the other hand, there are several categories of unaccented words. Some of these are inherently unaccented (enclitic pronouns and particles); others can be said to have "lost" their inherent accent. The latter type includes vocative forms (Whitney §§92a and 314) and "finite" verbs, i.e. verbs with personal endings, if they occur in certain syntactic or prosodic positions (Whitney §§92b, 591-598, 1082-1085).

The "inherent" accent is a "musical" or "pitch" accent, characterized by a high pitch (called उदात्त 'raised') and in principle contrasting with all unaccented syllables which have a low pitch (अनुदात्त 'not raised'). A reflex of this relatively simple system is found in the passages from the Maitrāyaṇī-Saṁhitā, where a raised vertical line indicates the accented syllable (as in वि॑ष्णुमुखा वै॑ देवा॑ ..., Selection XX:E3).

This system, however, has undergone a large number of changes and, as a matter of fact, the accentual system of the Maitrāyaṇī-Saṁhitā is quite complex, requiring a large number of different marks in written texts, which for typographic reasons had to be omitted in this Reader.

The most commonly encountered variant of this system is that of the Ṛg-Veda, which involves several changes and peculiarities:

> The high pitch of the accented syllable "spills over" onto the next syllable (if any) and combines with the low tone of that syllable into a falling tone, called स्वरित lit. 'resounding'.
>
> The syllable preceding the inherently accented syllable has an especially low tone, called अनुदात्ततर 'lower'. (In poetic texts, all unaccented syllables in a line before the first accented one are अनुदात्ततर.)
>
> In case of conflict between falling tone and lowest tone, lowest tone takes precedence.
>
> In written texts, it is these falling-tone and lowest-tone syllables which get marked, by a raised vertical stroke and a subscript horizontal stroke respectively; the inherently accented syllable is left unmarked. The MS passage वि॑ष्णुमुखा वै॑ देवा॑ thus would come out as विष्णु॑मुखा॒ वै दे॒वा.
>
> Further complications arise from two facts. First, just as there is sandhi between the vowels and consonants of adjacent words, so there is tone or accent sandhi, which may result in falling tones or "svaritas". (There are in fact yet other results of tone sandhi, one of which can be found in XX:H2, line 19, where the numeral १ is used to "support" the accentual marking.) The second complication consists in the fact that in the history of Vedic, some inherently accented vowels dropped out, so that the following falling tone or svarita is no longer derivable from a preceding high tone or udātta. (This is the case for instance for राज॒न्यं॑ in XX:G, verse 12.) The latter type of svarita is often referred to as "independent svarita".

The Śatapatha-Brāhmaṇa presents yet another variety of accent marking. The only marking used in manuscripts and printed editions is a subscript horizontal stroke, which in other traditions indicates the lowest tone. A recent study has established that this is in fact the value of the subscript stroke in the Śatapatha-Brāhmaṇa, even though at first sight it may appear to correspond to the inherent accent of the other Vedic texts. See the following comparison:

MS-type accentuation	RV-type accentuation	ŚB-type accentuation
वि॑ष्णुमुखा वै॑ देवा॑	विष्णु॑मुखा॒ वै दे॒वा	वि॒ष्णुमुखा वै॒ देवा॒

The latter impression is shown to be wrong by the evidence of words with "independent svarita", where the syllable preceding the independent svarita is marked by the subscript stroke, as in

RV-type accentuation	ŚB-type accentuation
राज॒न्य॑	राज॒न्य

The proper solution is, simplified, as follows. In the history of the Śatapatha-Brāhmaṇa tradition three events took place: (1) The svarita syllable received the highest pitch; (2) the syllable before the svarita (whether independent svarita or resulting from tone sandhi) received the lowest pitch, becoming anudāttatara; (3) all tonal distinctions between syllables other than the anudāttatara were lost, in favor of the high pitch of the svarita. As a result, only the anudāttatara syllables needed to be marked, anything unmarked having high pitch. (For further discussion see George Cardona, 'The bhāṣika accentuation system', *Studien zur Indologie und Iranistik* 18: 1-40, 1993.)

Glossary

Glossary

Although this Reader is intended as a supplement to Lanman's *Reader*, the Glossary has been organized so as to be self-contained. A few departures have been made from Lanman's citation practice. Most important is that Sanskrit forms are given in devanāgarī, not in romanization. For verb entries, principal parts (other than the present tense) are listed only as far as required for this Reader. Of the finite verb forms, generally only the third person singular is given; but third plural forms are provided where there is a different root shape or stem form, and a few other forms are given that might be difficult to recognize. In addition, as regards noun and adjective classes, the Glossary follows the Indian grammatical tradition by writing अच्, अत्, मत्, वत्, यस्, वस्, instead of Lanman's and Whitney's *-añc, -ant, -mant, -vant, -yāṁs, -vāṁs*. Similarly, pronoun entries are to be found under the citation forms of the Indian grammatical tradition, such as तद् for the demonstrative pronoun stem स/त; or त्वद् for the second singular personal pronoun. (Exceptions are the interrogative pronoun क, instead of the किम् of the Indian grammatical tradition, and the numerals.) In the case of proper names, no attempt has generally been made to provide a translation, even though names tend to have recognizable lexical meanings. Instead, the following abbreviations are used: PN = Proper Name; PNF = a name indicating ancestry or family affiliation, which in many cases can also be used as the name of an individual (see Whitney §§1204 and 1205 for the vṛddhi-derivation and suffixes employed for most PNFs). Most of the other abbreviations should be self-explanatory. Paragraph references in the Glossary refer to Whitney's *Grammar*. "Introduction" refers to the Introduction to this Reader, "Note(s)" to the Notes section, and "Grammatical Notes" to the notes on grammar at the beginning of the Notes section.

अ (before vowel अन्, §1121a) negative prefix

अ (pronoun stem, both enclitic and non-enclitic, see इदम् and Grammatical Notes, section 2)

अकार (m.) the sound अ (grammatical term; compare उकार, मकार)

अकृत्स्न (adj.) incomplete (कृत्स्न)

अक्षर (adj.) imperishable; (n.) syllable, esp. the sacred syllable ओम् / ॐ

अगृह्य (adj.) not graspable (neg. gerundive of √गृह्)

अग्नि (m.) fire, esp. sacred fire; the God of fire, Agni

अग्निहोत्र (n.) a sacrifice of or to fire, i.e. to Agni

अग्र (n.) front, beginning; tip, end

अङ्ग (particle) please, just

अङ्ग (n.) limb, body

अङ्गार (m.) coal

√अच् (अचति; pass. अच्यते) to bend
+ उद् to produce (lit. to bend up)

√अज् (अजति; gerund -अज्य)
+ उद् to drive up, drive out

अज (m.) goat, he-goat

अजर (adj.) not aging, ageless (जर)

अजा (f.) she-goat

अजातशत्रु (m.) PN (lit. without a born enemy)

अणिमन् (m.) subtle nature, subtle essence, atom (अणु)

अणु (adj.) small, tiny, fine, subtle

अतस् (adv., §1098) from that; thereupon, then

अति (prefix) beyond, exceeding

अतिघ्नी (f.) pinnacle or point of highest oblivion (from अति + घ्न, compound form of √हन्)

अतिमुक्ति (f.) highest/ultimate release; escape (√मुच् + अति)

अतिमोक्षा (f.) ultimate release (√मुच् + अति)

अतिव्याधिन् (adj.) piercing, sharp (fr. √व्यध् + अति)

अतिष्ठा (m.f.n., §348-354) superior in standing; surpassing (√स्था)

अतिसृष्टि (f.) highest creation (lit. beyond-creation; see सृष्टि)

अतीव (adv.) exceedingly (अति + इव)

अत्तृ (m.n.) eater (√अद्)

अत्र (adv., §502) here

अथ (§1101) now, so

अथर्वाङ्गिरस् (m., in pl.) Vedic name of the Atharva Veda (after its two components, the auspicious and black-magic hymns)

अथा (= अथ, §248a)

अथो (see अथ and उ)

√अद् (अत्ति, अदन्ति; inf. अत्तुम्, pple. अन्न) to eat

अदस् (dem. pron., §501, 503) that (yonder, over there); special use in असौ (द्यौः) yonder sky and as neuter अदः yonder (sky); (neut. also as adv., §1111a) over there, yonder

अदिति (adj.) without limit, unlimited; (f.) infinity, unboundedness, the Goddess Aditi
अदितित्व (n.) "Aditi-hood"
अद्य (adv.) today
अद्वितीय (adj.) without a second or partner (द्वितीय)
अधस् (adv.) below, down
अधस्तात् (adv., §1100b) below, (as adposition, w. genitive) under
अधि (adv.) above, beyond; also used as prefix
अधिज्य (adj., bahuvrīhi) with the bowstring (strung) up (अधि + ज्या bowstring)
अधिदेवतम् (adv., §1313) according to the deities (contrast: अध्यात्मम्)
अध्यर्ध (adj.) one and a half (अधि above + अर्ध half)
अध्यात्मम् (adv., §1313) according to the आत्मन् (contrast अधिदेवतम्)
अध्वन् (m.) way, road, path
अध्वर्यु (m.) the chief priest associated with the Yajur-Veda (Introduction, section 5)
√अन् (अनिति, अनन्ति, §631) breathe
  + प्र breathe forth, breathe (§192a)
अन (pron. stem; see इदम्)
अननूक्त (adj.) not studied (fr. अनूक्त ta-pple. of √वच् + अनु)
अनन्त (adj.) without end (अन्त)
अनारम्बण (adj.) without support (आरम्बण, fr. √रम्ब्/लम्ब् 'hang down, cling to' + आ)
अनिल (m.) wind; (earlier, literal meaning:) not resting
अनु (prefix) in accordance with, along with
अनुज्ञा (f.) assent, agreement (fr. √ज्ञा + अनु)
अनुव्याख्यान (n.) a kind of commentary (fr. √ख्या + अनु + वि + आ explain)
अनूचान (adj.) learnèd (perf. mid pple. of √वच् + अनु recite after, repeat, learn)
अनूचानतम (adj. compve.) more, most learnèd
अन्त (m.) border, limit, end; front, (loc.) in front of
अन्ततस् (adv., §1098) ultimately; in the end (अन्त)
अन्तर् (adv.) inside, within
अन्तर (adj.) inner, (n.) interior, middle
अन्तरतर (adj., compve., §471-473) innermost (अन्तर)
अन्तरतस् (adv., §1098) inside (अन्तर)
अन्तरा (adv.) inside, in between (अन्तर)

अन्तरिक्ष (n.) atmosphere, ether (the intermediate space between द्यौः heaven and पृथिवी earth)

अन्तरेण (adv.) inside, between (अन्तर)

अन्तवत् (adj.) having an end, finite, limited (अन्त)

अन्न (n.) food (ta-pple of √अद्)

अन्नाद (m.) eater of food; eater (fr. अन्न + अद eater, fr. √अद्)

अन्नाद्य (n. §1212) food (अन्नाद)

अन्य (adj., §523b) other

अन्यतम (adj. compve.) one of several, another

अन्यतस् (adv., §1098b) otherwise, elsewhere

अन्यत्र (adv., §1099) elsewhere

अन्योन्य (adj.) each other

अप् (f., usually in pl., §393) water (running, live water in contrast to standing, still water, or water as a substance)

अप (prefix) down, away

अपक्षीयमाणपक्ष (m.) the part (पक्ष) or fortnight of the lunar month in which the moon wanes (अपक्षीयते, see √क्षि + अप)

अपचिति (f.) veneration (√चि notice, observe + अप)

अपर (adj., §525a) behind, after, following; western

अपरपक्ष (m.) hind/later side; the second fortnight of the lunar month during which the moon wanes

अपर्यन्त (adj.) unlimited (पर्यन्त boundary, limit, fr. परि + अन्त)

अपात्त (n.) abundance (? — see Note on XVII:A, line 26)

अपान (n.) down-breath (see Note on X, lines 30-32)

अपार (adj.) boundless, infinite (पार other side, boundary)

अपि (adv., conj.) also, even; also used as prefix

अप्रिय (adj.) not dear, disagreeable (fr. प्रिय)

अबलीयस् (adj., comparative, §461,467) weaker (अबल weak, fr. बल)

अभि (prefix) to, unto; against

अभितस् (adv., §1098) on both sides, on all sides, around

अभिनन्द (m.) pleasure, enjoyment, incl. sexual (√नन्द् rejoice + अभि)

अभ्यवदान्य (adj.) depriving (√दा 2 cut + अभि + अव)

अभ्यारोह (m.) lit. ascent; see Note on III, line 3 (√रुह् + अभि + आ)

अभ्याश (m.) prospect (√अश् 1 + अभि)

अभ्र (n.) rain cloud

अमर (adj.) immortal (मर death, fr. √मृ)
अमानव (adj.) non-human, spiritual (मानव human, fr. मनु)
अमु (pron. stem; see अदस्)
अमृत (adj.) immortal; (n.) immortality (मृत dead, fr. √मृ die)
अमृतत्व (n.) immortality
अमृत्यु (m.) non-death, immortality (fr. मृत्यु)
अयन (n.) going, way (√इ go)
अयम् (see इदम्)
अयस् (n.) metal
अरण्य (n.) forest, wilderness
अरिष्टि (f.) uninjuredness = well-being (fr. √रिष् harm)
अरे (particle of address) my dear (tends to be condescending)
अर्क (m.) ray; fire; hymn
अर्कत्व (n.) "arka-hood"
अर्घ (m.) honor, hospitality
अर्चिस् (n.) flame
अर्ध 1 (adj.) part, half; (m.) the half
अर्ध 2 (m.) abode, place (in the Vedic language this has a different accent from अर्ध 1)
अर्वन् (m.) a courser, type of horse (√ऋ)
√अर्ह् (अर्हति) deserve; (w. infin.) be able
अर्हा (f.) honor, hospitality (√अर्ह्)
अलम् (adv.) ready, enough for (w. dative); enough of (w. instr.)
अलोक्यता (f.) worldlessness (लोक)
अलोमक (adj.) hairless (लोमन्)
अव (prefix) down, away
अवक्षयण (n.) decreaser, extinguisher (fr. √क्षि + अव)
अवाच् (adj., §408-409) downward
अवान्तर (adj.) intermediate (from अव + अन्तर)
अवि (m.) sheep; (f.) ewe
अविदित (adj.) unknown, not known (fr. विदित, √विद् know)
अव्याकृत (adj.) undifferentiated (व्याकृत, fr. √कृ + वि + आ)
√अश् 1 (अश्नोति, अश्नुवन्ति) to attain
√अश् 2 (अश्नाति, अश्नन्ति) to eat
अशन (n.) food (√अश् 2)

√अशनाय to be hungry (denom., अशन)
अशनाया (f.) desire for food; hunger (fr. √अशनाय)
अशनि (f.) thunderbolt
अशीर्य (adj.) indestructible (neg. gerundive of √शॄ crush, break)
अश्व (m.) horse
अश्वा (f.) mare
अश्वमेध (m.) horse sacrifice, Aśvamedha (मेध)
अश्वमेधत्व (n.) "Aśvamedha-hood"
अश्वल (m.) PN
अष्ट (numeral) eight
अष्टम (adj.) eighth
अष्टाक्षर (adj.) of eight syllables (fr. अष्ट + अक्षर)
√अस् 1 (अस्ति, सन्ति §636; perf. आस) to be
√अस् 2 (अस्यति; pple. अस्त; gerund -अस्य) to throw
+ प्र to throw
+ अभि + प्र to throw away
असकृत् (adv.) not once, often (fr. सकृत् once)
असङ्ग (adj.) without attachment (सङ्ग attachment)
असत् (adj.) not being, untrue; (n.) non-being, untruth (सत्)
असित (adj.) unfettered, unconstrained (neg. ta-pple. of √सा to tie, bind)
असुर (m.) a type of divine being opposed to the Gods
असौ (see अदस्)
अस्थन् (see अस्थि)
अस्थि (n., §343i, 431) bone
अस्मद् (pron., §491) we, us
√अह् (आह, आहुः; sg. 2 आत्थ, §801a) say, speak (perfect inflection, past or present-tense value)
+ प्रति to answer, reply
अहन् (see अहर्)
अहम् (pron., §491, see मद्)
अहर् (n., §430a) day
अहल्लिक (m.) prattler, fool
अहस् (see अहर्)
अह्न (n.) daily (course of the sun) (अहर्)

आ (adposition w. dat. or acc.) up to; also used as prefix
आकाश (m.) space, sky
आक्रम (m.) approach (√क्रम् + आ)
आघात (m.) one who beats or strikes upon (√हन् + आ)
आङ्गिरस (m.) PNF
आचार्य (m.) teacher (√चर् + आ)
आत्मन् (m.) body, spirit, self; character, nature; transcendental principle; also used as reflexive pronoun (§514)
आत्मन्विन् (adj., §1232) having a self, a body
आदित्य (m.) sun, the Sun God Āditya (lit. descendant of Aditi); (in pl.) a class of Gods of heavenly light
आदेश (m.) instruction (√दिश् + आ)
आनन्द (m.) happiness, bliss (fr. √नन्द् + आ); (n.) supreme bliss (an epithet of Brahman)
√आप् (आप्नोति, आप्नुवन्ति; aor. आपत्; pple. आप्त; gerund -आप्य; caus. आपयति) to reach, obtain; (caus.) make obtain, fulfill
+ अभि + प्र to reach
+ उप to obtain
+ प्र to obtain
आपयितृ (m.n.) fulfiller (√आप्, caus.)
आपस् (see अप्)
आपूर्यमाणपक्ष (m.) the part (पक्ष) or fortnight of the lunar month in which the moon waxes (आपूर्यते from √पृ + आ)
आप्ति (f.) attainment; power, control (√आप्)
आभूति (f.) power, control (√भू + आ)
आयतन (n.) abode, resting-place, foundation (√यत् + आ)
आयुस् (n.) life
आर (m.) name of a lake (√ऋ)
आरम्भण (n.) convention, lit. holding on to (√रभ्/रम्भ् to hold + आ)
आरुणि (m.) PNF
आरुणेय (m.) PNF
आर्तव (adj.) connected with the seasons (ऋतु)
आर्द्र (adj.) wet, moist
आवर्तिन् (adj.) revolving, returning (fr. √वृत् + आ)

आवृत्ति (f.) return (√वृत् + आ)
आशा (f.) hope; prospect
आश्रावण (n.) the call for the श्रौषट् (see Note on XIII:1, line 16)
आश्वतराश्वि (m.) PNF
√आस् (आस्ते, आसते) to sit
+ उप to attend to, to serve; to worship; to concentrate, meditate on
आसन (n.) seat
√आह् (see √अह्)
आहुति (f.) oblation (√हु + आ)

√इ (एति, यन्ति, §612; perf. इयाय, ईयुः ; pple. इत; gerund -इत्य) to go
+ अधि (mid) to study, learn
+ अभि + सम् + आ to come together, assemble
+ आ to come, come up
+ उद् to rise (of the sun)
+ उद् + आ to go up to
+ उप to go to (a teacher for instruction, ask someone to be one's teacher)
+ उप + सम् to go up to
+ उप + सम् + आ to come up to
+ परि to go around, surround
+ परि + अव to turn around, turn away; to pass, elapse
+ प्र to go forth, depart; to die
+ प्रति to return to
+ वि to go away, disappear
+ सम् to come together, come about
इतर (adj., §436b) other
इतस् (adv., §1098) hence, from here, from now
इति (adv., particle) so, thus; quotative marker (§1102a-c)
इतिहास (m.) story, legend (fr. इति + ह + आस 'thus indeed it was')
इत्थंविद् (m.) variant of एवंविद्
इत्थम् (adv., §1101) thus, so
इदम् (dem. pron.) this (close by), this here; special use in इयं (पृथिवी) this earth, and as neuter इदम् this (world) (§501-502 and Grammatical Notes); (neut. also as adv., §1111a) here, now
इन्द्र (m.) the God Indra
इम (see इदम्)

इयम् (see इदम्)
√इष् (इच्छति) to desire
इष्ट (n.) offering, sacrifice (√यज्)
इह (adv.) here, here on earth
इव (enclit. particle) as, like; as it were, so to speak

√ईक्ष् (ईक्षते; perf. ईक्षां चक्रे; ger. -ईक्ष्य) to reflect
+ अनु + वि to look around
+ उद् to notice, see
√ईर् (ईर्ते, ईरते; caus. ईरयति) to move
+ आ to send forth
ईर्म (m.) arm; fore-quarter of an animal
√ईश् (ईष्टे, ईशते) to rule, own
ईशान (m.) epithet of Rudra/Śiva (pres. mid. pple of √ईश्)
ईश्वर (m.) lord, ruler; (adj.) powerful, capable; likely (to happen) (√ईश्)

उ (enclit. particle) and, also, even
उकार (m.) the sound उ (grammatical term; compare अकार, मकार)
उक्ति (f.) expression, declaration (√वच्)
उग्रपुत्र (m.) son of a powerful person/powerful son; princely warrior (उग्र powerful + पुत्र)
उच्चावच (adj.) high and low; various (fr. उद् + च + अव + च, §1314)
उत (particle) and, also; perchance (in an ironic question)
उद् (prefix) up, forth; away
उदक (n.) water (as a substance)
उदङ् (adv., fr. उदच्)
उदच् (adj., §408-409) directed upward; north, northern
उदर (n.) belly
उदान (m.) up-breathing (see Note on X, lines 30-32)
उदीची feminine of उदच्
उद्गातृ (m.) the chief priest associated with the Sāma-Veda (fr. √गा 1 + उद्; see Introduction, section 5)
उद्गीथ (m.) Sāma-Vedic chant, a sāman, office of the उद्गातृ (fr. √गा 1 + उद्)
उद्ग्रहण (n.) grasping, taking up, lifting up (√ग्रह् + उद्)

उद्य (adj.) apparently a mistake for उज्ज्य with the bow-string (ज्या) away (उद्)
उप (prefix) to, toward, close to
उपकरणवत् (adj.) rich (lit. having उपकरण riches, possessions)
उपनिषद् (f.) esoteric learning (fr. √सद् + उप + नि)
उपमास (m.) additional, intercalary month (मास)
उपव्याख्यान (n.) explanation, discussion (√ख्या + उप + वि + आ)
उपस्थ (m.) lap
उपाय (m.) approach (√इ + उप)
उपायन (n.) approach (√इ + उप)
उभ (adj.) both (dual only)
उभय (adj.) both, of both kinds (sing. and plur. only, §525)
उरस् (n.) breast, chest
उल्ब (n.) enveloping membrane of an embryo
√उष् (ओषति) to burn
उषस् (f.) dawn

ॐ (variant of ओम्)
ऊर्णवाभि (m.) spider (from an obsolete √वाभ् to weave + ऊर्ण wool, lit. wool weaver)
ऊर्ध्व (adj.) upward; neut. also as adv.
ऊवध्य (n.) undigested grass
√ऊह् (ऊहति, -ते) to shift, move, remove
+ उद् to cast up or out
+ वि to spread out
+ सम् to bring together
+ सम् + उद् to move up together

√ऋ (ऋच्छति) to go, reach
ऋग्वेद (m.) the Ṛg-Veda (ऋच्)
√ऋच् (अर्चति) to sing, praise
ऋच् (f.) hymn of praise, verse; (collective pl.) the Ṛg-Veda
ऋतु (m.) season, fixed time, esp. for sacrifice
ऋत्विज् (m.) priest (ऋतु + √यज्)
√ऋध् (ऋध्नोति, ऋध्नुवन्ति) to thrive
+ अधि to make prosper beyond (no doubt made up to explain अध्यर्ध)
ऋषि (m.) seer, poet

एक (num. adj.) one; sole, only, alone
एकत्रिंशत् (numeral) 1 + 30 = 31
एकैक (adj.) one-by-one, every one
एजत् (adj.) moving, animate (pres. act. pple. of √एज् to move, stir)
एतद् (dem. pron., §499b) this, that (near by); (n. also as adv.) here, now
एतदनुकृति (adv., §1313) of that nature (एतद् + अनुकृति imitation, nature)
एतदात्म्य (adj.) having the nature of that (एतद् + आत्मन्)
एतर्हि (adv., §1103d) now (एतद्)
एतावत् (adj., §517) thus much (एतद्)
एध (m.) fuel, wood (√इध् to light)
एन (enclit. pron.) him, her, it, them (see §500, 502a, and Grammatical Notes)
एनस् (n.) transgression, sin
एव (emphasizing particle) just, exactly (often not to be translated)
एवम् (adv.) so, thus
एवंविद् (adj.) knowing thus, he who has this (esoteric) knowledge (एवम् + विद् 1 know)
एष (see एतद्)

ओम् (particle) Oh, yes; the most sacred syllable, also transcribed as ॐ (see Introduction, sections 2, 3.7)
ओषधि (f.) plant, herb

औपनिषद (adj.) related to or connected with the उपनिषद्, esoteric

क (interrog. pron.) who
कतम (interrog. pron., compve. §473b) who/which of several; precisely who/which
कतर (interrog. pron., compve. §473b) who/which of two
कति (interrog. pron., §519) how many
कथम् (interrog. adv., §1101) how
कनीयस् (adj. compve., §463) younger, smaller, less
कपूय (adj.) bad, evil (lit. badly stinking, from √पूय् stink + derogatory prefix क, see §§506, 1121j)
कम् (indeclinable) well-being; also used as postpositive emphasizing particle (§1111a)
√कम् (कामयते) to love, desire
कर्तृ (m.) doer, agent (√कृ)
कर्म (compound form of कर्मन्)
कर्मन् (n.) deed, work, action; sacrificial action (√कृ)

कल्याणतम (adj., superl.) most beautiful (कल्याण good, beautiful)
कात्यायनी (f.) PN(F), one of Yājñavalkya's two wives
काप्य (m.) PNF
काम (m.) wish, desire (√कम्)
√कामय (see √कम्)
कार्ष्णायस (n.) iron (कृष्ण + अयस्)
काल (m.) time, appropriate time
काश्य (adj.) of/belonging to काशी (Banaras/Varanasi)
किम् (interrog. pron.; see क); as adv. how, why
किल (postpositive emphasizing particle, §1122a)
कीट (m.) worm, insect, vermin
कीर्ति (f.) announcement, mention; good repute, fame (√कृ 2 recite, praise)
कुतस् (interrog. adv., §1098) whence, from where, why
कुमार (m.) boy, young man
कुरु (m. pl.) the Kuru people (≠ कुरु imperative of √कृ)
कुल (n.) family
कुलाय (n.) nest; receptacle; home
कुलीन (adj.) of/belonging to the family (कुल)
√कृ (करोति, कुर्वन्ति; perf. चकार, चक्रुः, sg. 1 चकर; aor. mid pl. 3 अक्रत; fut. करिष्यति; ta-pple. कृत; gerund कृत्वा, -कृत्य; pass. क्रियते) to do, make; to put
+ उद् + आ to drive up (lit. to make or put up to)
+ वि to change, divide
+ वि + आ to distinguish
+ हिम् to make the sound *him/hum* (in Vedic chant)
कृच्छ्र (adj.) pitiful, troubled, perplexed
कृत्स्न (adj.) whole, entire
कृत्स्नता (f.) entirety
कृन्तन (n.) cutter, cutting instrument (fr. √कृत् cut)
कृपण (adj.) pitiful, wretched
कृष्ण (adj.) black, dark
कौरव्यायणी (f.) PN(F)
क्रतु (m.) power, poetic power, inspiration

√क्रम् (क्रामति, mid. क्रमते; perf. चक्राम, mid. चक्रमे; aor. अक्रामीत्, normally अक्रमीत्; pple. क्रान्त) to step, stride
  + अति to go beyond, overcome
  + आ to approach
  + उद् to go out, depart (of vital spirit)
  + प्रति to go back to
√क्रुध् (क्रुध्यति; perf. चुक्रोध, चुक्रुधुः) to be angry
क्लोमन् (m.) the lung (often plural)
क्व (interrog. adv., §505) where, whither
क्षत्र (n.) power, dominion; (collect.) the kṣatriya caste
क्षत्रिय (m.) kṣatriya, member of the rulers' caste
√क्षि (intrans. क्षीयते) to wane, be diminished
  + अप to wane, dwindle away
क्षुद्र (adj.) small
क्षुर (m.) razor

ख (n.) sky, ether
खलु (postpositive emphasizing particle, §1122a)
√ख्या (ख्याति, intrans./pass. ख्यायते; fut. ख्यास्यति; inf. ख्यातुम्) to state, make known; (intr./pass.) be known
  + आ to tell, to name; to be known as
  + प्रति + आ to turn down, reject
  + वि + आ to explain

गणशस् (adv., §1106) in groups (fr. गण group, host)
गन्ध (m.) smell
गन्धर्व (m.) a heavenly musician, a Gandharva
√गम् (गच्छति; perf. जगाम, जग्मुः; fut. गमिष्यति; pple. गत; gerund गत्वा; caus. गमयति) to go
  + अभि + आ to go to, to arrive
  + आ to come
  + नि to go into, enter
  + सम् + आ to come together, meet; to engage in sexual union
गर्दभ (m.) donkey, ass

गर्दभी (f.) female donkey, ass
गर्भ (m.) womb; embryo; child
√गा 1 (गायति; pass. गीयते) sing, chant
+ आ sing up, obtain something by chanting
+ उद् chant the sāman
√गा 2 (जिगाति; aor. अगात्) to go
+ आ to come
+ उप + आ to go to, come to; to acquire
गाङ्गायनि (m.) PNF
गायत्री (f.) a Vedic meter, also the name of RV 3:62:10 (Selection XX:D), composed in this meter
गार्गी (f.) PN(F)
गार्ग्य (m.) PNF
गुदा (f.) entrail, intestine
√गुप् (गोपायति; fut. गोपायिष्यति; desid. जुगुप्सति) to guard against, protect
गुरु (adj.) heavy; wise; (m.) teacher
√गॄ (गृणाति, गृणन्ति) to call, to praise
+ प्रति (+ आ) to respond (an activity of the adhvaryu in the ritual)
√गृह (see √ग्रह्)
गृह (m. pl.) house
गो (m., f., §361c) cow, bull
गोत्र (n.) family, clan; family name (lit. cow pen)
गोप (m.) guard, guardian, protector
√गोपाय (see √गुप्)
गौतम (m.) PNF
√ग्रह् (गृह्णाति, गृह्णन्ति; pple. गृहीत; gerund गृहीत्वा; pass. गृह्यते) to take, to seize (the earlier form of the root is ग्रभ्)
ग्रहण (n.) seizing, holding
ग्राम (m.) village
ग्राहिन् (adj.) taking, deserving to take (fr. √ग्रह्)
ग्लाव (m.) PN

घन (m.) mass, accumulation (√हन्)
घ्रा (जिघ्रति) to smell (trans.)

च (enclit. conjunction) and, also; it turns preceding interrogatives into indefinite pronouns (§507)
√चक्ष् (चष्टे, pl. 3 चक्षते) to appear; to tell
+ आ to say; to call, name
+ वि + आ to explain
चक्षुस् (n.) eye
चण्डाल (m.) a Chandala, member of the lowest, most despised caste
चतुर् (numeral adj., §482g) four
चतुर्विंशति (numeral) 4 + 20 = 24
चत्वार् (see चतुर्)
चन (particle) not even; it turns preceding interrogatives into indefinite pronouns (§507)
चन्द्र (m.) moon
चन्द्रमस् (m., §§389b, 397a) moon
√चम् (चामति, only with आ) to sip, to drink
√चर् (चरति; caus. चारयते) to go, move
+ आ to perform; to associate with
+ उद् to move up, to rise
+ परि to go around, to attend, serve; caus. mid. have oneself attended to
+ वि + उद् to rise in different directions; to emanate
+ वि + निस् to emanate
चरक (adj.) wandering; (m.) wandering student (√चर्)
चरण (n.) wandering; conduct, life-style (√चर्)
चित्र (adj.) colorful; (m.) PN
चिद् (enclit. particle) it turns preceding interrogatives into indefinite pronouns (§507)
चिर (adj.) long (of time); (neut. also as adv.) for a long time, for a while
चेद् (enclit. conjunction) if

छन्दस् (n.) poetic meter
छाया (f.) shadow

जघन (m., n.) the rear; the buttocks
√जन् (intr. जायते; ta-pple. जात; caus. जनयति; gerund जनयित्वा) to be born; (caus.) to cause to be born, engender
+ अनु to be born after, along with
+ उप to be born, arise
+ प्र to be procreated, to procreate
+ प्रति + आ to be born again

जन (m.) man; (pl.) people

जनक (m.) PN of a famous king

जनपद (m.) a people, community, district

√जप् (जपति) to mutter (a form of Vedic recitation)

जर (adj.) old

√जरय (जरयति; fut. जरयिष्यति) to age, to become old (denom. fr. जर)

जातु (particle) at all, ever, indeed

जानपद (adj.) inhabitant of a country or region (जनपद, §1204)

जाया (f.) wife

√जि (जयति; fut. जेष्यति, जेता; pple. जित) to win, defeat, be victorious

+ अप to defeat

जित् (adj.) winning, conquering (in compounds, √जि, §345)

जिति (f.) victory, conquest (√जि)

जिह्वा (f.) tongue

√जीव् (जीवति; pple. जीवित) to live

+ उप live upon, depend on for one's living

जीवित (n.) life (ta-pple. of √जीव्)

जुहुराण (adj.) misleading, crooked (pres. mid. pple. of √ह्वृ/ह्वर् go crookedly)

√जृम्भ् (जृम्भते) to gape

+ वि to gape open

जैवल (m.) PNF

जैवलि (m.) (same as the preceding)

√ज्ञप्, ज्ञपय see √ज्ञा

√ज्ञा (जानाति, जानन्ति; aor. pl. 2 act. अज्ञासिष्ठ; pple. ज्ञात; pass. ज्ञायते; caus. ज्ञापयति/ज्ञपयति, perf. ज्ञापयां चकार; future ज्ञपयिष्यति) to know; (caus.) to make known, instruct, inform

+ अनु to assent, agree

+ आ (caus.) to command, invite

+ प्रति to promise

+ वि to distinguish, understand

ज्योतिस् (n.) light; (pl. also) heavenly bodies, stars

√ज्वल् (ज्वलति) to burn brightly, flame

+ उद् to flare up

ततस् (adv., §1098) thence; thereupon; compared to that

तत्र (adv., §1099) there

तथा (adv., §1101) so, thus; likewise; yes

तद् (demonstr. pron., §495) that, this; sometimes to be translated as definite article, or as third person pronoun; (neut. also as adv., §1111a) then, there, in this way, therefore, so, on this count

तन्तु (m.) thread (√तन् stretch)

√तप् (तपति; ta-pple. तप्त; intrans./pass. तप्यते) to be warm, to heat; (intr./pass.) to perform penance or austerities

+ अभि to perform austerities on something

तपस् (n.) heat, fire; asceticism, austerities

√तपस्य (तपस्यति) to perform austerities (तपस्)

तमस् (n.) darkness

तर्हि (adv., §1103d) then, at that time (fr. तद्)

तल्प (m.) bed

तस्मात् (adv., §1114a) therefore (तद्)

तात (m., voc. sg.) my dear

तावत् (adj., §517) so great, so much, of that extent; (adv.) so much, so far

तिरस् (adv.) through, across, away, beyond

+ √अस् or √भू to be(come) invisible, disappear

+ √धा to obscure

तिरोहित (pple.) obscure (तिरस् + √धा)

तिल (m.) sesame, sesame seed

तिसृ (see त्रि)

तीर्थ (n.) passage, way; correct, or traditional way (√तृ to cross over)

तुभ्यम् (see त्वद्)

तूष्णीम् (indecl.) silent, silently

तृण (n.) grass

तृतीय (adj.) third, one-third

ते (see तद् or त्वद्)

तेजस् (n.) brilliance

त्यद् (pron., §499a) this

त्रय (adj.) threefold, triune

त्रयस्त्रिंश (adj.) 33rd

त्रयस्त्रिंशत् (numeral) 3 + 30 = 33
त्रयोदश (numeral) 3 + 10 = 13; also ordinal, 13th
त्रि (numeral, §482e,f) three
त्रेधा (indecl., §1104) threefold
त्वद् (pron., §491) you (sg.)
त्वच् (f.) skin, cover

दक्षिण (adj.) able; right; south, southern
दक्षिणतस् (adv.) from the right/south
दक्षिणा (adv.) to the south
दक्षिणा (f.) fee or reward paid to a priest
दत्त (n.) (act of) giving (pple of √दा)
दन्दशूक (adj.) mordacious (√दंश् bite ?)
√दम् (दाम्यति) to be controlled
दम (m.) control
√दय् (दयते) to be compassionate
दया (f.) compassion
दर्व्य (m.) the दर्वीहोम, a sacrifice (होम) in which warm milk is given to the pitṛs in ladles (दर्वी)
दर्शन (n.) seeing, looking, beholding; appearance
दश (numeral, §483) ten
√दह् (दहति; pple. दग्ध) to burn
+ सम् to burn up; to consume
√दा (ददाति, ददति, mid. दत्ते, ददते; perf. ददौ, ददुः; aor. अदात्, अदुः; pple. दत्त, gerund -दाय; pass. दीयते) to give
+ अभि + वि + आ open one's mouth at someone (so as to devour)
+ आ (mid.) to take; to take away
+ परा to abandon
+ वि + आ to open one's mouth
दातृ (m.) giver
दान (n.) giving, the act of giving
दाल्भ्य (m.) PNF
दास (m.) servant, slave
दासी (f.) female servant, slave
दिक् (see दिश्)
दिव् (m., §361d) sky, heaven
√दिश् (दिशति; ta-pple. दिष्ट) to point, to direct

दिश् (f.) direction; cardinal direction, cardinal point
√दीप् (दीप्यते) to blaze, flame, shine
दीर्घ (adj.) long (of distance)
दुन्दुभि (m.) (kettle) drum
दुर्निष्प्रपतर (adj. compve.?) more difficult to evolve (fr. दुस् + √पत् + निस् + प्र)
दुस् (prefix) bad, badly; difficult
दुहितृ (f.) daughter
√दृ (द्रियते; gerund -दृत्य; used only with आ) to heed
दृप्त (adj.) proud, arrogant (√दृप् to be proud)
√दृश् (pple. दृष्ट; gerund दृष्ट्वा; present from √पश्;) to see, behold
दृष्टि (f.) seeing, look
देव (m.) divine being, God (दिव्)
देवता (f.) deity
देवत्रा (adv., §1099) among the Gods
देवयान (adj.) going to the Gods (यान going, path)
देवी (f.) Goddess
दैव (adj.) divine, belonging to the Gods
दोषा (adv.) at night
द्यावापृथिवी (du. f.) heaven and earth (dvandva fr. दिव् + पृथिवी, §1255)
द्यु (see दिव्)
√द्युत् (द्योतते) shine, gleam
  + वि to flash (of lightning)
द्यौस् (see दिव्)
द्रष्टृ (m.n.) seer (√दृश्)
√द्रु (द्रवति; perf. दुद्राव, दुद्रुवुः) to run
  + प्र to run forth/away; to flee
द्व (numeral, §482d) two
द्वात्रिंशत् (numeral) 2 + 30 = 32
द्वादश (numeral) 2 + 10 = 12
द्वार (n.) door, gate
द्वारगोप (m.) doorkeeper, guardian (द्वार + गोप)
द्वासप्तति (numeral) 2 + 70 = 72
द्वि (see द्व)
द्वितीय (adj.) second
द्वेधा (adv.) in two
द्वैत (n., , §1204) duality (द्वित second)

धनुस् (n.) bow
√धम् (धमते; pass. ध्मायते) to blow
धर्म (m.) established or proper conduct; duty, virtue
√धा (दधाति, दधति, mid. धत्ते, दधते; aor. (अ)धात्, aor. opt. pl.1 धेम; fut. धास्यति; ta-pple. हित; gerund धित्वा, -धाय) to put, place; to do, make
+ अपि to cover up
+ अभि + आ to put (fuel etc. on or in a fire), to set a fire
+ अव to put down into
+ आ to put on; to set (a fire, esp. in the ritual)
+ वि to arrange; to do, make
धान (adj.) containing; (n.) container
धाना (f.) grain, seed
धानारुह (adj.) growing from a seed (fr. धाना + आरुह, from √रुह् + आ)
धारा (f.) edge, blade
√धाव् (धावति) to run
+ अभि to run to
√धू (धूनोति, mid. धूनुते) to shake
+ वि to shake
धूम (m.) smoke, vapor
√धृ (धारयति, -ते, intr./pass. ध्रियते; perf. दाधार, mid. दध्रे; pple. धृत) (mid.) hold oneself (ready for), prepare oneself for; (intr./pass.) set out to, start to (w. infinitive)
+ वि hold/keep apart, separate
√धृष् (धृष्णोति; perf. दधर्ष, दधृषुः) to dare
ध्म (m.) blower (compound form, from √धम्)
√ध्माय (see √धम्)
√ध्या (ध्यायति; desid. दिध्यासते) think upon, meditate
+ नि think on; (desid.) to try to think on, pay attention

न (adv.) not
नक्षत्र (n.) heavenly body, star; asterism, constellation; (pl. also) the lunar zodiac
नख (m., n.) finger nail, toe nail
नदी (f.) river
√नन्द् (नन्दति) to rejoice, be glad
नभस् (n.) mist, cloud
नमस् (n.) honor, reverence
नमस्कार (m.) the act of doing reverence

नव (adj.) new
नव (numeral) nine
नवतर (adj., compve.) newer (नव)
नवम (adj.) ninth
√नश् (नश्यति) to perish
  + अनु + वि to perish along with
नस् (see अस्मद्)
नाडी (f.) tube, artery
नाना (adv.) separate, different
नाम (particle) indeed
नामधेय (n.) name-giving, name, appellation (नामन् + धेय, fr. √धा)
नामन् (n.) name
नासिका (f.) nostril
नि (prefix) down, in, into
निःश्वास (m.) breathing out, exhalation (√श्वस् to breathe + नि)
निकृन्तन (n.) cutting instrument, knife (√कृत् to cut + नि)
निविद् (f.) a short invocation in the ritual (√विद् 1 + नि)
निस् (prefix) out, forth; away
√नी (नयति) to lead, convey, take
नु (particle) now
√नु (नौति) to praise
  + प्र (प्रणौति) to utter the sound ओम्
नूनम् (particle) now; indeed
√नेद् (नेदति) to flow
  + अति to flow excessively (or make an excessive noise)
  + प्र to flow forth
न्यग्रोध (m.) banyan tree, *ficus indica* (√रुध् to grow + न्यच् downward, because it sends out roots from its branches; the tree is holy, its hanging roots being compared to the downward rays of the sun)

पक्ष (m.) wing; side, part
पञ्च (numeral) five
पञ्चदश (numeral) 5 + 10 = 15; (also adj.) fifteenth
पञ्चम (adj.) fifth
पञ्चाल (m., pl.) a people closely associated with the Kurus
√पत् (पतति; perf. पपात, पेतुः ; fut. पतिष्यति; caus. पातयति) to fly; fall; (caus.) make fly; divide
  + वि to fly apart; (caus.) to make fly or fall (apart); divide

पतङ्ग (m.) flying (insect)
पतञ्चल (m.) PN
पति (m.) lord, master, ruler; husband (§343d)
पत्त्र (n.) feather, wing; leaf (√पत्)
पत्नी (f.) wife, master
पत्र (alternative form of पत्त्र)
पथ् (see पन्थन्)
√पद् (पद्यते; perf. पेदे, पेदिरे; pple. पन्न; gerund -पद्य) to go
+ अभि to go to; to pervade; to seize
+ अभि + निस् to return (down) to
+ आ to come to
+ प्रति to return to; to reply; to perceive; to attain
+ वि + प्रति to go in different directions, separate
पद (n.) foot-step, step; foot trace; a quarter, hence a quarter of a verse, a line
पदनीय (n.) a foot trace (पद)
पन्थन् (m., §433) road, way, path
पर (adj.) surpassing, best, highest; other
परम (adj.) farthest, highest, supreme
परमता (f.) highest position or highest rank; highest end or aim
परश्वत् (m.) some kind of snake or other mordacious animal
परस्तात् (adv., §1100b) after
परा (prefix) away, beyond
परायण (n.) greatest goal (पर + अयन)
परार्ध्य (adj.) having the highest place (पर + अर्ध 2)
परावत् (f.) distance; long time
परि (prefix) around; from
परिधान (n.) clothing (√धा + परि)
परिमोषिन् (adj., m.) robbing, robber (√मुष् to rob + परि)
परिषद् (f.) assembly (√सद् + परि)
पर्जन्य (m.) God of rain; rain
पर्वत (m.) mountain
पर्वन् (n.) joint, knot
पर्शु (f.) rib
पवमान (adj.) being purified or strained (pres. mid. pple. of √पू); an epithet of Soma; name of stotras sung in the jyotiṣṭoma ritual dedicated to Soma

√पश् (पश्यति; the rest of the inflection from √दृश्) to see, behold
पशु (m.) cattle, cow; domestic animal; victim (in the ritual)
पश्चात् (adv., §1114c) behind, after; later; to the west of
√पा (पिबति) to drink
पाङ्क्त (adj.) fivefold (पञ्च)
पाजस्य (n.) hoof, lower part of an animal, (also:) belly, flanks, sides
पाणि (m.) hand
पाण्डुरवासस् (adj.) white-robed (पाण्डुर white + वासस्)
पात्र (n.) vessel
पाद (m.) foot; gold piece, coin
पाप (adj.) bad; (n.) evil
पापीयस् (adj., compve., §463) worse
पाप्मन् (m.) evil, sin
पायु (m.) anus
पारिक्षित (m.) name of a royal lineage
पार्श्व (n.) side, flank
√पालय (पालयति) protect, watch over
+ प्रति to watch out for, keep watch for
पिण्ड (m.) lump, ball, mouthful, dumpling, esp. one offered to the pitṛs
पितामह (m.) grandfather
पितृ (m.) father; (du.) parents; (pl.) ancestors ("pitṛs") to whom a special ritual is dedicated
पितृयाण (n.) going to the pitṛs (यान)
पित्र्यावत् (adj.) having property that is associated with the father or the pitṛs (पित्र्य related to the fathers or pitṛs)
पिपीलिका (f.) (small) ant
√पिष् (पिनष्टि, पिंषन्ति; present gerund -पेषम्, §995) to crush, to grind
+ आ to rub, touch
पुंस् (m., §394) man
पुच्छ (n.) tail
पुण्य (adj.) good, right, auspicious, meritorious
पुत्र (m.) son
पुनर् (adv.) again; but
पुमस् (see पुंस्)

पुमांस् (see पुंस्)
पुरस् (adv.) in front, before, forward; earlier; east
पुरस्तात् (adv., §1106b) in front, before; earlier; east
पुरा (adv.) formerly, before
पुराण (adj.) former, ancient, old; (n.) an account of the past, esp. of a sacred nature
पुरीतत् (m/n) pericardium or some other organ near the heart
पुरुष (m.) man; human being
पुरोनुवाक्या (f.) introductory verse (fr. पुरस् + अनुवाक्य introductory verse, ultimately fr. √वच्)
√पुष् (पुष्यति) thrive; (trans.) nourish
√पू (पुनाति, पुनन्ति, intr. पवते; ta-pple. पूत) purify, clarify; (intr.) become clarified or strained (of Soma)
पूत (adj.) pure (ta-pple. of √पू)
पूर्ण (see √पृ)
पूर्त (n.) public works (√पृ)
पूर्व (adj.) before, prior, preceding; east; (neut. also as adv.) before, earlier
पूर्वपक्ष (m.) front/earlier side; the first fortnight of the lunar month during which the moon waxes
पूषन् (m., §426a) the God Pūṣan
√पृ (पृणाति, पृणन्ति; pple. पूर्ण; intr./pass. पूर्यते) fill, satiate; (intr./pass.) become full
+ नि put down; pour out; offer (esp. to the pitṛs)
+ सम् (intr.) become full
पृथक् (adv.) separately
पृथिवी (f.) earth
पृष्ठ (n.) back of a human being or animal; top
√प्या (प्यायते) to swell, become full
+ आ to become full, rich in; to wax (of the moon)
प्र (prefix) forward, forth
√प्रछ् (पृच्छति; perf. पप्रच्छ; aor. अप्राक्षीत्; fut. प्रक्ष्यति; inf. प्रष्टुम्) to ask, to question
प्रजा (f.) offspring, descendant; creature; subject (of a king) (√जन् + प्र)
प्रजापति (m.) the creator God Prajāpati (lit. lord of creatures)
प्रणव (m.) the sacred syllable ओम् (fr. √नु + प्र)
प्रति (prefix) in return, back, again (corresponding to the Engl. prefix *re-*)
प्रतिगर (m.) the adhvaryu's response to the hotṛ (√गृ + प्रति)
प्रतिपद् (f.) approach, access (√पद् + प्रति)
प्रतिलोम (adj.) against the grain (said of the hide or hair) = contrary to established custom (लोमन्)

प्रतिष्ठा (f.) support, foundation (√स्था + प्रति)
प्रतिष्ठित (adj.) established, supported (ta-pple. of √स्था + प्रति)
प्रतीक (n.) initial part of a verse or paragraph, used as an "address" in recalling information from memory; hence topic, outline (प्रत्यच्)
प्रतीची (fem. of प्रत्यच्)
प्रत्यच् (adj., §408, 409) directed backward; west, western (प्रति)
प्रमायुक (adj.) liable to destruction, perishable, dying away (√मी diminish + प्र)
प्रवर (m.) retinue (√वृ 1 + प्र)
प्रवाहण (m.) PN
प्रशासन (n.) guidance, control, rule (fr. √शास् + प्र)
प्रश्न (m.) question
प्रस्तोतृ (m.) a priest, an assistant of the उद्गातृ; see Note on III, line 3 (√स्तु + प्र)
प्राक् (adv.) before; east (प्राच्)
प्राच् (adj., §408, 409) directed forward; east, eastern (प्र)
प्राची (fem. of प्राच्)
प्राजापत्य (adj.) descended from Prajāpati
प्राण (m.) out-breathing, breath, vital breath; life spirit; life (see Selection X, lines 30-32) (√अन् + प्र)
प्राणिन् (adj.) having breath, breathing, animate
प्रातर् (adv.) in the morning; on the next morning
प्रादुस् (indecl.) visible, (w. √अस्) to be visible
प्रिय (adj.) dear
प्रेयस् (adj. compve., §467-470) dearer (fr. प्रिय)
√प्सा (प्साति; gerund -प्साय) to chew
  + सम् to chew or consume completely

फल (n.) fruit; result (of an action)

बक (m.) PN
बत (exclamatory particle of joy, anger, etc.)
√बध्/बन्ध् (बध्नाति, बध्नन्ति; pple. बद्ध) to bind, tie
  + आ to attach, fasten
बन्धु (m.) connection; relative, friend; (at the end of compounds) related, but not identical, hence second-rate
बल (n.) strength

बलीयस् (adj. compve., §461) stronger

बस्त (m.) male goat

बहिष्पवमान (m.n.) a chant performed during the early morning pressing of Soma (पवमान), outside (बहिस्) the sacred enclosure

बहिस् (adv.) out, outside

बहु (adj.) much, many

बाणवत् (adj.) made of reed, shafted; arrow (बाण reed, shaft, arrow)

बालाकि (m.) PN

बाह्य (adj.) being outside, external (बहिस्)

बुडिल (m.) PN

√बुध् (बोधति, intr./pass. बुध्यते; caus. बोधयति, perf. बोधयां चकार) to awaken, (intr./pass.) to wake up, be awake

+ प्रति (intr./pass.) wake up (in response)

बृगल (n.) piece, fragment, morsel

बृहत् (adj., §450a) great

ब्रह्मग्राहिन् (adj.) (interested in) grasping, understanding sacred learning

ब्रह्मचर्य (n.) religious studentship

ब्रह्मचारिन् (m.) religious student

ब्रह्मन् (n.) sacred word, sacred formula, mantra; sacred learning, theology; the (impersonal) transcendental principle; (collectively) the brahmin caste

ब्रह्मन् (m.) the formulator of the ब्रह्मन् (n.); in the ritual, the brahman-priest, overseer of the Vedic ritual; the personified transcendental principle

ब्रह्मविद्या (f.) sacred learning or knowledge

ब्रह्महन् (m., §402) brahmin slayer

ब्रह्मिष्ठ (adj. superlative, see §§467-470) most brahmin(-like), most learnèd

ब्रह्मोद्य (m.) something to be said about ब्रह्मन् (n.); a learnèd riddle or disputation (उद्य gerundive of √वद्)

ब्राह्मण (n.) exegetical Vedic text (ब्रह्मन् n.)

ब्राह्मण (m.) somebody who studies the Vedic texts; a brahmin (ब्रह्मन् m.)

√ब्रू (ब्रवीति, ब्रुवन्ति, mid. ब्रूते, ब्रुवते) to speak, to say

+ अनु to recite after, repeat (esp. of mantras etc.), study the Veda(s)

+ प्र to proclaim, announce

+ प्रति to answer, reply

√भक्ष् (भक्षयति) to eat, consume

भग (m.) portion, share; fortune (√भज् to portion out, share, allot)
भगवत् (adj.) fortunate; often used as polite form of address (भग)
भगोः (Vedic shortened voc. sg. masc. of the preceding)
भय (n.) fear (√भी)
√भल् (भालयते) to perceive
+ नि to perceive
भवत् 1 (pres. pple. of √भू)
भवत् 2 (m., §456) polite form of address, usually construed as third person (reduced form of भगवत्)
भस्मन् (n.) ash, ashes
भाण् (onomatopoetic, supposedly imitation of breathing or hissing)
√भालय (see √भल्)
√भाष् (भाषते) to speak, to say
भास्वर (adj.) shining, brilliant (√भास् to shine)
√भिद् (भिनत्ति, भिन्दन्ति, mid. भिन्द्धे, भिन्दते; pple. भिन्न) to cut, break
√भी (भयते, alternat. pres. बिभेति; fut. भेष्यति, cond. अभेष्यत्) to fear, to be afraid
√भुज् (भुनक्ति, भुञ्जन्ति, mid. भुङ्क्ते, भुञ्जते) (act.) cause to enjoy, nourish, support; (mid.) enjoy, partake of
भुज्यु (m.) PN
भुवस् (indecl.) a sacred utterance (used in the formula भूर्भुवः स्वः)
√भू (भवति; perf. बभूव, बभूवुः, aor. अभूत्; fut. भविष्यति; pple. भूत, gerund भूत्वा; desid. बुभूषति) to be, become, come about; prosper; (desid.) want or try to be(come)
+ अभि + सम् to pass on to (and become one with)
+ आ to come about
+ वि to prosper
+ सम् to unite, couple with; to take form, come about
भूत (n.) being, creature; entity (ta-pple. of √भू)
भूमन् (m.) existence, world; abundance
भूमि (f.) earth
भूयस् (adj. comparative., §463) more, greater
भूयिष्ठ (adj., superl.) greatest, best (compare भूयस्)
भूर् (indecl.) a sacred utterance (used in the formula भूर्भुवः स्वः)
√भृ (भरति, altern. pres. बिभर्ति, बिभ्रति, §645); pple. भृत) carry, bear; endure; support
+ आ to bring forth
+ सम् to bring together
भृत् (adj.) carrying, supporting (in compounds, fr. √भृ, §345)

भोस् (indecl., §174b) exclamation of address (according to Manu 2:124-128, भोस् is the essence of names and can therefore be used instead of a person's name)

मकार (m.) the sound म् (grammatical term; compare अकार, उकार)
मक्षिका (f.) fly, gnat
मणि (m.) jewel; pearl, bead
मति (f.) thought, thinking (√मन्)
मत्स्य (m.) fish
√मथ् (मथ्नाति, मथ्नन्ति, mid. मथ्नीते, मथ्नते) shake, shake up, treat violently
  + वि to tear up
मद् (first person pron., §491, 494) I, me
मद्र (m.) name of a people
मध्य (adj.) middle
√मन् (मन्यते, alternative pres. मनुते, मन्वते; perf. मेने, मेनिरे; fut. मंस्यते; pple. मत; desid. मीमांसते) to think, believe; (desid.) seek to understand, consider, reflect, deliberate
  + अभि think about, plot against, kill
मनस् (n.) mind, intellect
मनु (m.) man, human being; Manu
मनुष्य (adj.) human; (m.) man, human being
मन्तृ (m.n.) thinker (√मन्)
मन्त्र (m.) sacred formula, verse, mantra
√मन्त्रय (मन्त्रयते; perf. मन्त्रयां चक्रे; ta-pple. मन्त्रित) recite; speak (मन्त्र)
  + अनु say something after/along with (something else)
  + आ speak to, address; greet
  + उप to address, invite
√मन्थ् (मन्थति) to drill, stir
  + अभि to drill (so as to produce fire)
मय (adj., at end of compound) consisting of; characterized by
मरुत् (m., pl.) the Maruts (Gods of the wind storm)
मर्त्य (adj.) mortal; (m.) man (√मृ)
मस् (m., §§389b, 397a) moon; month
महत् (adj., §450b) great
महा (compound form of महत्)
महामनस् (adj.) conceited (महत् + मनस्)

मह‍िमन् (m.) power, greatness
मा (prohibitive particle, normally used with injunctive, §§579, 587)
मांस (n.) meat, flesh (also used in pl.)
मातृ (f.) mother
मान (m., n.) arrogance, conceit (√मन्)
मानस (adj.) of the mind, mental, spiritual (मनस्)
मानिन् (adj.) considering, fancying oneself to be X; arrogant (मान)
मानुष (adj.) pertaining to man, human; (m.) man
माष (m.) bean, lentil
मास (m.) moon, month (मस्)
मिथुन (m., later n.) pair, couple; pairing, coupling
√मिह् (मेहति) to make water, urinate
√मीमांस (see √मन्)
मुक्ति (f.) release (√मुच्)
मुख (n.) mouth; face; head
√मुच् (मुञ्चति, intr./pass. मुच्यते) to release, free; (intr./pass.) become free
+ अति become free beyond, escape
√मुह् (मुह्यते; caus. मोहयति, redupl., caus. aor. अमूमुहत्) to be confused; (caus.) confuse
मूर्धन् (m.) head
मूल (n.) root
√मृ (म्रियते; pple. मृत) to die
मृत्तिका (f.) clay, soil
मृत्यु (m.) death (√मृ)
मृद् (f.) soil, earth (as a substance), clay
मृन्मय (adj.) made of clay (मृद् + -मय)
√मृश् (मृशति; pple. मृष्ट; gerund -मृश्य) to touch
+ अव to feel around, search for
+ वि to feel around for; to consider, investigate
मेघ (m.) cloud, rain (√मिह्)
मेध (m.) sap, essence (esp. of sacrificial victim); sacrificial victim
मेध्य (adj.) fit for sacrifice; pertaining to sacrifice
मेष (m.) ram, male sheep
मैत्रेय (m.) PNF
मैत्रेयी (f.) PN(F), one of Yājñavalkya's two wives

मोह (m.) confusion (√मुह्)

म्लुच् (म्लोचति) to sink, to set

+ नि settle down, set (of the sun)

य (see यद्)

यकृत् (n., §§398a, 432) liver

√यज् (यजति, यजते; perf. इयाज, ईजुः, mid. ईजे, ईजिरे; fut. यक्ष्यति, -ते; ta-pple. इष्ट; caus. याजयति) to sacrifice; (act. usually) to sacrifice for somebody else, serve as priest for that person's sacrifice; (mid.) to sacrifice for oneself, to commission a sacrifice (through a priest or priests); (caus.) to make somebody a यजमान, (hence) to serve as priest for somebody

यजमान (m.) sacrificer; usually a person who commissions a sacrifice (through a priest or priests) (pres. mid. pple. of √यज्)

यजुर्वेद (m.) the Yajurveda

यजुस् (n.) sacrificial formula; (collective pl.) the Yajurveda

यज्ञ (m.) sacrifice

√यत् (यतति; pple. यत्त) to stretch, strive

+ अनु + आ to be connected with, attached to; to depend on

यतस् (rel. adv., §1098) whence, from where

यतिथ (rel. adj., §1242d) "how-manieth", i.e. which one at the end of a series (यति how much, how many)

यत्र (rel. adv., §1099) where, whither

यथा (rel. adv., §1101) how, in which way; as, just as; so that

यथा- (at the beginning of compounds, §13113c) according to (as in यथाकर्म according to one's कर्मन्, यथाकामम् according to one's desire, यथाविद्यम् according to one's knowledge)

यद् (rel. pron., §509, 510) who, what, which; (neut. also as adv., §1111a) that, so that, considering that, concerning that, since; very often used in the meaning 'in so far as' (frequently with correlative तस्मात् or तेन therefore)

यदा (rel. adv., §1103a) when, if

यदि (rel. adv., §1103e) if

√यम् (यच्छति) to hold, extend; extend to, give

+ प्र to offer, to give

यम 1 (m.) The God Yama (ruler of the deceased)

यम 2 (m.) controller (√यम्)

यव (m.) barley
यशस् (n.) fame, honor
√यस् (यस्यति; pple. यस्त) to well up, be heated
  + आ to toil, be wearied, disturbed, agitated
√या (याति; fut. यास्यति) to go
  + उद् to go away, leave (see Note on V, line 1)
याजिन् (adj.) sacrificing (√यज्)
याज्ञवल्क्य (m.) PN
याज्या (f.) verse recited during the sacrifice (√यज्)
यान (adj.) going, leading; (n.) way, path (√या)
यावत् (rel. adj., §517) as much, as great; (neut. also as adv., §1111a) as long as, while
यावत्संपातम् (adv.) as long as the residue (of previous merit) (संपात residue fr. √पत् + सम्)
यावदायुषम् (adv.) as long as one's life (may last) (आयुस्)
√यु (युयोति) to repel
युष्मद् (pron., §491) you (pl.)
यूयम् (see युष्मद्)
योनि (f) womb, lap, vagina; home, foundation
योषा (f.) woman

रजस् (n.) dust
रथ (m.) chariot
√रम् (रमते; perf. रराम, रेमुः, mid. रेमे, रेमिरे) to stop, rest; enjoy
  + उप to stop, become silent
रमणीय (adj.) pleasant, enjoyable
रश्मि (m.) ray, beam
रस (m.) sap, juice; essence; taste
रसतम (adj., comparative) highest essence, quintessence (रस)
राजन् (m.) king
राजन्य (m.) older word for क्षत्रिय
राजसूय (m.) sacrifice at the consecration of the king (सूय, fr. √सु 2 or √सू to press out [the Soma, for the sacrifice])
राति (f.) giving, gift
रात्र (at end of compound = रात्रि)
रात्रि (f.) night

√राध् (राध्नोति; aor. subj. sg.2 (?) राधाः) to succeed
 + अप to blame, hold against someone
राये (see रै)
रुद्र (m) the God Rudra; (pl.) a class of Gods associated with Rudra
√रुध् (रुणद्धि, रुन्धन्ति; perf. रुरोध; fut. रोत्स्यति) to stop, come to an end
 + अव (tr.) to pen up, put into a pen, corral
√रुह् (रोहति) to grow
 + प्र to grow forth
रूप (n.) appearance, form; body
रेतस् (n.) semen, seed
रै (m.,f., §361b) wealth (see the Note on XIX, line 7)

लवण (n.) salt
लाह्यायनि (m.) PNF
√लिप् (लिम्पति, intr./pass. लिप्यते) to smear; (intr./pass.) to be covered, be stuck with
√ली (लयते, intr./pass. लीयते; ta-pple. लीन) to cling to, stay with
 + अनु + वि to dissolve along with
 + वि to dissolve
लोक (m.) world (often in plural)
लोमन् (n.) body hair; fur
लोह (m.) metal, esp. copper and iron; but also gold
लोहित (adj.) red, bloody; (n.) blood

√वच् (वक्ति, वचन्ति; perf. उवाच, ऊचुः; aor. अवोचत्; fut. वक्ष्यति; inf. वक्तुम्; ta-pple. उक्त; gerund उक्त्वा, -उच्य; pass. उच्यते) to say, speak
 + अनु to say after, repeat; to study
 + प्र to declare, proclaim
 + वि to tell apart, explain, solve
वचस् (n.) speech
वडवा (f.) mare, female horse
वत्स्य (see √वस्)
√वद् (वदति; perf. उवाद, ऊदुः; aor. अवादीत्, mid. अवदिष्ट, pple. उदित) to say, speak
 + अति to out-talk
 + अनु to speak after, repeat, reverberate
 + अभि to talk about
 + सम् (mid.) to speak to

वन (n.) forest
वनस्पति (m.) tree (वन + पति)
वयम् (see अस्मद्)
वयस् (n.) bird
वयुन (n.) sign-post
वर (m.) choice, wish, boon (√वृ 2)
वराह (m.) boar
वरुण (m.) Varuṇa
वर्ण (m.) color; category, kind; caste; speech sound (grammatical term)
वर्ष (n.) rain, rainy season; year
√वस् (वसति; perf. उवास, ऊषुः; fut. वत्स्यति; ger. उषित्वा; caus. वासयते) to dwell; (caus.) to house, accommodate
+ आ to take up one's abode (in a place)
वसति (f.) stay, visit (√वस्)
वसु (n.) good(s), wealth; (m. pl.) a class of Gods (the Vasus)
√वह् (वहति; ger. -उह्य) carry, convey;
+ प्रति to put back
+ वि + उद् to raise up, establish
वा (enclit. particle) or (not to be confused with वा, a sandhi form of वै)
√वा (वयति; pple. उत/ऊत) to weave
+ आ to weave back
+ प्र to weave forth
वाच् (f.) speech, voice, utterance (√वच्)
वाचक्नवी (f.) PN
वाचारम्भण (adj.) holding on by means of speech = based on conventions of language (वाचा instr. + आरम्भण, fr. √रभ् + आ to hold on to)
वाजिन् (m.) steed, race horse (from वाज swiftness)
वात (m.) wind (√वा to blow)
वाद (m.) player (√वादय)
√वादय (caus. of √वद्, वादयति, pass. वाद्यते) to play (an instrument)
वामदेव (m.) PN
वायु (m.) wind (√वा to blow)
वायुर (adj.) windy, airy (वायु)
वाव (postpositive emphasizing particle)
वासस् (n.) garment (√वस् to wear)

वि (prefix) apart, away, out
विकार (m.) differentiation, modification (√कृ + वि)
विचक्षण (adj.) brilliant; (n.) brilliance, light (√चक्ष् + वि)
विजरा (f.) name of a river (lit. unaging)
विजिज्ञासा (f.) desire to know, curiosity (fr. desid. of √ज्ञा + वि)
विज्ञातृ (m.n.) knower (√ज्ञा + वि)
विज्ञान (n.) understanding, knowledge (√ज्ञा + वि)
विज्ञानघन (adj.) having pure knowledge (घन)
वित्त (n.) property (ta-pple of √विद् 2)
√विद् 1 (वेत्ति, विदन्ति, mid. sg. 1 विदे; perf. (pres. value) वेद, विदुः, perf. (past value) विदां चकार; aor. pl. 3 अवेदिषुः; fut. वेदिष्यति; pple. विदित; gerund विदित्वा; gerundive वेदितव्य) to know
+ प्रति (mid.) to know, to recognize
+ सम् (mid.) to know fully
√विद् 2 (विन्दति, -ते; perf. विवेद, विविदुः; pple. वित्त) to find, obtain
+ अनु to find, find out
विद् (adj., at end of compound) knowing
विद (adj., at end of compound) knowing
विदग्ध (adj.) clever; also PN (?) (√दह् + वि)
विदुष् (see विद्वस्)
विद्या (f.) knowledge
विद्युत् (f.) lightning (√द्युत् + वि)
विद्वस् (adj., §461) knowing, wise, learned (perf. act. pple. of √विद् 1)
विध (adj., at end of compounds) having the disposition or nature of (विधा)
विधा (f.) disposition, proportion; kind, sort (√धा + वि)
√विन्द् (see √विद् 2)
√विश् (विशति; pple. विष्ट; ger. -विश्य) to enter
+ प्र to enter
+ सम् + उप to sit down together
विश् (f.) people, the common people; (collect.) the Vaiśya caste
विश्व (adj.) all, every
विश्वंभर (m.) all-carrying; fire (which carries (√भृ) everything (विश्व) in the sacrifice to the Gods)
विश्वे देवाः (m. pl.) the All-Gods
विष्टप (n.) acme, height

विष्फुलिङ्ग (m.) spark
विसर्ग (m.) voiding, evacuation (√सृज् + वि)
विसृष्टि (f.) creation (√सृज् + वि)
वीणा (f.) a stringed musical instrument, veena
वीर्य (n.) manliness, courage, strength, power
वीर्यवत्तर (adj., compve.) more powerful (वीर्यवत् powerful, fr. वीर्य)
√वृ 1 (वृणोति, वृणुते; pple. वृत) to cover, enclose; to guard
+ अप + आ to uncover
+ आ to cover
+ वि to open
+ सम् to close, cover
√वृ 2 (वृणीते; perf. वव्रे) to choose
वृक्ण (see √व्रश्च्)
वृक्ष (m.) tree
√वृत् (वर्तते) to turn; to become, exist, be
+ अनु + परि to turn around (in the cycle of incarnations) according (to one's prior actions, or in accordance with the discussion of the preceding text)
+ आ (w. पुनर्) to turn back, return
+ नि (w. पुनर्) to turn back, return
+ निस् to come about, evolve
+ परि to roam around
+ सम् to come about, happen, exist
√वृष् (वर्षति) to rain
+ प्र to rain (forth)
वृष (at end of compound; see वृषन्)
वृषन् (m.) male of the species, esp. the bull; mighty, strong
वृषभ (m.) bull
वृष्टि (f.) rain (√वृष्)
√वृह् (वृहति) to tear
+ उद् to uproot, tear out
वेद (m.) knowledge, esp. sacred knowledge; the Veda
वै (postpositive particle; generally to be left untranslated)
वैदेह (adj.) of/belonging to the Videha people
वैद्युत (m.) the area (or fire) of lightning (विद्युत्)

वैश्य (m.) a man of the third caste, a Vaiśya (विश्)
वैश्वदेव (adj.) connected with the विश्वे देवाः, (n.) a sacrifice to these deities
वैश्वानर (adj.) lit. relating to all (विश्व) men (नर); omnipresent; worshiped everywhere; a name of Agni (esp. as a transcendental principle)
√व्यथ् (व्यथते) to move back and forth, to waver
व्यष्टि (f.) (separate) obtainment; individual object (√अश् 1 + वि)
व्याख्यान (n.) commentary, explanation (√ख्या + वि + आ)
व्यात्त (adj.) opened (esp. of the mouth), the open mouth (√दा + वि + आ, ta-pple., see §§955f, 1087e)
व्यान (m.) diffused breath (see Note on X, lines 30-32) (√अन् + वि)
व्यावर्तन (n.) divergent return (√वृत् + वि + आ)
√व्रज् (व्रजति; perf. वव्राज) to wander
+ उद् to wander forth; to set out for
+ परि to wander around (esp. as students or mendicants)
√व्रश्च् (वृश्चति; pple. वृक्ण) to cut; to fell
व्रीहि (m.) rice
√शंस् (शंसति; perf. शशंस) recite, praise
+ आ to wish (for somebody); to hope
+ प्र to praise
√शक् (शक्नोति, शक्नुवन्ति; aor. अशकत्) to be able
शकुनि (m.) a (large) bird
शङ्ख (m.n.) conch, shell
शब्द (m.) sound, word
शर (m.) foam
शरीर (n.) body
शश्वत् (adv.) always
शस्त्र (n.) a mode of Ṛg-Vedic recitation (√शंस्)
शस्या (f.) verse recited during the ladling of soma (√शंस्)
शाकल्य (m.) PNF
शार्दूल (m.) tiger
√शास् (शास्ति, शासति; aor. अशिषत्; pple. शिष्ट; gerund शिष्य) teach, instruct
+ अनु teach
√शिक्ष् (शिक्षति) learn (old desiderative of √शक्)

शिरस् (n.) head
√शिष् 1 (शिनस्ति, शिंसन्ति, intr./pass. शिष्यते) leave; (intr./pass.) be left, remain
+ अव (intr./pass.) remain
√शिष् 2 (see √शास्)
√शी (शेते, शेरते, opt. शयीत; ger. शयित्वा) to lie, sleep
+ अधि to lie down
शुक्र (adj.) clear; (n.) essence
√शुच् (शोचति) to flame; to grieve
शुद्ध (adj.) pure (ta-pple of √शुध् purify)
शूद्र (m.) man of the fourth caste, a Śūdra
√शॄ (शृणाति, mid. शृणीते; pass. शीर्यते) to crush, to break
शृङ्ग (n.) horn
शौद्र (adj.) belonging to the Śūdra caste
शौव (adj.) canine (श्वन्)
श्रद् (indecl.) belief, faith (used with √धा)
श्रद्धा (f.) belief, trust, faith
√श्रम् (श्राम्यति, -ते; pple. श्रान्त) to be weary; to toil
श्रवण (n.) hearing
√श्रि (श्रयति) to lean on
+ उप + नि to lean on, resort to
√श्रु (शृणोति, शृण्वन्ति; perfect शुश्राव, शुश्रुवुः; pple. श्रुत; caus. श्रावयति) to hear, listen
+ आ (caus.) to call for the श्रौषट् (see Note on XIII:1, line 16)
+ प्रति to answer, reply
श्रेयस् (compve. adj., §403) better
श्रोतृ (m.n.) hearer (√श्रु)
श्रोत्र (n.) ear (√श्रु)
श्रौषट् (indecl.) a ritual particle, asking the deities to listen (√श्रु; see Note on XIII:1, line 16)
श्लोक (m.) fame, reputation; verse
श्वन् (m., §427) dog
√श्वस् (श्वसिति; pple. श्वसित) to breathe
+ निस् to breathe out

√श्वा (श्वयति; aor. अश्वत्; inf. श्वयितुम्) to swell
श्वापद (m.) some kind of wild animal
श्वेत (adj.) white
श्वेतकेतु (m.) PN

षष् (numeral, §483) six

स (pron., see तद्)
स (pref.) together with, co- (often used in bahuvrīhis such as सदेव with the Gods, (lit.) having the Gods with (oneself))
संरब्ध (adj.) holding on (to each other) (√रभ्/रम्भ् to hold + सम्)
संवत्सर (m.) year
संवृत (n.) a secret place, (lit.) closed up (ta-pple. of √वृ 1 + सम्)
सक्थि/सक्थन् (n., §§343i, 431) thigh
संकल्प (m.) will, intention, decision (fr. √क्लृप् to be fit (for) + सम्)
सङ्ग (m.) attachment (√सञ्ज्)
√सञ्ज् (सजति; intr./pass. सज्यते) attach; (intr./pass.) attach oneself
संज्ञा (f.) consciousness, understanding (fr. √ज्ञा + सम्)
सत् (adj.) being, true; (n.) being, truth (pres. act. pple. of √अस्)
सत्य (adj.) true; (n.) truth (सत्)
√सद् (सीदति; caus. सादयति, caus. gerund -साद्य) sit; (caus.) to seat, make sit
+ आ (caus.) to reach, come to
+ उप to attend to, call on
सदस् (n.) seat; settlement, abode
सदेव (adj.) together with the God(s), with its God(s)
सपत्न (m.) rival, enemy (back-formation from सपत्नी co-wife, who is considered the rival of the other wife or wives)
सप्त (numeral, §483) seven
सप्तति (numeral, §486b) seventy
सप्रतिष्ठ (adj.) with (its) support
सभाग (adj.) going to the assembly (सभा assembly + √गम्/गा)
सम् (prefix) together with; completely
समन्त (adj.) contiguous, complete (सम् + अन्त)
समर्धयितृ (m.n.) one who brings about an accomplishment (√ऋध् (caus.) + सम्)

समष्टि (f.) (joint) obtainment; aggregate (√अश् 1 + सम्)
समान (m.) common or equalizing breath (see Note on X, lines 30-32)
समिति (f.) assembly (√इ + सम्)
समिध् (f.) kindling wood, fuel
समुद्र (m.) ocean, sea
समूल (adj., bahuvr.) with the root (मूल)
समृद्धि (f.) accomplishment (√ऋध् + सम्)
संपद् (f.) success, result; enumeration (√पद् + सम्)
संपरिष्वक्त (adj.) closely embracing, clinging to each other (fr. √स्वञ्ज् to embrace + सम् + परि)
सम्भव (m.) growth
सम्राज् (m.) universal king, emperor (fr. √राज्)
सर्व (adj.) all, entire, every
सर्वदा (adv., §1103a) always, forever
सवितृ (m.) the God Savitṛ (lit. the impeller, fr. √सु 2)
सह (adv., postposition) together with
सहस्र (n.) thousand
सामन् (n.) (Vedic) chant; (collect. pl.) the Sāma-Veda
सामवेद (m.) the Sāma-Veda
सामश्रवस् (m.) PN (lit. having the fame of sāman)
सिंह (m.) lion
सिकता (f.) sand (grain)
√सिच् (सिञ्चति; aor. pl. 2 (?) असिषिक्त) to pour
सिन्धु (m.) river (esp. the Indus)
√सु 1 (सुनोति, सुनुते) to press out
√सु 2 (सौति, सुवति) to impel (different from √सू ?)
+ प्र to impel
सु (prefix) good, well
सुधन्वन् (m.) PN
सुपथ्/सुपन्थन् (m.) good path
सुपर्ण (m.) eagle (lit. having good feathers)
सुमेधस् (adj.) having good wisdom, wise (मेधस् wisdom)
सुरा (f.) alcoholic beverage, liquor
सुषुप्त (adj.) fast asleep, in deep sleep (सु + pple. of √स्वप्)

√सू (सूते; pple. सूत) to impel
  + प्र to impel
सूकर (m.) pig, swine; boar
सूत्र (n.) thread; rule; Vedic rule book, sūtra
सूर्य (m.) sun
√सृज् (सृजति, -ते; aor. mid. sg.1 असृक्षि; pple. सृष्ट; pass. सृज्यते) to let loose; create
  + अति to create in addition; to release beyond, to permit to go on
  + सम् to unite
सृति (f.) course, path (√सृ to run)
√सृप् (सर्पति, -ते; perf. ससर्प, ससृपुः; gerund -सृप्य) to creep, crawl
  + आ to "creep" up (in the ritual)
  + प्रति + अव to creep towards
सृष्टि (f.) creation (√सृज्)
सैन्धवखिल्य (m.) a lump (खिल्य) of salt (सैन्धव, fr. सिन्धु)
सोम (m.) a plant of controversial identification whose extract had some kind of hallucinogenic effect; the extract of that plant; the deified Soma
सोम्य (see सौम्य)
सौम्य (m., used in voc. sg.) gentle sir (सोम)
√स्तन् (स्तनयति) to thunder
स्तनयित्नु (m.) thunder (√स्तन्)
स्तब्ध (adj.) arrogant (pple. of √स्तभ्/स्तम्भ् to make firm, fixed)
√स्तु (act. pres. स्तौति, स्तुवन्ति §626; fut. स्तोष्यति, -ते) to recite, esp. to recite a स्तोत्रिया
  + प्र to recite a verse
स्तेन (m.) thief
स्तोत्र (n.) a form of sāman (√स्तु)
स्तोत्रिया (f.) a type of verse recited in the sacrifice (स्तोत्र)
स्त्री (f.) woman
√स्था (तिष्ठति, -ते; perf. तस्थौ, तस्थुः; aor. अस्थात्; ta-pple. स्थित; gerund -स्थाय) to stand; be situated; remain; exist
  + अभि + प्र extend, rise up to
  + उद् stand up (root-initial स् is lost if immediately preceded by this prefix, §233c)
  + उप + उद् stand or rise up to; confront
  + प्रति stand up, be established
  + सम् + उद् rise up, arise
स्थान (n.) standing; place, position; status, class, kind

स्थूल (adj.) thick, bulky, gross

स्नेह (m.) stickiness (√स्निह् to be sticky)

स्पर्श (m.) touch (√स्पृश् to touch)

स्म (encl. particle, slightly asseverative; in combination with present tense, it can yield a habitual past tense of the type 'used to do something', §778)

√स्मृ (स्मरति, -ते) to remember

√स्यन्द् (स्यन्दते) to flow

स्व (pron. adj.) one's own; (m.) one's self

स्वः (see स्वर्)

√स्वप् (स्वपिति; pple. सुप्त) to sleep, to dream

स्वप्न (m.) sleep, dream

स्वप्नयया (adv.) in dream (स्वप्न)

स्वर् (indecl.) a sacred utterance (used in the formula भूर्भुवः स्वः)

स्वर्ग (adj.) heavenly

स्वाध्याय (m.) reciting to oneself; study, esp. of the Vedas (स्व + अध्याय from √इ + अधि)

स्विद् (particle) perchance

√स्विद् (स्वेदति, -ते) to sweat

ह (enclit. particle, slightly asseverative, §1122a; generally to be left untranslated)

√हन् (हन्ति, घ्नन्ति; itr./pass. हन्यते) to strike, slay

+ सम् (intr./pass.) to solidify, congeal

हन्त (particle) come!, let's go!

हय (m.) a courser, steed (√हि)

हस्त (m.) hand

हस्तिन् (m.) elephant (because of its hand-like trunk)

हि (particle, §1122a) surely, indeed; because, for

√हि (हिनोति; perf. जिघाय, जिघ्युः) to set in motion, impel

+ प्र to send off

√हिंस् (हिनस्ति, हिंसन्ति; gerund हिंसित्वा) to harm, injure; to slay

हित (see √धा)

हिम् a sacrificial particle uttered in Vedic ritual, esp. in Sāma-Vedic chant

हिरण्मय (adj.) golden (see हिरण्य + -मय)

हिरण्य (n.) gold

√हु (जुहोति, जुह्वति; fut. होष्यति; pple. हुत) pour (libations); offer libations (in the ritual)

√हृ (हरति; perf. जहार, जह्रुः; caus. हारयति, caus. perf. हारयां चकार, caus. ger. -हार्य) to take, carry

+ अप to carry away

+ आ to bring hither; (caus.) to cause to be brought

+ उद् + आ to bring out; to utter, say

+ वि + आ to bring out; to utter, say

हृद् (n., §397) heart

हृदय (n.) heart

हो (a particle of address and surprise) hey

होतृ (m.) the chief priest associated with the Ṛg-Veda (Introduction, §5)

ह्रद (m.) pool, lake

ह्रस्व (adj.) short

ह्रादुनि (f.) hailstone

References

to

Resources

Editions

and

Translations

References to Resources, Editions, and Translations

Resource Tools

Bertold Delbrück, *Altindische Syntax.* (Syntaktische Forschungen, 5.) Halle: Waisenhaus, 1888. (Repr. 1968, Darmstadt: Wissenschaftliche Buchgesellschaft.)

Charles Rockwell Lanman, *A Sanskrit Reader: Text and Vocabulary and Notes*, Harvard University Press, 1884. (Reprinted 1996, Delhi: Motilal Banarsidass.)

A. Macdonell, *Vedic Grammar for Students.* London: Oxford University Press, 1916. (Repr. 1955 and later, Bombay/Calcutta/Madras: Oxford University Press.)

Sukumar Sen, *The Syntax of Cases in Vedic Prose.* Annals of the Bhandarkar Oriental Research Institute 8:347-78, 9:33-48, 91-170, 10:45-76, 219-34, 1926-30.

J. S. Speijer, *Sanskrit Syntax.* Leiden: E. J. Brill, 1886. (Reprinted 1973, Delhi: Motilal Banarsidass.)

William Dwight Whitney, *Sanskrit Grammar: Including Both the Classical Language, and the Older Dialects, of Veda and Brahmana*, Second edition, Harvard University Press, 1889. (Reprinted 1975, Delhi: Motilal Banarsidass.)

William Dwight Whitney, *The Roots, Verb-forms, and Primary Derivatives of the Sanskrit Language.* Leipzig, Breitkopf & Härtel, 1885. Repr. 1945, American Oriental Society. (Reprinted 1979, Delhi: Motilal Banarsidass.)

Editions and Translations

Upaniṣad-Collections

The Early Upaniṣads, edited and translated by Patrick Olivelle. Oxford University Press, New York, and Munshiram Manoharlal, Delhi, 1998.

The Principal Upaniṣads, edited with introduction, text, translation, and notes by S. Radhakrishnan, London, The Muirhead Library of Philosophy, 1953 (and later reprints).

The Twelve Principal Upaniṣads, text in devanagari with translation and notes by Raja Rajendralal Mitra and E. B. Cowell, second edition 1931. Reprint 1978, Delhi, Nag Publishers.

The Upanishads, translated by F. Max Müller, Oxford, *Sacred Books of the East* 1 and 15 = I and II, 1900.

उपनिषत्सङ्ग्रहः, in two parts [containing 120 + 68 Upaniṣads], edited in devanagari by Jagadīśa Śāstrī, Delhi, Motilal Banarsidass, 1970.

Śatapatha-Brāhmaṇa and Bṛhad-Āraṇyaka-Upaniṣad (Mādhyandina)

शतपथब्राह्मणम्, edited by Albert Weber, Berlin, 1855. Repr. 1964, Varanasi, Chowkhamba Sanskrit Series, No. 96. — The BAU parts are: BAU 1:1-2 = 10:6:4-5; BAU 1:3-6 = 14:4:1-4 ; BAU 2 = 14:5; BAU 3 = 14:6:1-9; BAU 4:1-2 = 14:6:10-11, BAU 4:3-5 = 14:7:1-3; BAU 5 = 14:8; BAU 6 = 14:9. (These comparisons are made with respect to the numbering system that appears on the odd-numbered pages of Weber's edition; the even-numbered pages follow a different system.)
A translation based on this edition, but omitting the Bṛhad-Āraṇyaka-Upaniṣad, was produced by Julius Eggeling in five volumes, *Sacred Books of the East* 12, 26, 41, 43, 44, 1882-1900; reprint 1963, Delhi, Motilal Banarsidass.

शतपथब्राह्मणम्, edited by Śrīdhara Śarmā (?) and published in five volumes by Gian Publishing House, Delhi, 1987. Unlike Weber's edition, this edition cites the text with the effects of consonant doubling and other features taught by the Prātiśākhya and does not try to impose its own theory on accentuation. There are also some differences as regards the placement of the daṇḍa (|) after the pratīka of a paragraph. Other differences are generally minor. — The BAU parts are: BAU 1:1-2 = 10:6:4-5 (in vol. 4); the rest of BAU = vol. 5, with BAU 1:3-6 = 1:1-4; BAU 2 = 2; BAU 3 = 3:1-9; BAU 4:1-2 = 3:10-11, BAU 4:3-5 = 4:1-3; BAU 5 = 5; BAU 6 = 6. (Again, the comparisons are made with respect to the numbering on the odd-numbered pages.)

Bṛhadâranjakopanishad, edited by O. Böhtlingk, St. Petersburg/Riga/Leipzig, 1889, with German translation. (Böhtlingk substitutes a superscript उ [for "udātta"] instead of the subscript anudātta stroke of the tradition. Some of the passages are left untranslated.)

Śatapatha-Brāhmaṇa and Bṛhad-Āraṇyaka-Upaniṣad (Kāṇva)

The Śatapatha-Brāhmaṇa in the Kāṇvīya Recension, ed. by W. Caland and Raghu Vira, Panjab Sanskrit Series, Lahore, 1926. Reprinted 1983, Delhi, Motilal Banarsidass.

शुक्लयजुर्वेदकाण्वसंहिता (= Vājasaneyi-Saṁhitā, Kāṇva recension), edited by Cintāmaṇi Miśra Śarmā and Divākaradāsa Śarmā, Varanasi, Sarasvatībhavana-Granthamālā 114, 1978. (Selection XIX of this Reader = 40:15-18.)

The Texts of the White Yajurveda or Vājasaneyā-Saṁhitā, translated by Ralph T. H. Griffith, 1899. Reprinted and enlarged edition, 1987, Delhi, Munshiram Manoharlal.

The Early Upaniṣads, ed. and transl. by Patrick Olivelle, pp. 36-165..

The Principal Upaniṣads, ed. and transl. by Radhakrishnan, pp. 149-333.

The Upanishads, transl. by Müller, II:73-227.

Chāndogya-Upaniṣad

छान्दोग्योपनिषत्, edited by E. Röer, Calcutta, Bibliotheca Indica 3, 1850. Reprint 1980, Biblio Verlag, Osnabrück. (The first printed edition, not always accurate.)

छान्दोग्योपनिषत्, published by the Ananda Ashrama, Ānandāśrama-saṁskṛta-granthāvali 14, reprint 1983.

छान्दोग्यब्राह्मणम्, part III, published by Sri Maharaja Sahib Govinda Deekshitar Punya Smarana Samithi, Kumbakonam, 1980. (The Chāndogya-Upaniṣad begins on p. 31 and goes to p. 156.)

The Chāndogya-Upaniṣad, text in devanagari with translation and notes by Swami Swahananda, second edition, Madras, Sri Ramakrishna Math, 1965.

Chāndogya-Upaniṣad, texte, traduction et notes par Fernand Hayot. Paris, Librairie d'Amérique et d'Orient, Jean Maisonneuve, 1996.

The Early Upaniṣads, ed. and transl. by Patrick Olivelle, pp. 170-287.

The Principal Upaniṣads, ed. and transl. by Radhakrishnan, pp. 337-512.

The Twelve Principal Upaniṣads, ed. and transl. by Mitra and Cowell, volume 3, pp. 8-275.

The Upanishads, transl. by Müller, I:1-153.

Other Texts and Translations

अथर्ववेदसंहिता, editions by R. Roth and W. D. Whitney, Berlin, 1855-1856 — Shankar Pandurang Pandit, Bombay, 1895-1898 — and many others. The best scholarly translation is that of William Dwight Whitney, *Atharva-Veda-Saṁhitā*, revised and edited by Charles Rockwell Lanman, Cambridge, MA, Harvard Oriental Series 7-8, 1905, Reprint 1962, Delhi, Motilal Banarsidass.

आश्वलायनगृह्यसूत्रम्, edited by Adolf Friedrich Stenzler in *गृह्यसूत्राणि: Indische Hausregeln Sanskrit und Deutsch*, Abhandlungen für die Kunde des Morgenlandes 3:4 and 4:1, 1864 and 1866 — another edition appeared in the Bibliotheca Indica, 1866-1869.

आश्वलायनश्रौतसूत्रम्, ed. by Maṇḍana Miśra et al., Saṁskṛta-Vidyāpīṭha-Granthamālā 48, Lal Bahadur Shastri Sanskrit Vidyapeeth, Delhi, 1984-1985.

ऋग्वेदसंहिता, editions by F. Max Müller, 1849 (6 volumes, with Sāyaṇa's commentary), second edition 1890-1874, and 1873 (without the commentary), reprinted 1965, Kashi Sanskrit Series 166-167 — Theodor Aufrecht, 1861-1863, Reprint 1968, Wiesbaden, Harrassowitz — and many others. The best scholarly translation is that of Karl Friedrich Geldner, *Der Rig-Veda aus dem Sanskrit ins Deutsche übersetzt*, Cambridge, MA, Harvard Oriental Series 33-35, 1951. A new English translation is under preparation by Joel Brereton and Stephanie Jamison.

ऐतरेयब्राह्मणम्, editions by Kāśinātha Śāstrī Āgāśe, Ananda Ashrama Series 32, 1896 — Theodor Aufrecht, Bonn, 1879, Reprint 1975, Hildesheim & New York, Olms — and others. The best scholarly translation is that of Arthur Berriedale Keith, *Rigveda Brahmanas: The Aitareya and Kauṣītaki Brāhmaṇas of the Rigveda*, Cambridge, MA, Harvard Oriental Series 25, 1920, Reprint 1971, Delhi: Motilal Banarsidass.

कौषीतकिब्राह्मणोपनिषत्, edited with an English translation by E. B. Cowell, Bibliotheca Indica, Calcutta, 1861, repr. 1968, Chowkhamba Sanskrit Studies, vol. 64, Varanasi — A slightly different edition in Śāstrī's उपनिषत्सङ्ग्रहः, I:194-207 — Edition and translation in Radhakrishnan's *Principal Upaniṣads* (pp. 751-791) and Olivelle's *Early Upaniṣads* (pp. 326-361) — The कौषीतकिब्राह्मणोपनिषत् constitutes books 3-6 of the शाङ्खायनारण्यक, published by the Ananda Ashrama, Ānandāśrama-saṁskṛta-granthāvali 90, 1922. — Translation by Arthur Berriedale Keith (*The Sankhayana Aranyaka*), London, Royal Asiatic Society, 1908, rep. 1975, Oriental Books Reprint Corporation, New Delhi. — Translation with commentary by Henk Bodewitz, *Kauṣītaki Upaniṣad: Translation and Commentary, with an Appendix: Śāṅkhāyana Āraṇyaka IX-XI*, Groningen: Egbert Forsten, 2002.

जैमिनीयं ब्राह्मणम्, critically edited by Raghu Vira and Lokesh Chandra, Nagpur, 1954, second revised edition, Delhi, Motilal Banarsidass, 1986 — *Das Jaiminīya-Brāhmaṇa in Auswahl*, selected passages with translation by W. Caland, Amsterdam, Verhandelingen der Koninklijke Akademie van Wetenschappen te Amsterdam, I, Nieuwe Reeks, XIV, No. 4, 1919 — See also Hendrik Wilhelm Bodewitz, *Jaiminīya-Brāhmaṇa I, 1-65: Translation and Commentary with a Study: Agnihotra and Prāṇāgnihotra*, Leiden: Brill, 1973.

जैमिनीयोपनिषद्ब्राह्मणम्, in *Jaiminīya Ārṣeya – Jaiminīya Upaniṣad Brāhmaṇas*, critically edited by Bellikoth Ramachandra Sharma, Tirupati, Kendriya Sanskrit Vidyapeetha, Tirupati Series 5-6, 1984 — Edition and translation by Hanns Oertel, *Journal of the American Oriental Society* 16:89-260, 1896 — Devanagari edition, based on Oertel's edition, by Rama Deva, Dayānanda Mahāvidyālaya Saṁskṛta Granthamālā 3, Lahore, 1921.

तैत्तिरीयसंहिता, edition in the Ananda Ashrama Series, 42-48, reprinted 1978 — Edition by Albrecht Weber, in *Indische Studien* 11 and 12, Leipzig, 1871-1872 — The best scholarly translation is that of Arthur Berriedale Keith, *The Veda of the Black Yajus School Entitled Taittiriya Sanhita*, Cambridge, MA, Harvard Oriental Series 18 and 19, 1914, Reprint 1967, Delhi: Motilal Banarsidass.

तैत्तिरीयारण्यकम्, an edition which contains the Taittirīya-Upaniṣad, Ananda Ashrama Series, 36, reprinted 1981.

तैत्तिरीयोपनिषत्, edition by E. Röer, Bibliotheca Indica, Calcutta, 1850, reprinted 1980, Biblio Verlag, Osnabrück — Edition and translation in Radhakrishnan's *Principal Upaniṣads* (pp. 525-563) and Olivelle's *Early Upaniṣads* (pp. 219-313).

मैत्रायणीसंहिता, editions by Leopold von Schroeder, Deutsche Morgenländische Gesellschaft, 1881, reprinted 1970, Frankfurt, Steiner — Śripāda Damodara Sātavalekar, Svādhyāya-Maṇḍala, Pāraḍī, reprinted 1983.

सुबालोपनिषत्, edition in Śāstrī's उपनिषत्सङ्ग्रहः, I:242-250 — Edition and translation in Radhakrishnan's *Principal Upaniṣads* (pp. 861-891) [This edition has numerous mistakes which have been corrected without comment in Selection XX:K of this Reader.]

Indices

Indices

Arabic numerals refer to page numbers; Roman numerals, to Text Selections. The order follows the conventions of the roman alphabet, with diacritics ignored for sorting purposes.

General Index

Language and Grammar Index